THE **COMPLETE IDIOT'S GUIDE®** TO

Planning a Trip Online

Julia A. Cardis and Kendall Smith II

que®

A Division of Macmillan Computer Publishing
201 W. 103rd Street, Indianapolis, IN 46290

The Complete Idiot's Guide to Planning a Trip Online

Copyright © 2000 by _Que_

International Standard Book Number: 0-7897-2168-6

Library of Congress Catalog Card Number: 99-63405

Printed in the United States of America

First Printing: October 1999

01   00   99   4   3   2   1

Trademarks

Warning and Disclaimer

Associate Publisher
Greg Wiegand

Acquisitions Editor
Angelina Ward

Development Editor
Sarah Robbins

Managing Editor
Thomas F. Hayes

Project Editor
Karen S. Shields

Copy Editor
Kitty Jarrett

Indexer
Kevin Broccoli

Proofreader
Tricia Sterling

Technical Editor
Robert E. Patrick

Team Coordinator
Sharry Gregory

Interior Designer
Nathan Clement

Cover Designer
Michael Freeland

Illustrator
Judd Winick

Copy Writer
Eric Borgert

Production
Dan Harris
Heather Moseman
Liz Johnston

Contents at a Glance

Contents

About the Author

Julia Cardis is an award-winning professional writer and official member of the BootsnAll.com Flip Flop Club. She has written about online business travel planning and co-authored a guide to building small business Web sites. Over the years as an armchair traveler, she has visited thousands of travel-related Web sites and has watched the Web evolve into a travel planner's paradise.

Kendall Smith II contributed to this book by providing creative direction, travel industry expertise, and personal travel experiences. Kendall has spent more than 25 years as the creative director at Indiana Design Consortium, Inc., a full-service marketing communications firm. He and his wife, Beatrice, also own and manage Lafayette Travel and Cruise, a 50-year-old travel agency. They have developed and manage several travel-planning Web sites, including **www.grouptravel.net**.

Contributors

Andrew J. Kunka and Carol Schuler contributed writing and research to several chapters. Andrew thanks Jennifer Liethen Kunka, Val Coit, and Michael Scholtz for their contributions. Carol thanks Katie and Houston.

Acknowledgments

First, many, many thanks to Angelina Ward for giving me a crack at my first major publication. And to Sarah Robbins, for helping me sort through the endless amount of travel information to develop the direction and content for the book. Thanks to Robert Patrick for making sure the information in this book is accurate and up-to-date, and to Karen Shields for moving the manuscript and art through production. Special thanks also goes to Kitty Jarrett for fixing little hiccups and fine-tuning my sometimes long-winded sentences. The Macmillan USA production team gets a pat on the back for translating a bunch of mysteriously coded electronic files into an attractive bound book. Thanks, too, to Sam Harper and Mark Grondin at Pyxis International, for their technical and travel reservation systems expertise. And to Emily Short, intern extraordinaire and diligent research buddy. Finally, a big thanks to the crew at Indiana Design Consortium.

The Web, It Is a-Changin'

While doing research for this book, I contacted a good number of Web sites for one reason or another. I was surprised at how many asked me to come back and re-review their sites in "a month or two—we're in the middle of upgrades and redesigns." Moral of the story? The Web is an ever-changing landscape, so please accept my apologies if a site listed in this book has moved to a new location, dropped off the face of the Web, or completely reinvented itself since I last visited and wrote about it.

Researching this book led to the discovery of a seemingly endless supply of travel resources and Web sites. If we missed a site that you'd like to recommend for future versions of this book, please let us know. Write to:

The Complete Idiot's Guide to Planning a Trip Online

Macmillan USA

201 West 103rd Street

Indianapolis, Indiana 46290-1097

Tell Us What You Think!

As the reader of this book, you are our most important critic and commentator. We value your opinion and want to know what we're doing right, what we could do better, what areas you'd like to see us publish in, and any other words of wisdom you're willing to pass our way.

As an Associate Publisher for Que, I welcome your comments. You can fax, email, or write me directly to let me know what you did or didn't like about this book—as well as what we can do to make our books stronger.

Please note that I cannot help you with technical problems related to the topic of this book, and that due to the high volume of mail I receive, I might not be able to reply to every message.

When you write, please be sure to include this book's title and author as well as your name and phone or fax number. I will carefully review your comments and share them with the author and editors who worked on the book.

Fax: 317-581-4666

Email: consumer@mcp.com

Mail: Greg Wiegand
         Associate Publisher
         Que
         201 West 103rd Street
         Indianapolis, IN 46290 USA

Introduction: Using the Web to Plan the Perfect Trip

When you're planning a vacation or travel adventure, one of the first things you do is gather information and answer some basic questions. Where are you going? How will you get there? How much can you spend? Do you need immunizations or special documentation? Then you need to find out about must-see attractions, such as lodging, transportation, exchange rates, entertainment, and dining. Regardless of the kind of trip you're taking, the planning stage requires careful thought and consideration.

Of course, travel agents have been around a long time to help plan and plot journeys. With expert advice and up-to-the-minute rates and availability, travel agents have provided brochures and helped check airfares, reserve hotel rooms, and find out about must-see attractions. Do-it-yourself types used to get travel guide and reference books from the library, made calls to visitors' bureaus, and relied on a good friend's advice to decide where to go and where not to go.

These days, though, all the old options are still available, and people are going online to become informed travel consumers by tapping into the ever-growing pool of travel resources available on the Web. Travel magazines, travel directories, online booking sites, travel newsgroups, and online travel gear stores provide all the tools we need to make the most of our trips and journeys. And all that information is in one place, accessible from the comforts of our own home, day or night.

Let's face it. You're not an idiot, because if you were, you wouldn't have picked up this really cool book. You've been hearing about all the great deals you can get on the Web, but you just don't know where to begin, or you just don't have the time to sort through the many, many travel sites. Well, you've come to the right place. This book will show you

> ➤ How to find travel deals available only to online travelers and how to scout out other travel bargains.
> ➤ How to use the tools of the Internet to do your own travel research and planning.
> ➤ How to create custom guidebooks and personal planners based on your unique travel needs.
> ➤ How to go online to preview your destination.
> ➤ How to find city and country guides, travel safety advisories, weather forecasts, and road maps.
> ➤ How to connect with other travelers for tips, advice, and insider information.
> ➤ How to use online reservation systems.

I assume that you have a computer, you know how to use it, and you know how to get onto the Internet. The first part of the book covers some online basics, but if you need help using your computer and the Internet, get your hands on a copy of *The Complete Idiot's Guide to PCs, Seventh Edition*, by Joe Kraynak, and *The Complete Idiot's Guide to the Internet, Sixth Edition*, by Peter Kent. And if you're traveling to Europe, I also recommend that you get a copy of *The Complete Idiot's Guide to Planning Your Trip to Europe*, by Reid Bramblett.

How to Use This Book

There are different kinds of travelers and different ways to travel. Whether you're looking for information on Las Vegas packages, senior travel, group tours, honeymoons, family vacations, or RV road tripping across the United States, this book has something for you. It's designed to help every kind of traveler use the tools of the Internet to plan better trips, find better deals, and connect with like-minded people for tips and advice.

You don't have to read this book from cover to cover, but you'll miss out on some good laughs and funny stories if you skip any part of it. If you're new to the Web, start with Chapter 1, "Going Online to Plan Your Travel." If you're new to travel planning on the Web, start with Chapter 4, "Traveler's Online Resources 101." If you're looking for destination information only, check out Chapter 8, "Using Destination Guides to Research and Plan Your Trip." If you want to know how to find the best deals on airfare, see Chapter 10, "Air Travel," which tells you how and where to look. Or maybe you're looking for the perfect cruise? Chapter 16, "Cruises, Cruises, and More Cruises," is the place for you. If you want to know the answer to an age-old question, you can find the secret in Chapter 23, "Are We There Yet?!."

Each chapter is broken down into distinct travel topics, with cross-references to related information in other parts of the book. To help you quickly find the information you need, I divided the book into the following four parts:

➤ **Part 1**, "**Using the Web to Plan the Perfect Trip**," covers the basics of using the World Wide Web and tools of the Internet to research your travel and find online travel resources.

➤ **Part 2**, "**Do-It-Yourself: Planning and Buying Travel Online**," equips you with resources to plan your own travel by using destination guides; online hotel, air, and car rental reservation systems; travel directories; and other online resources that'll help you become an informed travel consumer.

➤ **Part 3**, "**Cruises, Package Tours, Group Travel, and Custom Group Tours**," shows you how to locate tour group leaders, find cruise information, locate specialty travel agents, and go online to plan customized or package tours for your group.

➤ **Part 4**, "**Traveler's Toolbox: Checklists and Planning Tools**," covers the details of travel planning and gives you tips on staying connected on the road, keeping the kids happy in transit, shopping for travel gear and accessories, and just about everything you need to know to plan and prepare for your next trip.

And so you know, Web site addresses (URLs) listed throughout the book appear as **www.companyname.com**, rather than **http://www.companyname.com**. You will run across a handful of URLs that include the http://, but that's in case your browser doesn't autmatically translate that for you. In other words, if you have trouble accessing a site using only **www.companyname.com**, try adding on http://. And if you see an address in this book, type it in, just in case.

Conventions Used in This Book

This book is full of pearls of wisdom to make the book fun to read and easier to use. There are four kinds of boxes in this book:

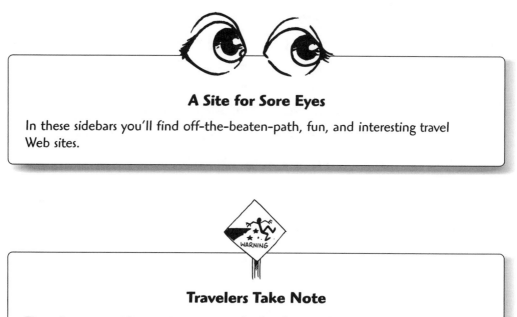

A Site for Sore Eyes

In these sidebars you'll find off-the-beaten-path, fun, and interesting travel Web sites.

Travelers Take Note

These boxes provide warnings, tips, and tales that can help make your travel planning and your actual trip better.

Tech Trek

The boxes give technical how-to's relating to travel Web sites, like how to post questions to travel newsgroups, use interactive atlases, and view online videos.

Straight from the Horse's Mouth

In these sidebars you'll find stories, tales, and advice from real travelers.

Part 1

Using the Web to Plan the Perfect Trip

So you've decided it's time for a vacation. Or maybe you have to go to Grandma's for her 75th birthday party. Perhaps the boss just promoted you to regional sales manager and you get to spend the next six months on the road, getting to know your territory. Just got married and need some honeymoon ideas? Sounds like it's time to do some travel planning. How will you get there? Where can you find the best deals on airfare? Can you find a B&B that allows pets? How can you find out about off-the-beaten-path attractions? What do real travelers think about the cruise you want to take?

Lots of questions, you're saying to yourself. Well, you'll find lots of answers when you go online to plan the perfect trip. It only makes sense that with a world of travel destinations and activities, all the information and tools we need are available on the World Wide Web. Also known as the Web. WWW. W3. Online. The Net. The Big W…okay, so no one actually calls it that. I'm trying to start a trend. Be the first on your block to say "I found cheap plane tickets on the Big W!"

This first part of the book introduces you to the Web and how you can use its many travel-planning tools and resources, and what types of travel Web sites are out there. I'll go over the basics of browsers, search engines, newsgroups, chat rooms, message boards, travel forums, and all the other basics you need to go online and become an informed travel consumer.

Chapter 1

Going Online to Plan Your Travel

In This Chapter

➤ How to make the Web work for you

➤ The travel industry meets the Internet

➤ Don't despair...Web sites, books, and resources for beginners

Travel planning takes thought and time. Unless you're a fly-by-the-seat-of-your-pants kind of road warrior, you probably like to know where exactly you want to go, how you're going to get there, where you're going to stay, what you're going to do, and how much it's going to cost. In fact, unless you're an experienced spontaneous traveler, basic safety precautions mandate that the wheres, whens, and hows of travel be decided before you set out on your journey.

Lucky for us, there's a lot of information available through the World Wide Web about nearly every subject under the sun (including the sun and the rest of the planets). One of the fastest-growing and most popular topics on the Web is travel, and there are thousands of sites dedicated to travel planning, travel sales, destination guides, and all kinds of other travel-planning tools and resources.

So if want to save time, possibly save some money, get detailed destination information, or get advice and tips from other travelers, the Web is a great place to start when you're making travel plans. Or if you just want to find a specialty travel agent, buy a guide book, or print out a map, you can do it all on the Web. This chapter offers some help to get you started.

Travel Sites: A Popular Destination

Online travel is the most popular and fastest-growing area in electronic commerce. Travel transactions account for about 50 percent of the money spent online. According to a report from Cyber Atlas (`www.cyberatlas.com`), a Web marketer's guide to online facts, 6.7 million American adults (9 percent of Internet users) have used the Internet to make travel reservations in the past year.

Getting Started on the Web

I'll just go ahead and say it. I just can't imagine life without the World Wide Web. That's not to say that I couldn't live without it because I did, in fact, live without it for a long time. And so did you. But now that it's here and it's getting better and easier to use every day, can you imagine living without it? When it comes to gathering information and communicating with friends (as well as strangers), there's nothing else like it.

*AOL's Family Travel Network (keyword: **Family Travel Network**) lets you search for family-friendly vacation destinations, talk to other parents and kids about their travel hits and misses, or take a virtual vacation to a far-away land.*

The World Wide Web gives us the tools and information we need to research, communicate, meet people with shared interests, comparison shop, purchase, reserve, bid, barter, offer advice, trade, sell, update, download, plug in, log on, post, send, receive information, and most of all, *learn*. And best yet, it's available from the comfort of our own homes at any time of the day or night.

How the Web Works

Walk into any bookstore and you'll find hundreds and hundreds of books on computers, the Internet, and the World Wide Web. Or log on to the Web, and you'll find lots of Web sites and tools to help you get started with your online adventures. But first things first. What is the World Wide Web and how does it work?

Although many people use the terms *Internet* and *World Wide Web* to mean the same thing, they are, in fact, different animals. The Internet, in a nutshell, is a network of networked computers. Every day, more and more people log on. And every day, more and more information is posted, emails are exchanged, databases are updated, and information is exchanged electronically across the wires from one Web server to the next and down the lines to desktops all over the world. But the Internet is not the World Wide Web—it's simply the system that connects us from server to desktop. The Web and Web browsers (more on those in Chapter 3, "Search Engines 101") are the beasts that allow us to view the data files and images that appear on our computer screens.

The World Wide Web is a collection of documents (text, pictures, sounds, video clips, animations, and so on) that are stored on Web servers all around the world. Each document can contain hyperlinks to other documents, so that when you click on a link, a new document appears. Every Web site has a unique address, like **www.yahoo.com**, and every page or document contained in the site has a filename, like **www.yahoo.com/r/tr**. When you click the hyperlink to the page you want to see, the new page appears on your screen.

It's really not as complicated as it might sound. In fact, the Web was designed to make seeing (and hearing) all those documents easy to do through an intuitive point-and-click system.

The Web site address, or URL (which stands for uniform resource locator), appears in the Location bar in your Web browser. Let's say you want to see what's in the travel category in Yahoo!'s directory. Just click on the text, and you'll go to the Web page that appears in the bottom of your browser.

How to Use the Internet

Accessing the World Wide Web and translating documents through Web browsers is not all the Internet is used for. When you withdraw money from an ATM, for example, your request is sent using the Internet. And there are other ways to use the Internet to exchange data and information. The following Internet tools are especially handy for online travel planning:

➤ **Email** is the most-used Internet service. Each day, billions of electronic mail messages are sent between family members, friends, and businesses each day. It's a great way to stay in touch when you're traveling or trying to arrange travel plans that require long-distance communication.

➤ **Chat** is another popular Internet service, but I find it a bit annoying and hard to follow, although there are some good travel chat rooms out there. I'll tell you more about those later.

➤ The **World Wide Web** (also called the Web, the WWW, and W3) allows images, text, sound, animation, and video files to be transferred using an intuitive (usually) hypertext-based, point-and-click system. Anyone with Internet access can build and post a Web document, and lots of people do just that.

➤ **Telnet** is another information exchange system that operates on a text-based menu command system, and is used to tap into data sources like library databases. It's not as widely used as the Web's hypertext system, but it can be useful.

➤ **Newsgroups** might be one of the most valuable online resources for non-commercial travel information and resource gathering. You can use them to connect with like-minded travelers across the globe or post a warning/complaint about the hotel in Borneo that "lost" your reservation, forcing you to sleep on the couch at the house of a nice man you met on the plane. There's a newsgroup for just about any travel topic or destination you can think of.

➤ **Emailing lists and Web forums** are similar to newsgroups in that you use them to connect with others based on a shared interest in the topic of discussion. Unlike a newsgroup, an emailing list runs through your email system and a Web forum is hosted within a particular Web site.

➤ **Email subscription newsletters or notifications** are automatically sent to your email inbox. They contain information about specific topics that you request. For example, you can sign up for weekly low-fare notices that some travel Web sites send to subscribers when the airlines announce reduced fares in an effort to sell unreserved seats. (After all, the airlines figure, it's better to get something than nothing, which is what they get if the seats are empty.) You'll learn more about getting insider tips like that later, too.

I'll go into more detail on how to use all these tools to plan your travel in Chapter 5, "Online Travel Communities 101."

Signing Up for Access to the Web

If you don't already have access to the World Wide Web, you'll need to locate an Internet service provider (ISP) in your area or get an account through an online service like America Online, AT&T, or Microsoft Network. You should be able to find the names and phone numbers of access providers in your phone book. I've found access through a local service provider to be more enjoyable, but AOL boasts about a 50 percent market share and has a pretty good toolbox of resources for travelers, so you might want to try it on for size if you're just getting started.

Travelocity was one of the first Web sites that allowed consumers a free and easy-to-use system to check flight information, compare rates, and make flight reservations. It also contains helpful travel tools to help you gather destination information, check out entertainment calendars, and preview attractions.

Longtime Friends: The Travel Industry and the Internet

If you're like me and you have a natural curiosity and a need to understand how things work, after you read this next section, you'll probably slap yourself on the forehead and say, "Oh! *That's* how they do that!"

My good buddy Mark Grondin of Pyxis International (**www.pyxis.net**), an Internet and e-commerce consulting company, was part of the team that helped build the Swissair Web site, so he knows a thing or two about how the travel industry uses the

Internet to exchange flight information and book seats. As Mark explains, the travel industry has always been a leader when it comes to using information technology, so it was no surprise when it became one of the first industries to use the Internet to exchange travel information. One of the first major online initiatives occurred more than 13 years ago: The EasySabre tool was created by Sabre (formerly a division of American Airlines) as a simple online extension of a computer reservation system (CRS) used by professional travel agencies.

Before the advent of EasySabre, airlines and travel agencies could only use a CRS by having a terminal connected to a nonpublic computer network. These terminals were used by the airlines, which in turn rented the terminals to travel agencies to provide agents with direct access to airline seating availability and flight schedules.

Although EasySabre provided more people access to information, it was difficult to use because it only provided a system for text-based interactions. For example, in order to book a flight from Chicago to Orlando on June 15 at 7:30 a.m., travel agents had to type in ORD,ORL,15JUN,730A. In most cases, it took a training class and a couple months on the system for agents to become proficient at using the system. And although EasySabre provided instructions for using this text-based system, it just wasn't user friendly, so it was phased out and replaced by the more easy-to-use systems we have today like Expedia and Travelocity.

The Travel Information System Grows Up

EasySabre provided a more convenient way for John Q. Public to book flights directly on the CRSs. Then, the next generation of travel Web sites, accessible by everyday airline customers, were built to use the full capabilities of the Internet and Web browsers to create graphical, user-friendly screens that users could easily use to search for and book travel. Two of the big names in this revolution were Travelocity (`www.travelocity.com`), built by Sabre, and Microsoft's Expedia (`www.expedia.com`), which uses the Worldspan CRS. These sites provide pictures, easy-to-read schedules, and advice for booking travel. They remain two of the most popular travel destinations on the Web today, and I'll talk more about them throughout the book. .

Behind today's cool, user-friendly travel Web sites is the same old CRS that uses text-based commands like ORD, ORL, 16JUN, and 730A. We just don't have to figure it out to make the online systems work for us. After Expedia and Travelocity developed their new systems, many new travel-booking Web sites emerged. Most airlines have their own Web sites that customers use to book their own flights, and other Web sites bring all the airlines together for quick, convenient one-stop shopping. Some sites even help users find the cheapest flight, or find flights based on how much money the person wants to spend. Some of the more popular one-stop airfare Web sites are the Internet Travel Network (`www.itn.com`) and Cheap Tickets (`www.cheaptickets.com`).

But it doesn't end there. Smaller travel agencies are using the Internet to research and book travel for their customers. These booking tools, while once costly and available only to large companies, are now available to all travel agencies. And because the costs have gone down over the years, today we have more competitive rates and an increased number of types of free travel-planning services on the Web.

This is good news for those of us who like to dig in and research our vacations and destinations or find a professional travel agent who specializes in California Boar Hunting expeditions. Somewhere among the thousands and thousands of travel Web sites, you'll most likely find the help you need to plan and book your travel.

FuzzyLu's Internet Playpen Ain't Just for Babies

You might not become a full-blown Web guru at FuzzyLu's Internet Playpen, but you will find lots of easy-to-understand tips and techniques to get started on the Web. A playful and funny beginner's site to visit, FuzzyLu's Playpen is for people who want to know a little something about the Web without having to feel like a complete idiot. It'll help you learn how to use your browser, bookmark pages (which is a good way to keep track of all the cool travel sites you'll want to come back to again and again), and find out how the Internet and Web started. There's even a cool diagram of the anatomy of a URL (or Web site address). You can begin your learning adventure at `www.fuzzylu.com/docs/home1.htm`.

Web Sites, Books, and Resources for Beginners

Even though all these travel-planning tools are out there on the Web, if you don't know how to use the Web, you'll have a tough time finding them. But don't despair if you feel like you've got some catching up to do to get up to speed with the information revolution. There are lots of online learning centers, a variety of books and other resources for helping "newbies" to the Net find their way around:

Newbie.net Cyber Course (`www.newbie.net`) A good starting point for newcomers to the Web.

Yahoo! How to (`howto.yahoo.com`) A tutorial covering the best online directory, Yahoo!, to help you learn your way around Yahoo! and the Web in general.

Web 101 (`www.hotwired.com/webmonkey/web101/`) From the Webmonkey folks; a fun, easy-to-follow guide to finding your way around the Web.

Books *The Complete Idiot's Guide to the Internet, Sixth Edition,* and *Sams' Teach Yourself the Internet in 24 Hours, Second Edition,* are good resources, both available at bookstores and online at `www.mcp.com/catalog`.

America Online (AOL) (`www.aol.com/nethelp/home.html`)   Another good place to start and a good, all-around resource for users at all levels.

Internet service providers   Many ISPs provide some "getting started" help to their members, and you can find this at the ISPs home page. You may even be able to sign up for a class or lesson through your ISP.

Libraries and clubs   Community colleges, libraries, AARP, clubs, and computer user groups often hold short training sessions for new Web users. A good place to start gathering information about Internet classes in your area is the local library or chamber of commerce.

The Least You Need to Know

➤   The way we research, plan, and buy travel has been revolutionized by the World Wide Web.

➤   The Internet provides lots of tools to help plan travel. The Web, email, newsgroups, chat rooms, emailing lists, and traveler's forums are good tools to help gather information about destinations or connect with people who share your interests.

➤   You can find resources to learn more about the Web on the Web, at your local library, and in books that explain how to use the World Wide Web.

Chapter 2

Browsers 101

> ## In This Chapter
>
> ➤ Pick a browser and stick with it!
>
> ➤ Who's Earl and what's a URL?
>
> ➤ How to use bookmarks and favorites to organize your travel planning and Web searching
>
> ➤ Prime your browser for action-packed surfing

A browser is a software application that allows you to view Web documents that are downloaded from Internet servers. If you're one of the bazillions of Americans who has bought a computer with Windows on it in the past few years, you already have a browser installed on your computer—Microsoft's Internet Explorer. Or if you got software from your Internet service provider, you probably got a version of Netscape Navigator when you signed up. Or if you're an AOL user, you have AOL's own browser.

Because browsers are like children (they grow up fast and get a lot smarter as the years go by), this chapter covers just the basics on getting your browser ready for travel surfing on the Internet. This chapter also includes ideas on how to organize your favorite sites and bookmark them to make your online trip planning a more enjoyable experience. Especially if you've decided to become your own travel agent, it's a good idea to set up a system for keeping track of all the great Web sites you'll find when you go online to do destination research, locate traveler tools, and set up member accounts at the online booking sites.

If you're using recent versions of Internet Explorer or Netscape Navigator, you probably already have all the plug-ins you'll need to take virtual video tours or hear sound files. But if you need help doing these techie things, there's plenty of support available: The information is conveniently located on your browser menu bar and at Web sites that are set up to help Web users get up to snuff on the tricks and tools of the Web. I'll tell you about those in a bit.

What Browser Should You Use?

That's a tough question to answer, but you do have choices when it comes to deciding which browser to use. If you use a PC that runs on Windows, it's probably easiest to use Internet Explorer. It's already installed, and all you have to do is click the icon, and you've fired up your browser. If you use a Macintosh, the choice is wide open.

I don't think it makes much difference which browser you use. The features and capabilities are upgraded so quickly, it would be useless to say which one is better. It simply comes down to a matter of personal preference. So, sorry, I'm not going to recommend one over the other, and you may encounter problems online if you use one exclusively over the other. For example, if you visit a site that uses Java programming, you might run into problems with Internet Explorer. If you go to Microsoft Expedia's Mungo Park (**www.mungopark.com**) and try to take a video tour using Netscape, you might run into problems.

I have both Navigator and Explorer on my machine and ready to go at any time. Some days I feel like Internet Explorer, but most days I use Netscape Navigator because I started out many, many years ago using Netscape, and I'm a sentimental gal. If you have the computer memory to have them both, go right ahead, but if you bookmark a lot of sites, it's probably best to use just one so that you're not always forgetting where you were when you bookmarked a certain site. But the moral of the story is, either one is fine, but you'll need to get to know your browser, and that's easy to do online.

Getting to Know Your Browser

Believe it or not, there are other browsers besides Microsoft's Internet Explorer (IE) and Netscape's Navigator. But because these two are the most popular and up-to-date, it's a good idea to stick with one or the other for general Web surfing. The competition between Netscape and Microsoft is so fierce that they're constantly pouring money and time into the development and improvement of their browsers. Version 3.0 or later of either one should work just fine for most of your online sessions.

Now let's talk about some of the standard features and tools you'll find on your browser.

Choosing Your Own Home Page

If you find yourself visiting the same Web site every time you log on, maybe you should make it your starting page, or home page. This is easy to do in IE and Navigator. Just go into the Preferences or Internet Options menu and enter the Web address (or uniform resource locator, abbreviated URL and pronounced "Earl") of the page you want to start each online session with. For example, my home page is ABC News, so I entered `http://www.abcnews.com` to launch each time I go online.

Speaking of URLs, you'll notice throughout this book that Web site addresses are generally listed as *www.companyname.com* rather than *http://www.companyname.com*. The reason the *http* isn't included is because most browsers don't require it to understand what you mean. Any Web addresses listed in this book, though, that include http:// may or may not require an http, so I included it just in case. In any event, if you have trouble accessing a site without typing http, try both ways before you throw in the towel. If *www.companyname.com* doesn't work, try again including http.

Making Your Favorite Travel Site Your Starting Page

You can choose any Web site as your home page to download every time you launch your Web browser. But if you're planning a trip to Ireland, for example, you could make The Irish Times your home page so you can read the day's news first thing when you go online. Or say you want to stay up-to-date on travel news—you could make CNN Travel your home page. It's up to you!

Icons and Status Bars

In the top of your browser window, you'll either see the Netscape logo or the IE logo. If you see shooting stars or revolving whirls, that means you're retrieving data from the server. At the bottom of the browser window you'll see a status bar, which lets you know the address of the site you're contacting and the size of the files you're requesting. If you're downloading a big image file, you can either wait for the file to download, or you can click the **Stop** button and turn off the **Auto Load Images** option. Your choice probably depends on what the image is. If it's a picture of a little street in Lisbon you want to visit on your trip, it might be best to wait. If it's a company's logo, you probably want to forget it. (If I see a file size above 75KB, I think twice about waiting for the file to download.)

The Location button tells the URL of the site you're currently visiting. The page title appears at the very top of the page (for example, Netscape: Welcome to GroupTravel.net!), and is what appears in your bookmarks or favorites folder if you add it to the list.

Toolbar Tools

There are more similarities than differences between IE and Navigator. Many of the features on the toolbar that appears at the top of the browser window are the same in both browsers:

➤ The Back button lets you click back to the previous page.

➤ The Forward button takes you back to the page you started on after you've clicked the **Back** button.

➤ The Home button takes you to your start page (in my case, Yahoo!).

➤ The Reload button (in Navigator) or the Refresh button (in IE) loads the Web page again. It is particularly useful if the page contains updated information such as weather, news, or rate information. It can also be used if a transfer is interrupted or all the images don't download properly.

➤ The Go pull-down menu is a running list of the Web sites you've visited during that online session. If you get lost, this is a good way to get back where you started.

➤ The Print button lets you print the page you're looking at. It's important to note that if you're at a Web site that is built with frames (or panes), and you want to print out the frame with the text, you need to open a new browser window. To do this, just put your cursor inside the window you want to print, hold down the right button (or click once on the Mac), and you'll have the option to go back or open a new window.

➤ Last but not least, the **Stop** button stops the file from downloading.

Fodor's Web site, like many others, is built in frames (panes), so if you want to print text, you need to open a new browser window, as shown this figure.

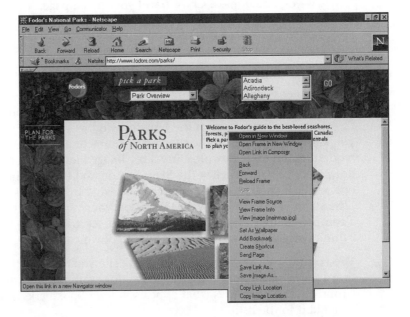

Buttons that are unique to Navigator include the following:

➤ The Images button lets you quickly access the option to turn off images and keep them from downloading, or to turn them on. If you're just looking for text-only information, turning off images can sometimes save time. Many Web pages don't have text-based navigation tools, though, so you might need to see graphics to find your way around the site.

➤ The Find button lets you search for a specific word in a Web document.

➤ The Open button lets you open a file on your computer's hard drive.

➤ The Bookmarks button leads to a collection of your favorite Web sites.

Buttons that are unique to IE include the following:

➤ The Search button takes you to Microsoft's Web site, from which you can quickly access directories and travel categories.

➤ The Favorites button is just like Navigator's Bookmarks button. It's an address book for your frequently visited or favorite Web sites.

➤ In IE, you can also click the **History** button to trace your online activity by date. That's cool!

➤ Finally, clicking the **Font** button increases or decreases the appearance of the text on your screen.

Getting to Know Netscape Navigator

To learn more about how Netscape Navigator works, go to the **Help** menu at the top of the screen. Choose **Help Contents**, and then click **Browsing the Web**. This is the best place to learn the ins and outs of your browser. It walks you through the basics of the Internet, how to search and find, what a link is, what a URL is, what bookmarks are for, how to change your preferences, what the security function is, and much more. You'll find everything you need to know about Netscape. Because the browser features are constantly being updated, it's best to go straight to the source for the latest features and tools available through Netscape.

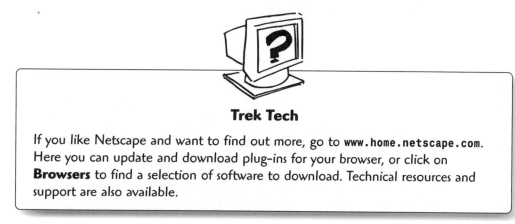

Trek Tech

If you like Netscape and want to find out more, go to www.home.netscape.com. Here you can update and download plug-ins for your browser, or click on **Browsers** to find a selection of software to download. Technical resources and support are also available.

Netscape's Navigator is one the most popular browsers. You can customize the appearance of the Browser toolbar to suit your tastes and surfing habits.

Getting to Know Microsoft Internet Explorer

To learn more about how to use Internet Explorer, go to the **Help** menu. Choose **Internet Explorer Help**, and a box will appear that explains the features of the browser. Learn what the new features of your version are, how to explore the Web, how to mark and retrieve your favorite pages, how to search, what you need to do to save and print, how to change your preferences, and what tips and tricks can save you time and make your surfing more fun. Also, there's a glossary with definitions and examples of tech terms. The help section is thorough and is a good place to start if you don't know much about browsers.

If you want to learn more about Microsoft Internet Explorer, go to **www.microsoft.com**. If you want to update your browser, click **Downloads**, and then choose **MSN Products**. Here you'll be able to download the latest version of Internet Explorer for your use—for free! Netscape offers free upgrades to its browsers, too. To get the most recent version, visit **www.home.netscape.com**.

Wanna Know More?

Here are some places to find tips and tech support for Netscape or IE:

➤ Browser News at **www.browserwatch.internet.com** provides information about browsers, plug-ins, and ActiveX controls. Choose **Browser Boulevard** and the type of computer you use (or platform, like Windows or Macintosh), and you'll find a list of browsers to choose from. Each browser then has a link that you can click to find out more.

➤ *The Complete Idiot's Guide to the Internet, Sixth Edition*. It's available in bookstores or online at Macmillan's Web site at **www.mcp.com/catalog**.

Microsoft's Internet Explorer History feature tracks online activity and favorites by date, which is a cool feature if you can't remember what you do from day to day.

Packing Your Browser Bag for Travel Surfing

Knowing how to organize your favorite travel Web sites when you're doing online research can save time and make finding things later on easier. This section shows you how to get your Favorites or Bookmarks folders ready for online travel research and how to keep things organized as you go about your online travel planning and research. You'll also learn about plug-ins, cookies, and how to download audio and video files for an interactive and exciting online experience.

Get Those Bookmarks and Favorites in Order!

There are lots of interesting travel sites on the Web, and you could spend hours and hours and hours visiting them all and then trying to get back to the ones you especially like. But most of us don't have an endless amount of online time. Something you can do to find sites you want to revisit is make use of your browser's *Favorites* tool (Internet Explorer) or *Bookmarks* tool (Navigator) to organize your list of favorite sites. I'm going to use Internet Explorer as the example to explain this process, but it's nearly identical to the process you use in Navigator. (If you need a little extra help setting up your Bookmarks in Navigator, click the **Help** menu and select **Browsing the Web**. You'll find a thorough and easy-to-understand explanation of how to organize your bookmarks.)

Whatever you do, don't let your Bookmarks file end up like mine was when I first started surfin' the Net.... It contained about 200 links to sites dealing with all kinds of unrelated topics, and if the page name wasn't clearly labeled, I had no idea what the site was or why I'd bookmarked it. And keep in mind that one of the reasons you're going online to do your travel research and planning is to save time and become a smarter traveler, so it pays to be smart about your browsing habits.

21

The Favorites feature is designed to save your favorite Web site addresses so you don't have to remember them all. Basically, it's a menu that you can add and delete links from as you go about your research and planning. The first thing to do when you start your online travel research is think about what kind of information you're looking for. Depending on what stage you're at in the planning process, you may want to create topic folders for each subject you plan to research. You can do this by clicking the **Favorites** menu, **Add to Favorites**, and the **New Folder** button, and then typing a name for the new folder.

For example, some of the travel site folder names I have in my Favorites list are Hotels and Lodging, The Big Boys (for xxx), which includes airfare compare sites and multi-purpose travel sites, Campgrounds, My Trip to Ireland, Travel Tools (which includes links to currency converters, weather reports, maps, and so on), Destination Guides (like Fodors, Lonely Planet, Rough Guide), E-Zines (travel magazines), Airlines, and Cruise Finder. You get the idea, don't you?

I have folders in my Favorites menu organized by travel topics so I can stay on track when I go online to do research. I occasionally move URLs into the proper folders—before I get too many to remember what each one is for!

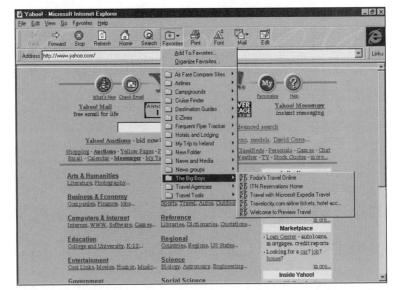

Let's say you've found Fodor's Web site (**www.fodors.com**) and you want to save it in your Favorites list because it's full of useful information and links to tons of travel sites, and you know you'll refer to it often. You can use a keyboard shortcut (Shift+A in Windows and Apple+D on a Mac) to add the address to your Favorites menu, or you can select the **Favorites** pull-down menu, and then click **Add to Favorites**. The Add Favorites dialog box appears and gives you the option to name the URL. Notice in the top of your browser bar that there's a page title; this will automatically be saved as the name of the Web page you're saving. But say the page title doesn't describe the contents of the page. Maybe it's named FAQs, but doesn't say what Web site the FAQs belong to. All you have to do is change it to something that's easier to remember, and then click **OK** to save the page, descriptive title and all, to your Favorites.

Bookmarking Before You Visit

You don't even have to visit a Web site to add it to your Favorites or Bookmark folder. Say you're at Fodor's Resource Center and you're reading descriptions of the sites and the links to those pages, but you don't have time or don't need to visit every link listed (like the weather site, the currency converter site, and mapping site). Just move your mouse over the link, right-click, and then choose **Add Favorite** from the pop-up menu.

That's one of the great things about the Web: When you find a valuable resource like Fodor's, a lot of the research legwork has already been done for you. Why the heck should you go out and try to find the best of the best Web sites when someone else has already done it for you? In fact, I recommend bookmarking link pages and directories rather than, for example, bookmarking the URL of each airline. If you can go to one site and use that as a jumping-off point, you can save the time it would take to find and manage a long list of links.

Organizing AOL Favorite Places

Whether you search the Web for travel information or stay in the AOL Travel section, you'll want to make use of your Favorite Places to stay on top of all the great travel sites online. To create Favorite Places folders, click the **Favorites** icon (or the folder with the heart) on the toolbar, and click **Favorite Places** in the drop-down menu. Your Favorite Places list opens up, and then you click the **New** button. Then click the **New Folder** button, type a name for the folder, and click **OK**. A new folder is created, and you then click each item and drag it into the appropriate folder.

If you want to modify your Favorite Places, click the **Favorites** icon (or the folder with the heart) and click **Favorite Places** to see the drop-down menu. Click to highlight the item you want to change, and then click **Edit**. Type the new name or address, and then click **OK**.

Throughout an online session you can save as many favorites as you want. Just remember to take a minute to organize Favorites into the topic folders you've set up. There's even an Organize Favorites dialog that has all the tools you need to do this: create folders, rename folders, move to folders, and delete. (Taking advantage of this dialog will save time later on—trust me!) Next time you log on and want to resume your travel planning, just click on the **Favorites** menu, and a list of submenus will appear. Just drag your mouse to the Web site you want to revisit, click, and there you are—right back where you wanted to be. And remember that any time you need help, you can just click on the question mark icon or the **Help** button.

Taking Bookmarks and Cookies with You

What if you're using an older version of IE or Navigator and you're ready to take the leap to download the updated version. What about all the work you did, though, researching your trip to Ireland, carefully setting up bookmark or favorite folders and keeping your Web addresses in a neat and organized fashion? Won't it all be lost when you download the new version? Absolutely not. In fact, all your preferences and settings will automatically be transferred to the new version.

Even if you switch from Navigator to IE (version 5 and higher), your bookmarks and cookies will be transferred. The Import/Export Wizard is one of the new features in IE 5, and it's used to import existing Navigator bookmarks or cookies to Favorites.

Plug 'Em In and Watch 'Em Go

Yet another goofy Internet term plug-in. It's an add-on piece of software that you plug in to extend your browser's capabilities (such as watching videos or hearing sound). Many plug-ins are compatible between Netscape and Microsoft, but some won't run on both. For the most part, though, you'll be able to view multimedia files without really having to worry about those specific plug-ins.

If you're using the 4.0 version or higher of IE or Netscape, it's likely you've already got the plug-ins plugged in to view videos and animation, or hear sound files. But if you're working with version 3.0 of IE or Netscape, you'll need to do some tooling to get the plug-ins installed and running. First, look to see if you have a folder on your computer for downloading files from the Web: This type of folder is usually in the `C:\temp` directory. If not, create one and be sure to go back and delete the files and folders once you've installed the plug-in, as the folder can get pretty big if you download a lot of software.

If you're running an older version of IE or Navigator, you might need additional help installing plug-ins. For help or more information on plug-ins, check out these online tutorials:

➤ You can get a good tutorial on what plug-ins are, why you want them, and how to use them from **www.learnthenet.com/english/html/56plugins.htm**. This site also describes several plug-ins and directs you to the links to download them and how to install them.

➤ Internet.com's Browser News has an extensive list of plug-ins at **www.browserwatch. internet.com/plug-in.html**. You can look through a long list of plug-ins or browse by category (such as multimedia, graphics, sound, or document). You can also search through plug-ins by platform, such as Windows or Macintosh. This site has plug-ins for everything you need, complete with instructions on downloading and using them.

Looking for a Virtual Video Tour?

If you want to get in a little practice using multimedia features of the Web and downloading plug-ins, be sure to stop by Preview Travel's Destination Guide Virtual Video Gallery at **www.previewtravel.com**. Just enter the Destination Guides section and click the video gallery icon for more than 100 tours of cities in Europe, the United States, the Caribbean, Canada, Mexico, Central and South America, Asia, Africa/Middle East, and the South Pacific.

Netscape Navigator Plug-Ins

Navigator plug-ins have to be downloaded and installed. If you get to a Web page with a sound or video file that requires a plug-in to be viewed or heard, a message box will say to download the plug-in. Just click the **Get Plug-in** button, and you'll be taken to the Web site of the maker of the plug-in (for example, Shockwave or Real Audio). You'll be told how to download it to your computer. It's actually much easier than it sounds, and the most grueling part can be waiting for the file to download. If your Internet connection is slow or the file is large, it can take awhile for the data to make it across the wires to your desktop. Remember that patience is a virtue and good things come to those who wait and all those other clichés.

After you've downloaded the plug-in file to an empty temporary directory, you need to install it. Close all running applications on your computer and double-click the icon to install it. Oftentimes, the installation is automatic, but sometimes you'll run into a file that needs to be decompressed before installation. But don't worry. Just look for an **install.exe** or a **setup.exe** file icon on your desktop, and double-click on that.

Internet Explorer Plug-Ins

Leave it to Microsoft to make using plug-ins easy. Most of the plug-ins people commonly need come with IE version 4.0 and up and are automatically installed to your hard drive when you install the browser. Also, Microsoft has developed a plug-in, ActiveX, that requires virtually no work on your part to download or install. If you use IE but don't have ActiveX, and you visit a Web page that has a file requiring the ActiveX plug-in, IE automatically installs it for you. When this happens, you get a warning message letting you know that a control is about to be installed. Voilà! The control installs and plays the file without you having to do a darned thing. Pretty simple, huh?

Cookies, Just the Way Grandma Makes 'Em

Cookies are tiny bits of data that a Web site sends to your hard drive. You'll get the full scoop on cookies in Chapter 6, "Before You Buy...Protecting Yourself Online," but since you have to do some work in your browser to manage cookies, I'll give you the quick 1-2-3 on how they relate to planning a trip online.

Web sites use cookies to identify you when you return. This is useful when you're required to register as a member or user to access the information, which is usually the case on travel booking sites and online storefronts. For example, if you visit Travelocity's Web site, you'll be asked to register in order to access airfare information or check out hotel availability. After you fill out the online registration form and choose a username and password, you can enter the site to compare fares or book your travel plans. At this time, Travelocity sends a cookie to your hard drive so that when you return, you don't have to register again. Also, if you use your credit card to pay for your travel services and supplies, you won't have to reenter that data next time you order something.

See Chapter 6 for more information on cookies and other online security and privacy issues.

Behold the Sights and Sounds of the Web

You can download RealAudio and RealVideo from RealNetworks at **www.real.com**. These programs allow you to listen to sound and view video on the Web, and although there are other multimedia plug-ins you can use for sound and video, you'll run into these the most. To download these programs, click the **Free RealPlayer G2 Download now** button. After doing that, you have a choice: You can download Realplayer G2 for free or you can download Realplayer Plus G2 for a fee. The Plus version includes controls for brightness and tint, adjustments for sharpness and contrast, a 10-band equalizer, built-in support for MP3, and free RealJukebox. I recommend the free version, because I'm a cheapskate and because it gets the job done. If you plan on using the Web to do a lot of destination previewing of videos and "guided tours," you may want to consider the enhanced version. Otherwise, you should be fine with the free plug-ins.

Download This: How to Print Travel Necessities

Printing maps, documents, itineraries, confirmations, directions, and other kinds of Web documents is a cinch. Just click the **Print** button on your browser toolbar or use a keyboard shortcut (Ctrl+P in Windows or Apple+P on a Mac), and in your document select **Print** or hit **Enter**. You can control many printing features, such as the orientation of the paper if you need longer, wider printouts instead of the standard tall orientation. For example, sometimes maps print better on a short, wide page. Just go into the print command, and select landscape or portrait orientation.

The Least You Need to Know

➤ You can download free versions of the most recent browsers for optimal Web surfing.

➤ You can use your browser to view Web documents, view videos, hear audio files, and organize your online travel–planning sessions.

➤ You can keep track of the addresses of your favorite Web sites by using the Bookmark or Favorites feature in your browser.

➤ You can print maps, itineraries, confirmations, and Web documents by using the Print button on your Browser toolbar.

Chapter 3

Search Engines 101

In This Chapter

➤ Get started on your online travel planning using search engines and Web directories

➤ Learn about the major search engines and some exciting up-and-comers

➤ Learn how to find hard-to-find information

When you go online to research travel, one of the first things you'll notice is that there are lots and lots of sites devoted to travel. To find specific information about your travel plans, you can use some cool Web tools called *search engines* and *Web directories* to find detailed information to help plan your trip. The first thing you'll want to do is become fast friends with at least one of these fabulous tools.

There are dozens of search engines and Web directories, and they each have their own peculiar techniques and tricks, although they operate on the same basic principle: You enter a keyword (or keywords), and the engine scours the Web and brings back documents that match what you're looking for. Or if you're using a Web directory, you find a general category on the topic you're looking for and click through subcategories until you find the exact topic you want to learn about.

Suppose you started a search with the keyword **travel**. I wouldn't recommend doing such a thing because the topic is so broad that you're going to get results of every document containing the word *travel*. Just for fun, and to prove my point, I went to Yahoo! and entered **travel** as my keyword. The results? 137 category matches, 19,542 site matches, and 5,169,645 Web pages. You think that's bad? I did the same thing at AltaVista and got 20,374,214 Web documents containing the word *travel*. Don't worry. In this chapter, I'll show you how to conduct effective searches, give you an overview of the features of the major search engines, introduce some up-and-coming engines, and even show you how using advanced search techniques can help you find even the hardest-to-find information.

Don't Get Lost on Your Online Travel Planning Adventure!

There's a lot of information on the Web, and it's very easy to get off track when you go searching for information. One of the cool things about planning your trip online is that you'll search and find a site on your travel topic that has links to other Web sites related to the travel topic you're looking for. So you start visiting all the linked pages, and you forget where you started!

Don't worry. Browsers keep track of pages you've visited so that if you need to backtrack, you can find a trail of visited Web sites in the **Go** pull-down menu of Netscape, and in the **History** tab in Internet Explorer. Internet Explorer even tracks your activity and saves it each day, so if you start searching on Sunday, but can't get back online until Wednesday, it's okay. You can use your History folder to find out where you were Sunday. Cool, isn't it?

The Top Search Engines and How They Work

There are search engines and then there are Web directories, and then there are search tools like Yahoo! that combine the features of both. Throughout this book, though, I use the term search engine to refer to any tool that uses keyword matching and other filtering devices to help you locate documents on the Web. In a nutshell, a search engine lets you search a database of Web pages, while a directory is a neatly categorized list of Web pages that you can click through to subcategories to find Web pages and Web sites related to the category you're looking in.

For example, when you look for travel information in Yahoo!, you'll find it under the primary category Recreation and Sports. Travel is a subcategory, and from there you'll find sub-subcategories of things like cruises, business travel, convention and visitors bureaus, family travel, lodging, travel magazines, and travel. From there, you can click any of the subcategories to get even more detailed listings for the type of travel you're looking for.

Letting Your Browser Do the Walking

You can also use the location box in your browser to initiate a search. In Netscape, just type in keywords, and the browser will automatically turn your search over to its selected search engine. In Internet Explorer, type **find** before the keywords in the location box (for example, **find national park directories**).

AltaVista, on the other hand, is a searchable database of millions and millions of Web pages. Type in the keywords **honeymoon specials**, and you'll get Web documents that contain the words *honeymoon* and *specials* (you might get information on furniture closeout specials, or the ska band The Specials), but not necessarily *honeymoon specials*. (I'll show you how to find the exact phrase you want in just a minute, though.) Another cool feature of AltaVista is that you can begin your search by asking a question: **Where can I find honeymoon specials?** Or better yet, you can ask **Where can I find honeymoon specials in the Caribbean?** to match with more detailed results.

Search engines and Web directories help you find information by letting you

➤ View a directory of categories, subcategories, and sub-subcategories.

➤ Search an index of subjects by typing in a keyword and clicking the **Search** button (or pressing Enter).

➤ Search an index of Web pages, as in AltaVista.

➤ Search regional directories, such as Yahoo! Chicago or Excite Italy.

The Skinny on Search Engines

Search engines and Web directories are in constant development, with new features, tools, and other bells and whistles added regularly. Besides search and directory functions, some engines provide free email accounts, email news reports, reminder services that send you an email when it's your mom's birthday or when it's time to mail your student loan payment. And as you'll read later in this chapter, new search engines with advanced features are popping up all the time.

At www.learnthenet.com you can take a virtual tour to learn how search engines work, plus find lots of other helpful information if you're new to the 'Net.

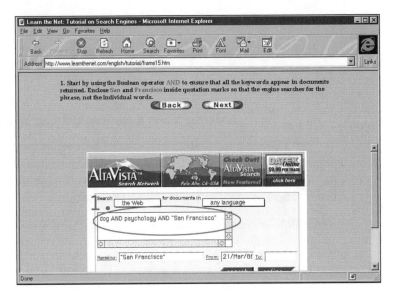

My advice to you, if you're new to doing research on the Web, is to pick one or two engines and get familiar with the techniques to make effective use of your time trying to hunt down information. Each search engine Web site's home page has a help section that will teach you the ins and outs of how to use it, plus tips on how to be a smarter "information detective."

This list of the more popular and easy-to-use engines and their URLs will help get you started with your travel research. Each site has links to travel related sites, so use the directory features or do a keyword search to find what you're looking for.

➤ **Yahoo!**   www.yahoo.com

➤ **InfoSeek**   www.infoseek.com

➤ **Lycos**   www.lycos.com

➤ **Excite**   www.excite.com

➤ **HotBot**   www.hotbot.com

➤ **AltaVista**   www.altavista.com

Can You Search the Web from AOL?

Online services such as AOL, Microsoft Network, Prodigy, and CompuServe (now part of AOL) are similar to private communities in that you have to be a member to access their content. Although you can get to the Web from an online service, you can't get to the private community/online service unless you're a member. And yes, you can search the Web from AOL—just use the AOL's NetFind search engine or Internet Explorer or Netscape if you prefer those browsers. And if you're looking for travel bargains, you can choose the link on the NetFind main page that goes to AOL's Time Savers Travel section. There you can sign up for email notifications of low airfare bargains, great cruise specials, and other great travel bargains.

AOL has a keyword search engine to search for documents only in AOL, and a Web search engine that lets you search for documents on the entire Web.

The New Generation of Search Engines

Younger, faster, smarter, more. These up-and-coming search engines can do some pretty fancy stuff. Just like the traditional search engines, take a few minutes to read the FAQs or help section of these search engines just to make sure you get the most out of your time researching online.

➤ **Looksmart (www.looksmart.com)** A rather large category-based Web directory created by editors whose sole job is to search for and index the best of the Web. Looksmart also goes to great lengths to make sure the sites it links to are pornography-free and family-friendly with good tips for parents.

➤ **Direct Hit (www.directhit.com)** Ranks search results based on popularity. Its computers watch search results in other search sites and studies which links users follow. It returns only site findings that have been popular with other users.

➤ **Ask Jeeves (www.askjeeves.com)** A fun search tool that lets you ask a question, and then supplies answers and multiple Web references based on the input of real-life editors who build a database of the most frequently asked questions and their answers. For fun, I asked Jeeves, **Why do birds sing?** and got answers (links) to Web sites on birds, singing, the album *Why Do Birds Sing?*, and news-groups dealing with birds.

Looking for Mr. Goodbar?

Not only can you find information and Web pages using search engines, you can also find people. Besides the people search features you'll find in most search engines, you can use **www.realwhitepages.com**, **www.bigfoot.com**, or People Finder at **www.peoplesite.com** to find Mr. Goodbar, an old boyfriend or girl-friend, or your third-grade teacher.

You should use the search engine you're most comfortable with, but sometimes depending on the kind of information you're looking for, some engines have more filtering tools to help you get better quality results. For example, HotBot provides pull-down menus you can use to limit your search; for example, you can search for documents created in the past three months, six months, year, and so on; for documents only in English; or for documents containing only images. But what do I know? Try them all on for size. I've been using Ask Jeeves quite a bit lately, just for the variety and quality of search results, and because I can ask it goofy questions like,

How much wood would a woodchuck chuck if a woodchuck could chuck wood? Are you dying to know what the answers were? Well, besides being matched with an encyclopedia article on woodchucks, I got this match: **How much Web would a Web browser browse, if a Web browser could browse Web?** It was an AOL member's personal page of tongue twisters. Touché, Mr. Jeeves.

Enter your keywords into the search boxes; then use the filter pull-down menus and check boxes to modify your search results.

HotBot lets you limit your search criteria by language, date created, and matching exact phrases, all the words, any of the words, page title, or links to the URL. Your results can include full-site descriptions or only URLs.

Getting the Inside Scoop

Even though I'll tell you more about newsgroups and other online communities in Chapter 5, "Online Travel Communities 101," because we're talking about searching for information on the Web, I'll mention here that you can also search for postings from fellow travelers in any of the hundreds of travel newsgroups. Go to **www.deja.com** and enter your travel topic in the search bar. You'll get a list of communities, discussions, and threads relating to your travel interest, and you can click through to see what people have to say. If you want to post a reply or your own question, you have to join the newsgroup, but that's easy to do, as you'll discover in Chapter 5. You can also go to **www.reference.com** to check out mailing lists, travel forums, and newsgroups.

Tips for Conducting Effective Searches

As I mentioned before, each search engine is a little bit different from the next, but luckily for you, help is available to teach you how to use each engine and get the most from your searching sessions. Just look for a help button or FAQs (which stands for frequently asked questions) button when you enter the search engine site.

A word to the wise: Read the instructions for the search engine you use—it'll save you time in the long run and help you find more detailed information to tailor your travel plans. And if you're trying to find hard-to-find information, the best thing is to familiarize yourself with the advanced search techniques of your search engine of choice.

Here are some general tips for getting more detailed search results:

➤ Try using multiple keywords, such as **family travel road trips**.

➤ Type a plus (+) between keywords so that you only get documents containing all the keywords together, rather than any document containing any of the keywords (for example, **senior + travel + discounts**).

➤ Put titles in quotes, like **"Road Trip USA"**, and proper names in capital letters, like **Positano**.

➤ Use *AND*, *OR*, or *NOT* between strings of words, like **Caribbean sailing AND charter OR lodging NOT hotels**.

➤ Unless you're looking for a proper name or title, use lowercase letters, like **family travel**. This search will also pull uppercase matches, but the opposite is not true. If you type in **Family Travel**, you won't get results unless the words appear in uppercase in the document.

At Web Tools, you can get lots of helpful information on how to search the Web. Visit www.thewebtools.com/ tutorial/tutorial.htm.

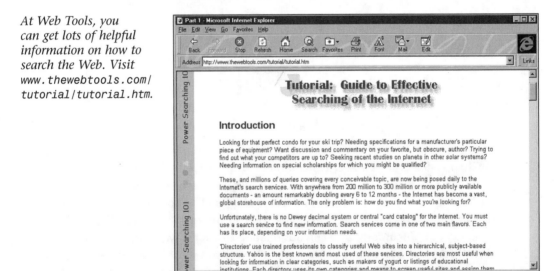

Keeping Track of Your Findings

Say you're looking for information on California boar hunting expeditions, and you start your search at Yahoo! by typing **California + boar + hunting** in the search box. This yields more results than you expected.

Instead of going to each site one at a time, you can bookmark the results page, or read through the site descriptions and pick the ones you want to visit later and add them to your favorites or bookmarks folder. You do this by holding your cursor over the hyperlink (the underlined, colored text that turns your cursor into a hand shape). Then just right-click and a dialog window will pop up, giving you the option to add to your favorites (in Internet Explorer) or add a bookmark for this link (in Netscape). Then, when you want to visit each site, just go into your **Favorites** menu or **Bookmark** menu, and all the sites you pegged as worthy of checking out will be there. Try to keep things organized using folders, as discussed in Chapter 3. And when you decide you don't want to go boar hunting after all, you can easily delete the folders!

The Least You Need to Know

➤ You use search engines and directories to locate Web documents and sites based on keyword or category searching.

➤ You can start a search with keywords or by browsing through directory categories.

➤ You can find people, tips from other travelers, telephone numbers, and specialty travel sites using search engines and directories.

➤ Advanced search techniques help you locate hard to find information, get better results, and save time.

Chapter 4

Traveler's Online Resources 101

In This Chapter

➤ Get up to speed on what's in the online travel information jackpot

➤ Whether you're looking or booking, find out what's available at online booking sites, one-stop-shopping sites, and travel auction Web sites

➤ Get a head start and save time using travel directories and search engines

➤ Get consumer opinions and tips and flip through online travel magazines

➤ Read reviews of travel software packages that bring trip-planning information and tools to your desktop

The online travel landscape is certainly a sight to behold. All the information you need to plan, pay for, and prepare for your trip is right there at your fingertips. How do you locate all these wonderful online resources? Easy. Read this chapter, and you'll soon discover that when it comes to travel Web sites (or any Web site, really), content is king. It's the first sign of a good Web site. Why? Think about it. Simply because it's so easy to gather complementary resources for its site visitors, a good Web marketer knows what it takes to draw an audience and keep it coming back. The Web is based on that principle—gathering information to make the site visit a worthwhile experience. And for you, the travel planner, that's good news.

This chapter introduces the most popular online travel resources and the top sites in each category. But keep in mind that it would be nearly impossible to catalog every travel site that's worthy of being catalogued. There are just too many. Most of these sites, though, have information beyond what you expect when you clicked the link to get there. You'll find links to other travel resources to help you plan your trip, and that's what makes going online to plan your trip such a refreshing experience.

What Travel Information Is Out There?

I'd like someone to tell me what travel information *isn't* out there. For an idea of the types and amount of travel resources available to the online community, just go to your favorite search engine or Web directory, and click the **Travel** category. You'll find online magazines, destination guides, mapping services and driving directions, tips on traveling with pets or kids, consumer support and advice, and traveler reviews of hotels, airlines, and activities. There's just so darned much information that it's tough to know where to begin. And depending on what stage of the planning process you're in, you may want to just jump in to book a flight or get hotel rate information. Whatever your information needs, chances are pretty good you'll find it online.

Most travel Web sites fall under one (or more) of the following categories, which are described in detail in this chapter:

➤ Online reservation systems

➤ One-stop-shopping

➤ Travel auctions

➤ Destination information and travel guides

If nothing else, you can do a quick search using the keywords that describe the type of information you're looking for.

Online Reservation Systems

If you remember in Chapter 1, I talked about the evolution of travel reservation systems and how they've been developed for use by the travel consumer and travel agent alike, and that it used to be that only travel agents and travel providers like airlines and hotels had access to global travel reservation systems. With the advent of online consumer booking sites, though, this information has been made available to the do-it-yourself type of traveler who wants to act as his or her own travel agent. Or if you simply want to compare rates and prices, this information is now available online to help you become a smart traveler. And that's a good thing, because nobody likes a dumb traveler!

If you're researching airfare information, of course you can always go directly to an airline's Web site, but if you want the option to compare rates or look for the best deals, it's best to use a system that has information for more than one airline. For tracking frequent flyer miles, or if you use one airline and one airline only, stick with the source. For a complete list of airline Web sites and more detail on these online booking sites, see Chapter 10, "Air Travel," or take a quick peek at the Airlines of the Web airline directory at **www.flyaow.com**.

The information and updates of flight schedules and hotel rooms all over the world are managed by global access, real-time, and online data systems. They are accessible to travel agencies, hotels, airlines, car rental agencies, and now even consumers.

Many online systems—including Sabre (the majority of which is ownership by American Airlines), WORLDSPAN (owned by affiliates of Delta Airlines, Northwest Airlines, and Trans World Airlines), Galileo (a European consortium of airlines and hotels), and Amadeus (a Global Distribution System (GDS) started by a group of European airlines)—are used to exchange reservation information. Now that travelers themselves have access to these systems, you can go online to preview availability, compare rates, and book your airline tickets and hotel room or other lodging yourself.

The Web's Most Popular Travel Web Sites

If a Web site is popular, does that mean it's good? Probably. But what qualities does a Web site need to have in order to be considered *good*? I look for quality and quantity of information. I look for content, as well as ease of use and navigation. I also prefer sites that aren't heavy on the advertising, but that's something you eventually just get used to (those pesky banner ads haven't always been around, you know). But one traveler's trash is another traveler's treasure, right?

For a hot list of the top 100 travel Web sites, be sure to check out 100 Hot at www.100hot.com to get a jump start on finding the most heavily trafficked sites. If other travelers think these sites are cool, won't you, too?

When you're hot, you're hot. You can get an up-to-date list of the hottest travel sites at www.100hot.com.

One-Stop-Shopping Sites

Although you can book a flight or hotel room at many online reservation sites like Expedia and Travelocity, they often collect and provide lots of other travel planning tools and information to help you plan your trip. From these one-stop sites, you can access destination information, currency converters, weather and map information, packing tips, travel reviews, articles, news, and plenty of other helpful links to get you started on your trip planning.

Don't Duplicate Your Efforts

Many travel companies on the Web partner with a single supplier of travel information, so it's possible for you to access the same information from several different sites. If you go to the American Express travel site, for example, you'll be using the same data source you'll find at the Expedia site, but in these partnering situations, you'll see logos and "powered by" statements on the home page.

Here's a quick list of the top one-stop-shopping sites, which are presented in no particular order:

➤ **Microsoft Expedia (www.expedia.com)** A site where you can book a flight or reserve a hotel room or a rental car. Easily one of the most popular all-around travel sites, Expedia connects you to the same information travel agents use to plan travel. It also gives you access to other useful travel information and is a good starting point. Expedia's real-time reservation system powers plenty of other travel sites, such as American Express Travel, so if you see the Expedia logo, you'll know that the information you're getting is the same as what you'd get at **www.expedia.com.**

➤ **Travelocity (www.travelocity.com)** A multipurpose travel site that can handle all your travel-planning and booking needs. The interface is similar to what you'll find at the other top online booking sites, plus plenty of travelers' resources are gathered to save you time. You'll find the Travelocity system at plenty of other travel-booking sites and search engines; if you see the Sabre logo on other travel sites, you'll know not to duplicate your efforts searching the same source for travel information.

➤ **The Trip (www.trip.com)** Powered by IntelliTrip, a reservation and fare-tracking system you'll find at other online travel ticket sites like Web Flyer (**www.webflyer.com**), which is a great system if you're a frequent traveler.

Another highlight of The Trip is the FlightTracker feature, which allows you to track, in real-time, the arrival and departure of a given flight. Say your mom is due in on the 3:00 from Tampa. You can check the arrival time and gate to make sure her flight is on time, and if the flight is running behind schedule, you can be notified via email when it lands. Cool.

➤ **Preview Travel (www.previewtravel.com)** The highlight of this online booking system is a feature you won't find on any of the other booking sites. Preview Travel's Farefinder collects fare information based on the airport of departure. It lists schedules and prices for every flight leaving a particular airport and lets you get fare information without also having to enter a destination or even a particular travel date. You can look for low fares up to three months in advance, and get a comparison of current prices compared to a three-month average, which makes it easy to locate rates that drop 5 percent below the three-month average. The Fare Alert service notifies you via email if the fare you want to pay is found, and gives the details on the restrictions and requirements. I'm planning a trip to Florida to visit my mom and I just got an email notice saying I could get a roundtrip ticket from Indianapolis to Tampa for less than $150, which is what I said I was willing to pay. I think I'll take that trip!

➤ **1travel.com (www.1travel.com)** Named *PC Computing*'s #1 Travel Bargain site in June 1999. This airline savings toolkit features airline news, expert advice, information on alternative airports, a drive-and-fly guide, a low-fare airline directory, information on pricing strategies, and a flight check that helps you find out whether a flight is on time. You'll also find extensive links to sites featuring information on travel activities, destinations, lodging, weather, yellow pages, currency exchange, and maps. You can also sign up for low-fare notification.

➤ **Airlines of the Web (www.flyaow.com)** A clearinghouse for airline information and a one-stop shop for air travelers. The first index of airline sites on the Web, the new version of Airlines of the Web was created as a joint effort between Internet Travel Network (**www.itn.net**) and Marc-David Seidel, the site's original creator. Airlines of the Web provides Seidel's extensive airline information and Internet Travel Network's complex online reservation systems for airlines, consumers, travel agencies, and corporations.

➤ **Internet Travel Network (www.itn.net)** This site has a quick and painless log-in process that takes you to Internet Travel Network's airfare selector wizard. You can get quick results and low fare results even if they're lower than what you tell the wizard you want to pay! You can also use this nice site to book hotel rooms and reserve rental cars.

If you're looking around for one booking site to meet all your needs, it's worth taking the time to visit more than one of these sites to find out which one is easiest for you to use and provides the most complete information based on your travel-planning and information needs. And remember that many of these Web sites are discussed throughout the book, so if you're using these sites to compare rates or get information, just refer to the chapter that covers the service you're looking for, be it airfare, hotels, car rentals, or destination information.

Go Ahead. Register. It's Easy.

If you plan on paying for your travel through a secure online booking system, you might as well go ahead and register as a user when you visit one of these sites. It's usually free to do, and you'll save time later on by not having to register every time you visit the site (see Chapter 2, "Browsers 101," to refresh your memory about cookies and why you need to set your browser to accept them). You'll also be able to establish an account history of your travel itineraries and purchases for record-keeping purposes. It's a sometimes tedious but painless process, so if you're sure you want to become your very own travel agent, take a few minutes to register. And if you're asked if you want to receive periodic emails on products or information of interest, beware that you're opening the flood gates for possible junk email.

Travel Auction Web Sites

Travel auction sites are a somewhat new development in the travel commerce industry, and more keep cropping up. There are different types of auctions. Some sites ask you to post the amount you're willing to pay for a room or air ticket and travel agents bid to win your business. Others work similarly to real-world auctions—buyers bid on offers made by the seller, and the highest bid wins.

One of the most heavily promoted online auction sites is Priceline at **www.priceline.com**, with the luminous William Shatner as your lovely spokesmodel. (I couldn't locate him anywhere on the site, so if you're going there looking for Captain Kirk, you won't find him.) The way Priceline works, in a nutshell, is that you name the price you want to pay for a flight or hotel room, and if a travel agent or travel supplier is willing to match your offer, you've bought the goods. You have to give your credit card information just to post your offer, and once it's posted and the price is met, there's no turning back. It's yours. Another possible drawback is that you don't know which airline you're flying on until the deal is done, and you're at the seller's mercy schedule-wise. You might have layovers in seemingly out-of-the-way cities, but you can get good deals, so you need to be sure you really want to buy it if someone can match your offer. And if you're taking out a second mortgage to pay for your vacation, you can get home refinancing through Priceline. Honestly, that kind of irks me, but who am I to say what Priceline can and cannot sell you?

Another contender in the online travel auction business is the Travel Bids discount auction at **www.travelbids.com**. Travel Bids is a reverse online auction. You enter your name, address, credit card number, a one-line description of your travel needs, the number of passengers, and how long you'll give the agents to respond. Then several different travel agencies bid on your vacation, and you get to pick the best trip. There's a $5 fee to use this service.

And then there's the most popular auction site on the Web, eBay, at **www.ebay.com**. I recently saw a listing for round-trip airfare for $12. You had to purchase hotel rooms from the seller, but even that price was reasonable. Most of the offers are posted by travel agents and tour operators, and the restrictions, guarantees, and other "fine print" is spelled out clearly, so be sure to read up on what you're getting before you place your bid. And as always, be skeptical of too-good-to-be-true deals. Keep in mind, too, that eBay can't screen every seller that posts items for sale on the auction. There are buyer reports and ratings of sellers, but even that information can be manipulated. In other words, do some follow-up before you send off your money, and don't ever give credit card information as payment, unless you are certain the item is being sold by an actual company or travel agency.

A new player in the online auction arena is Amazon.com (**www.amazon.com**), which is attempting to move beyond the title of World's Largest Bookstore to World's Largest Web Site. What will they think of next? Just click on the **Auctions** link, then **Other Goods and Services**, and then the **Travel** link to access this easy-to-use feature.

Amazon.com has travel items for sale in its online auction. Travelers can bid on tour packages, airfare, hotel rooms, and even luggage and other goods.

For more information on how to use online travel auction sites, the Help or FAQs section of each site should walk you through the process and explain the rules of the game. You should probably read this information even if you think the auction system is self-explanatory.

> ## The Inside Scoop on Discount Airfares, Delivered Straight to Your Inbox
>
> Airlines would rather sell a seat for a song than leave the seat empty. So, come the middle of the week, the airlines are scrambling to get warm bodies in unsold seats. This is good news for the spontaneous traveler, so if you're ready to take off with just a few days' notice, signing up for low-fare notification via your email account is a great way to get the inside scoop on deep discounts. Many of the regular booking sites and airline home pages offer such low-fare notification services. You just have to find them. See Chapter 10 for more information on airlines and low-fare notification services.

Destination Information and Travel Guidebooks

Chapter 8, "Using Destination Guides to Research and Plan Your Trip," is dedicated to travel Web sites that provide online destination information, so be sure to take a look if you've already answered the question of where to go. But even if you haven't yet decided where you want to go and you need ideas, one of the most complete destination guides on the Web has to be the Tourism Offices Worldwide Directory at **www.towd.com**, where you get a complete listing of official tourism sites around the world. The site promises no gimmicks, no travel agencies, no tour operators, and no unofficial sites. The links to the official tourism sites need a little tweaking, but otherwise, it's a darned good place to start.

City and regional information is another easy-access information source. From these types of sites you can often find out about entertainment, weather, restaurants, attractions, activities, special events, and a little bit of history to add a special touch to your visit. Some of the most popular city sites are City Search at **www.citysearch.com** and Kasbah's destination search feature at **www.kasbah.com**. I like the Travel Channel, too, which you can find at **www.travelchannel.com**.

Kasbah Gets a Five-Star Rating

One of the best places to start your online travel planning adventure is the Kasbah Travel Search Engine and Directory at **www.kasbah.com**. You can use the site to locate just about any kind of travel site using the search tools, or browse through the directory categories that include listings for online reservation sites for flights, hotels and other lodging, car rentals, business travel, last-minute travel, cruises, budget travel, and B&Bs. Or if you're interested in activity travel, Kasbah can help you locate winter sports, golf, adventure, scuba diving, eco-travel, and outdoor travel sources. Kasbah also has links to currency converters, maps, weather, health information, ATM locators, and travel advisories.

If you can't find your destination city in a destination guide, try your favorite search engine's regional directory and enter the name of your destination city (and state, to further filter your results) as the keywords. You're sure to find something using this powerful search engine and travel directory.

Directories of Travel Suppliers and Travel Agents

A quick stop online is the fastest and easiest way to gather contact information when you're looking around for travel agents or travel suppliers. And what better way to request information than through email? You can do this any time of the day or night, and you'll save on long distance charges. (Be sure to read Chapter 8 for the skinny on requesting literature and downloading brochures from the Web.) You'll also find directory references throughout the book, so if you're looking for a list of B&Bs in New England, be sure to read Chapter 15, "Alternative Lodging: B&Bs, Hostels, Furnished Rentals, and Campgrounds." If you're looking for a directory of airlines, see Chapter 10, "Air Travel." Chapter 7, "So, You Want to Be Your Own Travel Agent?" also discusses in detail how to use general travel directories to begin your travel research or locate important information.

If you have specialty travel plans in mind and you can't find an agency in your area to help with the details of your itinerary, you can easily use the Web to locate one that can help you with your trip-planning needs. It's a cinch to go online for listings of travel agencies in your area or anywhere in the world! You can find travel agents all over the Web, but it's a good idea to know the credentials of the agencies you're thinking about using. Regulatory associations make sure the member agencies play by the rules, which means you have less fact-checking to do. Try these sites, which feature directory listings of members and search tools to help you find an agency or agent in your area:

➤ **The American Society of Travel Agents**　`www.astanet.com`

➤ **Institute of Certified Travel Agents**　`www.icta.com`

➤ **American Express Travel Office Directory**　`www.americanexpress.com`
(Use the site map to locate the Travel Office Directory.)

➤ **International Airlines Travel Agent Network**　`www.iatan.org`

If the travel agency you're looking at hiring doesn't belong to at least one of these associations, you should think twice about handing your money to them. Another way to find out if the travel agency you're looking at is up-to-snuff with the tools and information available on the Web is to simply ask which travel Web sites the agency uses to help its customers plan better trips. If the person you ask doesn't know the names of Web sites or the Web addresses, that could be a bad sign. If they do mention their favorite travel sites, go check them out to see if the source is sound.

The American Society of Travel Agents lists members and contact information, including email and Web addresses.

Opinions, Reviews, and Consumer Tips

We all know that online information posted on commercial Web sites is probably not the complete picture of what you want to know about a place before you go. Even at official travel and tourism sites, you have to imagine that the sponsoring government that considers its country or city to be generally safe doesn't want you to know the nitty-gritty of crime statistics, disease, or traffic problems. They want you to come spend your money, so important information about safety and other travel concerns may not be made readily available. But you can read traveler reviews and opinions in newsgroups, message boards, chat rooms, online magazines, travelogues, and other online communities, or in the following Web sites, which are consumer-oriented and exist simply to help travelers avoid scams, raw deals, and other travel disasters:

➤ **Ticked-Off Traveler (www.ticked.com)** The writers at this site have a few things to say. And if you're unfortunate enough to be into the ticked-off traveler category or want to take steps to avoid problems or travel disasters, take a look at this candid and revealing source of travel advice. It contains information such as what countries to steer clear of and which airlines are notorious for providing lackluster service. You can also get the lowdown on the difference between a so-so hotel chain and a truly fantastic bed and breakfast. Read what these experts on travel are so ticked off about...you won't find any watered down stories to placate the Ticked.com advertisers because they don't accept ads from the travel suppliers they write about, and that's pretty cool, isn't it?

➤ **1000 Tips for Trips (www.tips4trips.com)** Are there really 1,000 tips at this site? I lost count after 645, but it wouldn't surprise me if there really are 1,000 tips for travelers. Get advice from real travelers on traveling with pets, tips for the disabled travelers, hints on traveling with children, packing tips, regional tips, safety ideas, and more.

➤ **Condé Nast Travel (www.travel.epicurious.com)** Has an awesome consumer help section. If you're looking for good advice or have a travel problem you can't solve, be sure to read the online version of the Perrin Report, by Condé Nast Traveler's consumer news editor, Wendy Perrin, who tackles the toughest travel questions. Or post a Question of the Week in the Ask Wendy Yourself forum. There's also a special Ombudsman section, which features Condé Nast Traveler's famous dispute-mediation service. Read about travel nightmares and how these problems get straightened out. The question-and-answer section has answers to real travel questions, taken from the pages of the printed version of the magazine.

Maps, Weather, Safety, and Language

Once again, the Internet comes through as the most cost-effective and efficient way to gather important information—this time on maps, weather, safety, and language. Imagine having to rely on news reports or radio or TV when planning your trips for up-to-the-minute weather, traffic, or safety information? Well, thanks to the Web, you don't have to go through the hassle. It's as easy as pie to go online and get essential travel information.

For point-to-point driving directions or door-to-door how-to-get-there info, check out these popular mapping sites:

➤ **Mapquest**   www.mapquest.com

➤ **Mapblast**   www.mapblast.com

➤ **Yahoo!'s mapping service**   maps.yahoo.com

➤ **Maps On Us**   www.mapsonus.com

You can also use CD-ROM mapping software, like DeLorme's Map'n'Go or Rand McNally's TripMaker, which I'll discuss later in the chapter. Or you can go to the Rand McNally site for your mapping needs.

For foreign language information, your best bet is to start at Travlang's site at **www.travlang.com**. Fodor's Resource Center also has links to useful language information. Visit **www.fodors.com/resource** for a jumping-off point to other language sites of interest. Also be sure to read Chapter 22, "Staying Connected: Locating Email and Internet Access Providers," for the scoop on international travel resources.

The weather conditions at your destination or along the way play a big part in the success of your trip. Although you can't control the weather, you can prepare for it. Be sure to check out Intellicast's real-time weather forecasts at **www.intellicast.com** before you hit the road. Most of the major booking sites and popular online traveler resources have direct links to weather sites, so you should have no trouble getting current conditions in your destination.

Having Trouble Printing a Web Page?

Say you stumble across some cool and valuable information and you go to print it out, only to discover that the only thing to print is the navigation tools on the left or right side of the page. The problem is that you're at a Web site built with *frames* (the navigation tools or frame contents are the same throughout the site), and you're only printing the frame page, rather than the content page. No problem—you just have to get rid of the frame. In Navigator, put your cursor inside the frame you want to print and hold down the mouse button. You'll see a dialog box that says Back, Forward, or New Window with This Frame. Select the **New Window with This Frame** option, and a new browser window opens up, showing just the contents. Now you can print the text from the new window! In Internet Explorer, you can do the same thing by right-clicking and selecting the **Open in New Window** option.

News and Reports

You can go online to get today's news about your destination or read about developments in the travel industry. What if there's a threat of a walk-out at the airline you're planning on using next week to get to Grandma's? There's so much news to report, it's impossible to find everything you want to know by reading a newspaper or magazine, or by watching the local or national news. But going online is a good way to stay on top of current events that could affect your travel plans. My favorite source for travel news is CNN Travel, at **www.cnn.com/TRAVEL**. *USA Today's* Travel section, at **www.usatoday.com**, is good, too. MSNBC has a great travel news section as well: Just go to **www.msnbc.com** and click on the Travel icon. For a complete list of online news sources, go to Yahoo!, which lists the Web addresses and site descriptions for TV, radio, and newspapers across the globe. Just click the **News and Media** link in the Travel category.

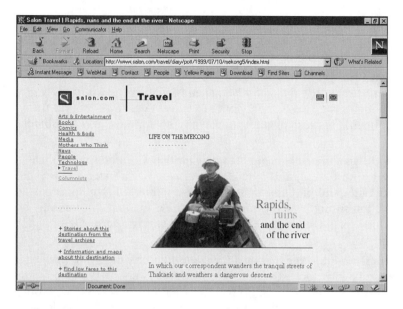

Salon.com's travel section features smart and well-written travelogues and destination reviews from writers like Rolf Potts.

Travel Magazines

I like online travel magazines (also known as *e-zines*), and I'm going to list some of my favorites here for you. Although they mostly contain destination information, I make a distinction between travel magazines and travel destination guides based on the writing style and the type and amount of information you'll find. Whereas travel magazines often focus on feature stories, a destination guide has archives of many, many city or country guides, and the information often originates from some type of official source, such as a tourism board or visitor's bureau.

Most major travel publications have wisely made the transition to online publishing of stories, reviews, tips, and everything else that usually appears in print publications. There are also online magazines that have sprouted up since the Web came to be. Either way you slice it, online magazines are excellent resources for helping you plan your trip. For a thorough listing of online travel magazines, see Yahoo!, go to the **Recreation** category, click **Travel**, and click **Magazines**. You'll get a list of more than 100 online travel publications. Here are some of my favorite travel magazines:

➤ **American Park Network** (**www.americanparknetwork.com**) From the publishers of visitor magazines for America's top national parks, this site has extensive resources for trip planning, park information, and even a link to Mapquest to provide driving directions from your door to the park of your choice.

51

➤ **Best Fares Magazine** (www.bestfares.com) Everybody likes a bargain, and if air travel is in the plans for your trip, be sure to check out this site—the definitive resource for air travel information and the latest scoop on deals, tips, tricks, and secret bargains the industry has to offer.

➤ **Condé Nast Traveler/Epicurious Travel** (www.travel.epicurious.com) Will you be reading the same articles and information that you find in the newsstand version? Not really, but you'll find more here than in the print version. You can get tips and advice or participate in online travel forums. There's also a direct link to Expedia, so if you're inclined to book a trip, you can do it all right here. As far as travel resources go, this is a good place to start.

➤ **Journey Woman** (www.journeywoman.com) Winner of Apex 1995, 1996, and 1998 Awards of Excellence, the quarterly is packed with exciting gal-friendly city sites, an international travel tips bazaar, women's travel tales from around the world, love stories, what to wear, and Journey Woman's online travel classifieds and links.

➤ **Leisure World Online** (www.ompc.com/leisureworld/) Connects you to feature articles, travel information, and advice from *Leisure World* magazine writers, plus lots of great stories and pictures. *Leisure World* is published five times per year for a half-million subscribers and members of the Canadian Automobile Association. Leisure World Online is published by the Ontario Motorist Publishing Company.

➤ **Mysterious World** (www.mysteriousworld.com) A quarterly online journal that explores ancient and exotic locales around the world. Mysterious World provides you with historical, archaeological, and travel information, as well as biographical information about famous people and artifacts related to the famous locales featured in this travel e-zine. Whether you're planning a dream trip to Egypt or looking for an interesting nearby destination for a simple day trip, Mysterious World covers it all.

➤ **National Geographic** (www.nationalgeographic.com) Nothing beats the print version of this popular and reputable source for exotic world travel destinations, and for travel-related articles and excerpts from the print magazine, and lots of other online travel tools, this site is a must read. The *National Geographic* site also has a cool cruise finder tool and many, many other travel tools to help you plan your trip.

➤ **Outpost Magazine** (www.outpostmagazine.com) Takes an adventurous and realistic look at the world and how people travel through it. At the Outpost site you get the good, the bad, and the ugly about travel, told in an honest, sometimes irreverent, tone.

These Monks Chant and Rant from the Road

As long as their cats Nurse and Nurse's Aid are on board, the Mad Monks will forge ahead on their path to success as roving and twisted road reporters—and you can watch them do it at www.monk.com. If I had a '72 Econoline van at my disposal, I might just follow suit and sell my every worldly possession—throw it all away for the glam, glory, and profit of this off-the-beaten path adventure across the United States. For alterna-reviews of San Francisco, Portland, Seattle, New York, Tahoe, and Los Angeles, take a peek at the Mad Monks' site.

Travel Software

You might be wondering why I'm including software in this book, when all the travel planning tools you need are online. Well, it may all be online, but it may not necessarily be located at one single Web site, and some people prefer a single-source solution for getting help with their travel planning. The software I'm talking about is neato torpedo: Randy McNally's TripMaker and DeLorme's AAA Map'n'Go 5.0. I've road-tested both of the following titles, and can't really say which one I like the best. It's darned good stuff, so you might want to check out the online demos and product information for each to put in your travel planning arsenal of tools—you can even order them online.

Rand McNally's TripMaker

TripMaker Deluxe 1999 Edition has an easy-to-use interface to help you plan the perfect vacation and print customized maps with detailed directions. It features information on weekend getaways and day trips to help you gather ideas for day trips, side trips, and weekend adventures, complete with driving directions, restaurant and lodging suggestions, and attraction recommendations. These vacation ideas, courtesy of the Rand McNally travel editors, are great for last-minute trips or to help make family vacations more fun.

If you own a PalmPilot or Palm III, you can download directions, itineraries, and address information so that this kind of information is always in a convenient place. TripMaker also has updated features, like Searchable Street-Level Detail, which lets you search for exact addresses, cross streets, and major points of interest in 82 cities. And it offers something no other trip planning software has: The RoadSense Intelligent Routing Wizard lets you create the optimal route based on road construction, seasonal road closures, and your personal preferences.

If you're traveling by RV, you can use the Commercial Campgrounds and RV Support Finder to get information on services and amenities available at thousands of commercial campgrounds and RV parks across the country.

TripMaker also provides thousands of hotel and restaurant listings along your route. If you need to find a good Italian restaurant in an unfamiliar city, the Mobile Travel Guide Information guide is there to help. For restaurant and lodging information based on location, amenities, price, cuisine, and the Mobile Travel Guide's One- to Five-Star Rating System, this guide has the answers. And the Searchable Exit Service Information Wizard lets you search for specific restaurants, lodging, fuel, hospitals, and other services available at exits along the U.S. Interstate Highway System. If this sounds like the kind of travel software for you, order online at **www.randmcnally.com** or visit any computer or bookstore that stocks software.

Map-Master Rand McNally Adds Worldwide Mapping and Other Cool Traveler Tools

www.randmcnally.com just keeps getting better. Besides the cool travel tips and mapping tools already available at their top-notch Web site, Rand McNally recently added some new and improved features, including an address-to-address driving direction tool that lets you enter two locations and create your very own map with turn-by-turn directions. Print out this easy-to-read map, and you're on your way.

Or say you want to measure distances between two points anywhere in the world. No problem. The world mapping feature works from a database of 1.5 million places and lets you view 3D maps of the world. Or you can download color maps of the U.S. states and thematic maps of the world. Still prefer old-fashioned maps? You can order them at the site. For ease of use and content, this site gets my stamp of approval! Check it out for yourself.

DeLorme's AAA Map'n'Go 5.0

You know if AAA puts its stamp of approval on this software, it's got to be good stuff. AAA Map'n'Go 5.0 is another easy-to-use trip-planning software package that brings all the travel information you need right to your desktop. The dashboard welcome screen is a great place to begin exploring the many features of the program, and if you get stuck, the easy-to-follow interactive tutorials help you discover the best ways to use the program.

A new feature in the 5.0 version is the Travel-Time Planner. Just enter the number of hours or miles you want to drive each day, and it automatically calculates where your stops will be along the way. Or say you want to preview your destination before you go (or when you get back, for that leisurely stroll down memory lane). Map'n'Go includes a multimedia display of more than 1,300 points of interest so you can get a sneak peak at the fun and interesting places to visit on your trip. And when you get back, you can use the Slide Show feature, which accepts images from digital cameras and digital photo-finishing services so you can save a slide show and email it to family and friends. It sure beats making them come over to your house to sit through hours and hours of slides while little Joe makes shadow bunnies across the screen.

Mac User? Too Bad, So Sad

I'm a Mac user, and I must admit I was saddened to discover that these super-cool travel planning software packages only run on Windows machines. (Lucky for me, though, I have access to a Windows PC, so I got to have all kinds of fun test-driving these software packages.) The folks at DeLorme tell me that if there's enough interest in a Mac version of the software, they'll try to find a Mac programmer to do the work.

Another cool feature is the Via Router, which helps you avoid urban areas of decay, like construction zones and travel zone nightmares. A simple right-click of the mouse tells the program to go around it. And if you have a laptop, you can use the Global Positioning System to track your whereabouts and progress in real-time. If you're a solo driver, you can click the spoken directions feature and let the computer do the talking. It even answers back, so go ahead and ask, "What is the meaning of life?" (just kiddin').

The Least You Need to Know

➤ The online travel landscape is full of free and valuable travel information and advice.

➤ Online travel magazines include destination and restaurant reviews, and often include links to related Web sites, making your online travel research a breeze.

➤ You can check out travel agencies and travel suppliers by visiting travel agency association Web sites for member listings, or to find a specialty agent to help with your unique travel plans.

➤ One-stop multipurpose travel sites include tools to book travel, compare rates, and gather important travel information.

➤ Trip-planning software brings technology to your desktop and is used with real-time reports from the Internet to help you plan your trips.

Chapter 5

Online Travel Communities 101

WELCOME! C'MON IN.

In This Chapter

➤ Get down-to-earth advice and travel tips from other travelers using newsgroups and message boards

➤ Meet other travelers through travel networks and get the scoop on the secret rites of initiation when you join a travel club (just kidding)

➤ DON'T SHOUT. Learn proper Netiquette for posting your questions or answers in newsgroups, chat rooms, and message boards

Going online is a great way to get up-to-the-minute information and meet people who can give you tips and advice on your travels. Besides visiting commercial Web sites to gather information and travel advice or request printed materials, you can learn from real travelers in online communities how to make your trip even more enjoyable and unique.

One of the coolest features of planning your travel online is using newsgroups, travel networks, mailing lists, and message boards to meet, swap information, share experiences, and get advice from other travelers. When you participate in online communities, you connect with travelers from around the world who can answer your specific questions, give you the inside scoop on off-the-beaten-path attractions, warn you about shoddy hotels or restaurants, and give you a real traveler's view on how to make the most of your travel adventures.

Introducing Newsgroups

A *newsgroup* is a virtual gathering place for people with shared interests to read and post both public and private messages on specific topics, such as European travel, women's travel, family travel, airlines, camping, RVing, and motorcycle road trips. There are thousands and thousands of newsgroups on any imaginable topic, but luckily for you, they're neatly categorized in one easy-to-use Web site, Deja.com (`www.deja.com`). Deja.com archives the daily discussions found in Usenet newsgroups and in various other forums.

In the Beginning, There Was Usenet

Usenet (which stands for *users' network*) is where newsgroups began. It is a distributed bulletin board system that began long before the World Wide Web came along. Today, it's the largest collection of message boards, discussion rooms, and newsgroups in operation. It's also available on non-Internet network systems.

Deja.com archives tens of thousands of newsgroup communities, forums, and discussions.

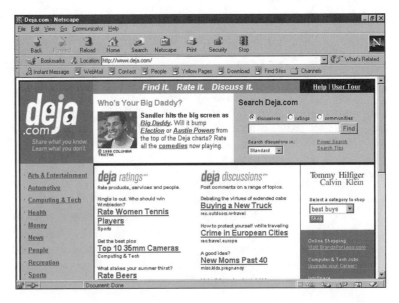

Your Internet service provider (ISP) might subscribe to newsgroups not available through Deja.com; you can find out by looking at your ISP's home page. If you see an icon that says something like News, Message Boards, or Forums, you're at the right place. Other Web sites, such as CNN, Yahoo!, MSNBC, and lots of other popular stopping points on the Web, also offer such links to newsgroups or have newsgroups and forums just for their site visitors.

To participate in a newsgroup, you use a *newsreader*, which is built in to Microsoft Internet Explorer, Netscape Navigator, and AOL. AOL users can access newsgroups only open to AOL users (called *message boards* on AOL), or they can head on over to Deja.com to connect with the newsgroups on the World Wide Web and Usenet groups.

Somebody's Posted a Reply, Somebody's Ringin' Your Bell!

One of the cool things about Deja.com is that you can post a question or message, and when someone replies to your post, you get an email from Deja.com that lets you know someone has responded. That way, you don't have to keep going back and checking for a response. You can also choose whether to put your email address on your posting so that people can reply to you personally, rather than just to the discussion board.

Getting Your Newsgroup Feet Wet

To help you learn more about how newsgroups work, Deja.com has put together a tutorial to guide you through the technology and terminology of newsgroups. Go to the Help section of the Deja.com Web site at **www.deja.com/help/help_index.shtml**, and you'll find everything you need to know about newsgroups. You can even take a guided tour of Deja.com to see exactly how it works and discover how you can use travel newsgroups to get the inside scoop from other travelers.

To get started, here are some commonly used newsgroup terms and helpful hints:

➤ *Channels* are the most popular topics and interests in Deja.com. Using channels, you can browse through discussions, ratings, and communities quickly to find the topic you're looking for. The main Deja.com channels are arts and entertainment (books, movies, music, TV), automotive (driving, maintenance, motorcycles, RVs), computing and technology (cameras, software, Internet services, audio and video equipment, computers and tech support), health (immunizations, allergies, nutrition), money (bonds, economy, currency exchange, stocks, employment), news (media, issues, world events), people (culture, kids and families, relationships, education), recreation (arts, hobbies, home, outdoors), sports (football, baseball, soccer), and travel (accommodations, destinations, transportation).

➤ *Cross-post* means you're posting a single message to several forums. If you're looking for tips on taking a European vacation, you might want to post a message in forums on world travel and miscellaneous travel.

➤ *Discussions*, also known as "conversations" or *threads*, are ongoing chains of messages on a single topic, and are useful in tracking multiple replies to messages or ongoing discussions on a particular topic.

➤ A *discussion forum* is an online gathering of people communicating with each other. Discussion forums include newsgroups, Usenet, and mailing lists.

➤ An *emoticon* (sometimes called a *smiley*) is a symbol you can use to indicate an emotional state in email or in a newsgroup. To read these emoticons, tilt your head to the left. : -) is a smiley face that indicates humor, laughter, friendliness, or sometimes sarcasm. : - (is a frowny face for sadness, anger, or being upset. ; -) is a half-smiley, a winky face, or a semi-smiley, and means only half-serious or ha-ha. : - / is a wry or ironic face and it means something like, "Have you always been so smart?"

➤ *FAQs* are lists of frequently asked or answered questions. You'll sometimes see FAQs in high-volume forums to discourage the same questions being posted over and over by new users. You'll also see the term *FAQs* on Web sites, and it generally functions in the same way by providing answers to common questions. It's a good place to start if you're visiting a site for the first time or need help figuring something out.

➤ *Flame* means to post a message intended to insult, offend, or provoke.

➤ A *followup* is a message generated in response to another message, and is broadcast for all to see. It differs from a *reply*, which goes through email to a single user.

➤ A *handle* is your online nickname, much like a CB radio handle, like Silver Bullet, in this friendly CB warning: "Hey there, Silver Bullet, you got a smokey comin' in your back door." Translated: "Excuse me, sir—you driving the orange 18-wheeler—there happens to be a state trooper approaching your vehicle from behind. You may want to slow down to avoid being issued a moving violation."

➤ *Netiquette* involves the conventions of politeness and courtesy used in discussion forums, like not plugging commercial sites or pushing a product unless it's in a business or new product forum. It also involves stylistic issues with the way you post your messages. For example, if you type in UPPERCASE LETTERS, IT'S CONSIDERED YELLING.

➤ A *newbie* is a beginner. If you haven't used a newsgroup before, you're a newbie. It's best to *lurk* for a bit and read the *FAQs*.

➤ *Post* means to broadcast a message to an entire forum.

➤ Besides being a tasty lunch "meat" item, *spam* refers to any unwanted message. It often refers to commercial postings in a newsgroup or messages of little or no interest to the topic of the forum. It also applies to junk email.

➤ Even if you don't want to post messages or reply to newsgroup postings, you can *lurk* to see what other people have to say. Oftentimes, you'll find the answer to your question or find information you weren't even looking for that can add a new twist or some insight to your travel plans. Lurking is recommended when you begin using newsgroups or chat rooms so you can get a feel for the style, tone, and personality of the other newsgroup members.

What the Heck Is rec.travel.misc?

Newsgroups are identified by a hierarchical naming system, with the first name being the top level. That's how you know what the topic of discussion is. The following parts of the name give the specifics of the newsgroup discussion. For example, **rec.outdoors.rv-travel** is a forum on recreation (rec), the outdoors (outdoor), and RV travel (rv-travel). The forum **rec.travel.caribbean** deals with recreation (rec), travel (travel), and the Caribbean (caribbean). Table 5.1 is a list of the most common newsgroup top levels:

Table 5.1 Newsgroup Naming System

Level	Description
comp	Topics include computer science, software sources, and information on hardware and software systems.
rec	Groups interested in hobbies and recreational activities.
sci	Discussions covering special knowledge of research in or application of the established sciences (but not astrology or science fiction, which you'll find under alt, misc, or soc).
soc	Groups that discuss social issues, socializing, and world cultures.
Talk	Long-winded discussions and debates with very little useful information. Talk about all the things your mom told you to keep your trap shut about around strangers, like politics, religion, or anything else controversial. To warm your hands by the flame (as it were), visit one of these discussions.
News	Groups concerned with the newsgroup network, group maintenance, and software.
Misc	Groups addressing themes that don't really fit into any of the other headings or that include themes from multiple categories. Subjects include fitness, job-hunting, law, and investments.
Alt	Alternative subjects that may be considered bizarre, inappropriate, or obscene.

Using Other Discussion Groups: Message Boards and Mailing Lists

As if the thousands of newsgroups in existence aren't enough to keep you busy, there are other online groups—mailing lists and message boards—you can use to gather travel information, make friends, get travelers' reviews, and get up-to-the-minute information to help plan your trip. Message boards are probably the most manageable, but there is a convenience factor involved with mailing lists—the information comes right to your email inbox, so you don't have to go check out replies to your message board posting. The difference between newsgroups, message boards, and mailing lists is the way in which messages are distributed. Newsgroups are distributed and accessible using a news-reader and a system set up specifically for their use; message boards are hosted on Web sites, and you post a note or question using a Web-based form; and mailing lists are distributed through email.

Reference.com makes it easy to find newsgroups, message boards, and other online communities.

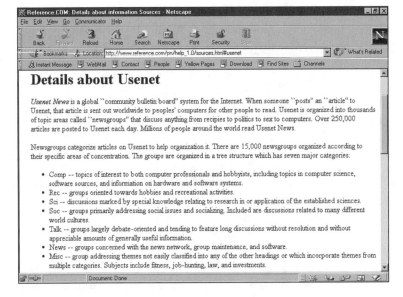

Get Help Using Online Communities at Reference.com

`www.reference.com` makes it easy to find, browse, search, and participate in more than 150,000 newsgroups, mailing lists, and Web forums. You can search for your topic of interest and find out how to locate and use the specific newsgroup, message board, or mailing list to become one of the 40 million users of online communities.

Should You Join a Travelers' Network?

Travelers' networks are meeting places for specialty travelers, women travelers, adventure travelers, Jewish travelers, backpackers, solo travelers, and many other special-interest travelers. The networks are set up so that members can enter personal profile and contact information into the member database, and then exchange emails (or letters or phone calls, although it makes sense to use the Internet to do this) with other members. Members hook up with like-minded travelers to share tips, get advice, offer a place to stay, or meet for coffee or dinner to share information about a particular destination or activity.

The member databases are usually monitored by the administrator of the network, and access to the personal information in the database is not made available until a membership application has been approved. Then, the first contact is usually made through email. Members aren't required to do anything beyond answer an email, although the point in joining a travelers' network is a willingness to help other travelers have a more unique, affordable, or meaningful travel experience.

Most of the travelers' networks are put together by real travelers—not by travel agencies or tour operators. You will find that some travel agencies refer to themselves as *travel networks*, and by definition, I suppose they are. But the *travelers' networks* that are set up by travelers aren't really trying to sell you anything. For that reason, there's usually an annual membership fee to help offset the costs of hosting and maintaining the Web site and the member database—usually between $10 and $50 a year.

You may even meet someone in one of these networks who's willing to let you camp out on their couch. Even though you need to exercise common sense when you make connections with strangers through travelers' networks or any other means, there's no harm in exchanging an email or two, or meeting for a cup of coffee or pint of beer. If you do decide to take someone up on an offer to let you stay at their place and want some added security, you should be able to contact the travelers' network administrator and ask for references from other people who have met and stayed with the person, just to be on the safe side.

So remember, when it comes to getting the inside scoop on your travel destination, nothing compares to advice that comes straight from the horse's mouth!

Membership Has Its Advantages

Chris Heidrich, a founding member of the BootsnAll.com (**www.bootsnall.com**) Travellers' Network knows from experience that membership has its privileges. His story goes something like this: "The last time I came to the U.S. from the U.K. via Canada, a U.S. Customs agent took exception to my perfectly legitimate visa and would not let me in. So, I was stuck in Vancouver, missing my connection to Seattle. I had never been to Vancouver before and had nowhere to stay. I called the BootsnAll headquarters and found out that a guy in Vancouver had signed up as a member just the day before. An hour later, I had a phone number and was able to get in touch with Ian. We met at a pub, had a few beers, and talked soccer. He thought I didn't look like the dangerous type and said I could crash at his place. In the following two days, Ian drove me to the airport a few times while I was battling U.S. Customs, let me get online, joined in my swearing sessions, and gave me beer. He was a great host, especially considering that he'd never met me before."

The BootsnAll.com Travellers' Network has three levels of membership, based on how you want to participate in the group.

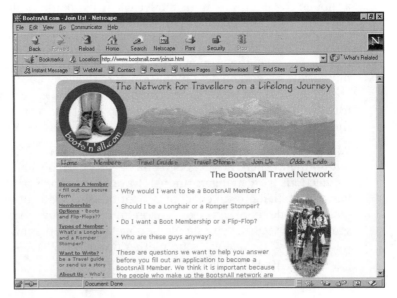

To get a glimpse of how travelers' networks operate and to find out what kinds of people belong to these groups, check out some of these cool travelers' networks. But remember, don't sign up for membership in any of the networks unless you match the member profile and are seriously interested in being an active member of the group:

➤ **Connecting...Solo Travel Network** (www.cstn.org) Offers tips and tales on singles tours, cruises, destinations, and activities that are designed for or are sensitive to the needs of people who travel alone. Here, solo travelers can network with an international member database of people who travel without a partner, or post an ad to find a companion traveler. Members can also read unbiased reports on travel options, travel companies, and lodging alternatives, and they can get tips from other solo travelers, like how to make friends on the road.

➤ **BootsnAll.com** (www.bootsnall.com) A network made up of folks who love traveling, learning, and meeting people from different cultures. In the password-protected Members Only section, members share email addresses and agree to be contacted by other members who may need advice or tips on coming to the member's area. There's no obligation to do more than just answer the email, and members can designate whether they're willing to offer a place to stay, meet for coffee to share insider knowledge, or give a guided tour of their region.

➤ **HERmail.net** (www.HERmail.net) A free email-based travel directory of international women travelers. The network search features allow members to enter their destination city and find matches with two contacts who can share advice on female-friendly B&Bs, vegetarian restaurants, what clothing is appropriate according to culture and weather, and other helpful hints for women travelers.

➤ **Jewish Travel Network** (www.jewish-travel-net.com) Seeks and offers homes and contacts worldwide for Jewish travelers. Hospitality exchanges include hosting travelers for special holiday meals or Sabbath, and companionship or information exchange. The network also offers an information service to help members locate synagogues, agencies, organizations, contacts, lodgings, and kosher facilities, and to research other specialized travel requests.

➤ **Hospitality Exchange** (www.goldray.com/hospitality/index.htm) A hard-copy traveler's directory of members who offer each other the gift of home-cooked hospitality. Members like to travel, be hosted by other members, and, in turn, host traveling members themselves. Each directory contains listings of the membership and provides details on each member's interests and the hospitality they can provide.

➤ **Globetrotters Club** (www.globetrotters.co.uk) At 50+ years, the Globetrotters Club is one of the oldest travel networks for independent travelers and travel enthusiasts of all ages. Members network, exchange information, and help each other to get the most out of their travels and to venture off the beaten path. Members have access to the Globe membership list to share information and sometimes hospitality. The club is nonprofit and run by volunteers.

You Don't Need a Secret Password to Join a Travel Club

You'll find dozens and dozens of travel clubs online, and they generally offer similar membership benefits—discounts on hotels, rental cars, and airfare, with some even offering cash-back bonuses on travel services purchased through the club. Annual dues range from $25 to $75. Should you join? It depends on how much you spend on travel per year, and whether you have the time and patience to go out and find similar discounts yourself. It might be a good idea to do some comparison shopping, using online booking systems, discount travel sites, and other online resources.

You can locate listings of travel clubs in your favorite search engine, and as an example, Yahoo!'s Travel section has links to more than 40 clubs, some specializing in cruise travel, European travel, business travel, family travel, and senior travel. And of course, if you belong to AAA or AARP, you're already eligible to receive travel club member benefits, so see what's included with membership in those organizations before you join something else.

Wanna Be a Mad Chatter?

Chat rooms allow participants to "talk" in real-time to other people through typed dialogue. As soon as you type your message and press **Enter**, your message is displayed on the chat screen for all the chat room visitors to see (and respond to, if they choose). Certain chat rooms require special software to use the chat service, but if that's the case, you can find directions on how to download the software you need. Most chat rooms don't require any special software, but your Web browser does need to be Java enabled. Netscape Navigator 2.0 and Internet Explorer 3.0 versions and later are Java enabled, so if you're using a version that predates those, you'll need to download a more recent version.

Double Up on Your Browser Selection

Depending on what chat room or live Internet event you want to participate in, you'll want to have both Netscape Navigator and Internet Explorer ready in case the room or event doesn't give you a choice of which one to use. Although most chat rooms don't care which one you use, others only work with Internet Explorer, so it's best to have both on your system. You can get the most recent versions of both browsers for free, and downloading is as easy as 1–2–3.

I'll tell you off the bat that I haven't come across very many *unmoderated chat rooms*, which are rooms where it's up to the chatters to direct the course of discussion, that have much to offer except a meeting place for participants to exchange silly and hard-to-follow blurbs with each other. Besides the fact that there is little substance to the dialogue in chat rooms, the chatter often doesn't have anything to do with the topic of the room. So, generally speaking, I don't find unmoderated chat rooms to be of much use, especially to find travel information. If you want to learn more about free-reign chat rooms, you'll find information at places like Yahoo!, Microsoft Network, and AOL—Web sites that host a vast assortment of unmoderated chat rooms.

Moderated chat rooms, which are monitored by a chat host to keep the conversation on track and decide which questions are answered, and live Internet events, on the other hand, can be fun to participate in or just observe. In a moderated chat room, there are usually two active chat windows. In the Ask Question box, a host or moderator, who chooses which questions or comments to post to the chat board, filters your comments. There's also a Chat box, where you can chat with other people in the room but your questions and comments are only seen by the people who have entered the chat area. If an annoying chatter does show up, you can block that person's postings, and sometimes even have the person banned from the room if warnings to stop being a nuisance are ignored. For a wonderfully enlightening explanation and answers to FAQs of chat and live Internet events, visit Yack! at **www.yack.com/editorial/reference/reference_chat.html**. You'll learn how to find live chat events, how to set up a chat alias, and how to use the features and tools of chat rooms.

Be Nice and Show Some Netiquette

The first time you enter a chat room, spend a few minutes getting familiar with the flow of information and the general feel of the group users. The last thing you want to do is start a flame war or upset other users, so make sure you're up to snuff on the topic at hand and that you don't say something you know is going to upset another chatter. If you're having a bad day and feel like kickin' up some dust in a chat room, think twice and log on another time! And remember, don't type your posts in UPPERCASE LETTERS because it's considered yelling.

Smaller groups of users can set up private chat rooms that function like online conference calls or meeting rooms. Using chat rooms in this way can be an ideal way to connect with a group of friends or family members to make travel plans, send updates from the road, or just stay up-to-date on events and important news. Oftentimes, these private chat rooms are hosted by a Web site or travel network, but you can also set up your very own chat room at Yahoo! (**www.yahoo.com**), Yack! (**www.yack.com**), About.com (**www.about.com**), and MSN (**www.msn.com**). Setting up your very own chat room is easy to do, but it's slightly different at each of the hosting Web sites, so if you need assistance, just look for the Help button.

The Least You Need to Know

➤ You can participate in online travel communities, such as newsgroups, message boards, and mailing lists, to get tips, advice, and insider information, and to meet other travelers.

➤ Travelers' networks connect like-minded travelers using member databases and email to exchange information.

➤ Chat rooms and live net events can be fun and easy to participate in.

Part 2

Do-It-Yourself: Planning and Buying Travel Online

Going online to plan your trip sure beats the pants off the old way of do-it-yourself travel planning. Thanks to today's online travel tools, we can plan travels from the comforts of home…any time of the day or night, weekends included. For the most part, the travel information you'll find online is absolutely free. And if you know where to look, you can even save money on special deals, super-low airfares, and other deep discounts that are given only to online shoppers. Even if you don't want to shop online, you've got a roadmap to the top sites for do-it-yourself trip planning. (Speaking of roadmaps, you can find those online, too.)

This part takes you through the online tools and travel resources available to help you do your own travel planning. You'll learn how to use online reservation and booking systems for air, hotel, and car rentals. You'll learn how to research the place you're visiting by using destination guides, and create customized miniguides based on your tastes and interests. You'll learn how to gather road trip information and get point-to-point driving directions using online mapping systems, and gather train and bus schedules—even purchase rail passes online.

As my mom used to tell me, "If you want it done right, you'll have to do it yourself!"

Chapter 6

Before You Buy...Protecting Yourself Online

In This Chapter

➤ How to protect your privacy and personal information online

➤ The tell-tale signs of shopping at a secure site

➤ If it seems too good to be true, it probably is

➤ Reading the fine print to get the scoop on cancellation policies, refunds, and changes to your travel plans

➤ Getting trip cancellation coverage, just in case

Lots of folks these days are logging on to the Web in hopes of finding rock-bottom-priced airline tickets, or hotel rooms and car rentals at unheard-of prices. In fact, just the other day, I heard three radio commercials in a row hawking online travel booking sites, each claiming to offer the lowest fares or the best services. Many people are logging on to check out travel sites—a good number of them are just looking, but some are making purchases, too. Whether you go online to look or book, you still need to know some basics about privacy and security. This chapter deals with making sense of all the hype surrounding online travel purchases and how to be a savvy shopper when it comes to do-it-yourself travel planning.

Hopefully by now you're comfortable with going online and can find your way around to the various travel-related Web sites. This chapter will help you get ready to make online transactions using your credit card to pay for travel-related goods and services. For even more detail on shopping online, be sure to read Chapter 20, "Finding and Shopping for Special Gear and Accessories," which deals with how to purchase hard goods and products—like luggage, clothing, mosquito nets, and other travel accessories—that can be returned if necessary. And if you're going online to find specialty travel agents, tour operators, or cruise packages, first check out Part 3, "Cruises, Package Tours, Group Travel, and Custom Group Tours," where I give tips and resources for those facets of travel.

I'll Show You My Privacy Statement If You Show Me Yours

Be sure to read the posted privacy statements at Web sites before you complete any forms, questionnaires, surveys, or polls. Don't give out your social security number, phone number, mother's maiden name, passwords, or other private information to any Web site, chat room, or newsgroup. And if the Web site asks you for information that doesn't really relate to the product or service it's selling, such as your income or age, either leave it blank or make something up if you don't want to share this information.

You'll notice that some *fields* (the boxes where you type in your information) are required and others are not. Required fields are usually noted with an asterisk or are highlighted. If you skip a required field, you often will get an error message telling you to go back and fill in the information that's missing. But the fields that aren't specified as required aren't, and you're under no obligation to fill them in. Most sites, too, have a button you can click that says something like, "Do not contact me with special information or news."

How to Protect Your Privacy

Because we go online from the comfort and privacy of our homes or offices, we're under the impression that visiting a Web site is an anonymous act. If you don't fill out a form or enter any information, no one ever knows you visited, right? Wrong. Contrary to popular belief, your activity and identity can be tracked from the moment you enter a Web site, and even before you arrive at the Web site. "They" know what pages you visit, how long you stay on a certain page, whether you bookmark the site, whether it's your first time visiting, how you found the site..."they" know pretty much everything about you except what you had for lunch today.

Is this giving you the heebie-jeebies? The point is to teach you how you can protect your privacy when you go online. The Internet and electronic commerce are very interesting subjects to marketers and advertisers. With the predicted growth of online sales, some Web-based businesses invest a great deal of time and money in studying and tracking your online activity. Why? Because they can, and because they use that information to customize your online experience (in other words, to direct advertising at you based on your age, income, gender, buying habits, and so on).

If you know how market researchers and advertisers use the information they collect from you or about you, you'll know what information you should and shouldn't give, who you should give it to, and how to make sure your information won't be shared or sold to another company.

Making a Name for Yourself

If you participate in chat rooms, message boards, or newsgroups, consider making up an onscreen pen name for yourself, like hooliana99, so that stalkers and other unwanted folks don't know your real identity. You can also get a free email account, like hooliana99@yahoo.com from Yahoo! (`mail.yahoo.com`), HotMail (`www.hotmail.com`), and a host of other email services. Even though the accounts are free, there is a price to pay. Your inbox can get flooded with spams (unsolicited emails) if you agree to accept any news or promotions when you sign up for your new, free account.

Also, you shouldn't give out your phone number or address, or otherwise identify yourself to strangers online. You just don't know who's out there.

With all this interest in electronic commerce and online business, it's good to know that there are consumer-oriented Web sites that explain in detail how to protect your privacy online and what to look for when you go online to make a purchase. They may even be able to help you out of an online jam. If you're concerned about online privacy and security, I strongly suggest you visit these sites to get the full story on online consumer protection:

➤ **Better Business Bureau Online** (`www.bbbonline.org`) Offers consumer tips on giving out personal information, password privacy, credit card caution, ethical electronic commerce, smart shopping, kids online, and Web site address verification. You can even file a complaint with the BBBOnline.com Privacy Program Intake Center against an organization or a company that may have misused information collected about you online.

The Better Business Bureau's online resource center helps consumers become informed online shoppers.

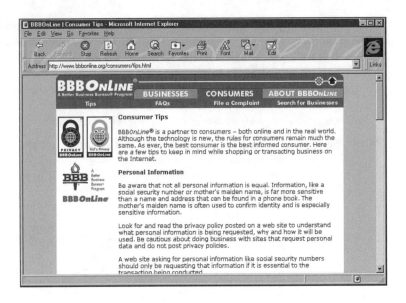

➤ **TrustE (www.truste.org)** An independent, nonprofit organization that deals with online privacy and works to build users' trust and confidence on the Internet. Web sites that meet certain security and privacy criteria are issued a TrustE seal that backs up the Web site's credibility, so users are more comfortable making online purchases or providing personal information. TrustE offers an extensive list of consumer protection tips and advice, as well as a list of participating online businesses. But because TrustE is not a mandatory program and most credible Web sites clearly state their privacy policies, don't be alarmed if a Web site you're dealing with isn't listed with TrustE.

➤ **Consumer Reports (www.consumerreports.org)** Provides access to many of its print magazine feature articles, and offers lots of tips on what to look for when shopping online. You'll also find lots of travel tips and advice, and company and service ratings, but you'll have to subscribe and pay a monthly or yearly access fee to get that information. It's worth it...for a few dollars a month, you get peace of mind and lots of free consumer and product advice. I'll talk about this site later in the chapter, so hang on.

If You Opt Out, Will Your Information Remain Private?

When you're checking out a Web site's privacy policy, look for information on an "opt-out" policy. This says your information will not be sold to any other party, even if you unsubscribe to an online newsletter, service, customer account, or anything else you may have agreed to participate in at any point. If you don't see an "opt-out" policy, send an email to the Web site administrator or call to find out what the policy is.

The Federal Trade Commission Web site (`www.ftc.gov/privacy/protect.htm`) has sample letters you can use to request that your personal information not be shared or sold, and how to contact credit reporting bureaus and direct marketers. Believe it or not, you can put an end to "preapproved credit card" offers, other direct mail, and those pesky telemarketers. (And you thought you'd just get advice on travel planning in this book!)

You can learn more about the choices you have to protect your personal information at the Federal Trade Commission's Web site.

What to Do with Cookies

Dunk 'em in a tall glass of milk. Make a pie crust? What do cookies have to do with online privacy? A *cookie* is a tiny piece of data that's sent to your computer's hard drive when you visit certain Web sites—especially electronic commerce sites—to help personalize your shopping experience. Imagine not having to check in with your username and password every time you visit your favorite online store. Or what if you didn't have to type in that super-long credit card number every time you order a new book, CD, or airline ticket? That's what cookies can do for you.

Cookies can be useful, and sometimes required, to make a transaction online or to reenter a Web site as a registered guest or customer. The cookies placed on your hard drive when you visit a Web site are checked regularly by Big Brother and Web marketers to track your online activities, what pages you visited, what items you bought, and so on. It's another thing to give you the heebie-jeebies, I know. But you can monitor what cookies are being sent and even set your browser preferences to not accept them, or to warn you before sending, so that you know what's being sent to your hard drive.

To Accept or Not to Accept Cookies: That Is the Question

You can tell your browser not to accept cookies if you don't want them. Or you can ask to be warned before allowing one to be sent. You can also choose to only accept cookies from the originating Web site, meaning if a banner ad appears on a page you access, a cookie can't be sent by the advertiser.

In Internet Explorer, go to the **Preferences** menu, and click **Receiving Files**. Then click the **Cookies** button. You'll get a list of cookies that have been sent, where they came from, and how to delete them if you want. In Navigator, you can set your browser preferences to accept, accept with warning, or decline all cookies.

For the whole scoop on cookies and to get details on how they work with your browser, check out **www.cookiecentral.com**.

The Tell-Tale Signs of Shopping at a Secure Site

Now comes the easy part. If you're ready to use your credit card online to make purchases or reservations, identifying secure sites is pretty easy to do. All Web sites that offer secure transactions are stored on secure servers, which means they use an encryption technology that scrambles your data when you place an order using your credit card. The way you know if the Web site is secure is to look at your browser's bottom-left corner. If you see a locked lock icon or an unbroken key icon, the site is secure. You may also see **https://www.company.com** in the location bar instead of just **http://www.company.com**.

You'll also be greeted with a security alert window that tells you you're about to enter a secure section of the Web site, assuring you that any information you exchange in the ordering system of the Web site cannot be seen by anyone else on the Web. The security statement, along with the privacy statement, should be easy to find when you enter the site. If you can't find a statement saying the site is secure and your transaction is safe, move on to another Web site. If you're still skeptical, make your first online shopping transactions at well-known merchants like L.L. Bean, Patagonia, major airlines, and companies you've dealt with in the real world. These guys have worked long and hard to earn your trust (and your business) and stand to lose a lot if customers feel unsafe and therefore unhappy.

There's Extra Protection Paying by Credit Card

If you use your credit card to pay for your travel expenses and you don't get what you were promised, your credit card might protect you when you dispute the charge. This doesn't mean they'll necessarily back you if you are dissatisfied with what you got—only if you didn't get what you were told you'd get. For example, the description in a brochure or an ad said there are tennis courts and saunas at the hotel. But when you got there, the sauna was out of order and the tennis courts were closed. So you check into a better hotel, making sure to take photographs of the unusable facilities, so that when you demand a refund, you can prove that the brochure didn't live up to its promise. If the hotel disagrees, you can refuse to pay the charge to your credit card and turn the dispute over to your credit card issuer. Plus, if some goon steals your credit card, you're protected, which may not be the case with a debit card. Check with your financial institution to see what kind of theft protection coverage you have with your debit card, (even though I've found many sites can't accept debit card payment).

After selecting my flight information, I entered the secure ordering section of www.travelocity.com to make my purchase. Note the locked lock icon in the lower-left corner.

How to Avoid Scams and "Too-Good-to-Be-True" Travel Deals

Keeping scam artists at bay is really a matter of keeping your eyes peeled and questioning deals that seem too good to be true. Vacations can be a pretty big investment, so it's important that you're working with businesses you know to be on the up and up. A good rule of thumb for any offer is that if they came looking for you, you should be cautious. Unsolicited emails, vacation coupons, time-share offers, or other "unbelievable travel deals" can be scams in disguise (and sometimes not even a very good disguise). For the low-down on down-and-dirty Internet scams, check out **www.internetfraudwatch.com**.

I'll talk more about working with travel agents and tour operators in Part 3 of this book, but here's a good bit of advice whether you're a do-it-yourself travel shopper or if you prefer to work with travel agents: If you're not familiar with the travel club, airline ticket consolidator, or travel agent, you have every right to ask for references. You can also check with the Better Business Bureau, or post a question to a travel forum or message board, asking if another user has ever worked with the company. Of course, don't take one person's word for it. This is just another thing you can do to check out a company you haven't worked with before.

Wendy Perrin's Ultimate Guide to Becoming a Smart Traveler

Wendy Perrin, *Condé Nast Traveler's* consumer travel expert and ombudsman, shares knowledge and insight on how to be a smart traveler. Using real stories from real travel nightmares, *Wendy Perrin's Secrets Every Smart Traveler Should Know* reveals how to handle airline mishaps, car rental foul-ups, travel scams, and much more. This book is recommended reading for every traveler—it'll improve your trip-planning skills and help you learn how to solve many potential travel disasters. You can find it in bookstores or online.

As I mentioned a little earlier in the chapter, Consumer Reports Online (**www.consumerreports.org**) is a good source of information on what you can do—and what signs of trouble to look for—when you go online to buy travel. You can also get the latest scoop on online travel scams by visiting the National Fraud Information Center at **www.fraud.org**. Here's a summary of NFIC's tips for protecting yourself against online travel fraud:

➤ **Beware of "free" offers or "great deals."** Especially be careful if the offer seems unreasonably priced. Don't respond to any offers like this until you get everything in writing—costs, conditions, and cancellation policies. Then take the time to thoroughly check it out.

➤ **Don't be pressured into buying NOW!** The reason they want you to respond to the offer now is because by the time you figure out what hit ya, they'll have closed shop and taken your money to the tracks. What's good today ought to be good tomorrow. If you ask me, I wouldn't even give these high-pressure offers a second thought.

➤ **Avoid offers that say you have "18 months to take the trip."** By the time you get around to taking the trip, the company could be out of business. The more time there is to deliver on the promises, the more time there is to stall. And if they stall long enough...oops, your time has expired. Also, travel fares and rates fluctuate on an hourly basis, so how can you be promised low prices if you choose to travel at the peak of the tourist season?

➤ **Get it in writing.** Get the price of the package and exactly what is and what isn't included. Get specific names of hotels, airports, airlines, restaurants, or any other part of the package deal. Get the phone numbers for these establishments yourself, rather than from the travel company (you can get business phone numbers at **www.bigyellow.com** or **www.411.com**) and call each establishment to confirm your reservation and verify that they are familiar with the company offering you the package.

➤ **If the package doesn't include air travel or hotels, do you have to purchase that through the company or can you arrange your own travel?** Sometimes companies sell you the cruise or package at cost, and then hit you where it hurts when it comes time to buying plane tickets or hotel rooms that you can only purchase through them...at a ridiculous mark-up.

➤ **Check prices with trusted, local travel agents.** After you've gathered all the information (in writing), shop around to see if a local travel agent can match the offer. They'll also be able to point out hidden charges or unexpected expenses. And just to be nice, if a local travel agent protects you from a scam, book your trip with them and then be sure to write a nice thank-you letter and recommend the agency to all your friends and family!

One consumer responded to a "great travel deal" and set off for vacation— a trip that took her to hell and back. Besides having to pay $500 in unexpected fees, her hotel reservation was switched from a nice hotel to a truckers' motel.

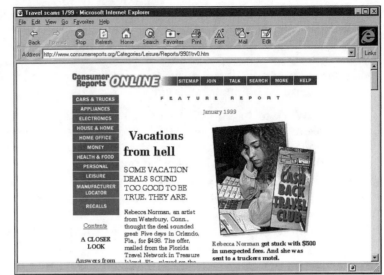

The following sections offer ideas about some other things to keep in mind when you go online to plan your trip.

Beware of Hidden Costs and Restrictions

Even though some of the super deals you find online appear to be better than what you'd pay if you called the carrier directly or worked with a travel agent, you might not be able to get a refund on the ticket if you can't make the flight. Or you might have to pay a rescheduling fee or cancellation fee if you break your reservation. Sometimes with bargains and deals, the restrictions may be so prohibitive that it's just not worth it. And sometimes things like frequent flyer miles don't count on super-discount fares. You really have to read the fine print to know if you're actually getting a good deal. I'll give you the details on this throughout the rest of the book.

Cancellation Policies and Trip Insurance

Generally speaking, when it comes to protecting your travel investment, you should strongly consider purchasing trip insurance to cover costs associated with unexpected trip expenses, trip interruption, medical expenses when traveling outside the United States, and other unforeseen disasters. First, though, check your existing homeowner's insurance and health coverage to see if they cover expenses for injuries or illnesses when traveling.

Be sure to shop around at established insurance companies or travel clubs like AAA to get the skinny on coverage and rates. Don't buy add-on protection directly from the cruise line or tour operator, because if they go out of business, you lose your money anyway. Visit these Web sites to learn more about travel insurance, and refer to Chapter 24, "Health, Wellness, and Online Information" for more details, especially if you're traveling overseas. You'll need a plan that includes medical and travel assistance coverage. Here are some travel insurance providers' sites you can check out, and be sure to ask your travelin' amigos who they use for travel insurance coverage:

➤ **Access America** (www.accessamerica.com) Offers consumer policies and corporate coverage. Visit the frequently asked questions (FAQs) page for answers to many of the most common travel insurance questions.

➤ **Travel Secure** (www.travelsecure.com) Answers travel insurance questions, too, and even includes a pricing chart. Most of the other travel insurance sites I've visited required an email or toll-free call to request a quote. So if all you want is an idea of how much travel insurance costs, this is the place to go.

➤ **Triple AAA** (www.aaa.com) Find the AAA branch in your area, and call to get a quote on travel insurance.

The Least You Need to Know

➤ You can protect your privacy online by visiting legitimate online businesses that clearly post a privacy statement and by using a credit card.

➤ Don't give out personal information online, and think up an onscreen pen name to protect your identity.

➤ Online consumer protection agencies can give you information on protecting your travel investment.

➤ You can get added protection with trip cancellation and emergency medical coverage insurance.

Chapter 7

So, You Want to Be Your Own Travel Agent?

In This Chapter

➤ Saving time and money making your own travel plans

➤ Using travel directories to locate travel suppliers and information sources

➤ Tapping into the resources and links found at major online booking Web sites

➤ Using lifestyle directories and resources to locate the trip options based on your unique needs and interests

Hopefully by now you're comfortable with the Web and electronic commerce, and I'm sure you've noticed that there's a good deal of advertising and promotion of travel Web sites. There's a very good reason for that. Travel is big business, and everyone wants a piece of the pie. Web marketers who understand how the Internet is used and what makes a good Web site (information, good design, easy to find, easy to navigate, and so on) take advantage of the ease of accessing information; they pull it all together so it's easier for us, the consumers, to find the goods and buy them. Well, that's not all travel sites are about, but if you've decided to become your very own personal travel agent, it's best to equip yourself with the most powerful tools of the trade so you can go online to save time and money to do your travel planning.

Whether you go online to buy travel or just to do research, it's never been easier to tap into the variety of travel resources to turn yourself into a smarter traveler, a more informed consumer, and a user of the greatest information system the world has ever seen. Fortunately, there are also some excellent starting points and general planning tools that can get you started more efficiently and make you smarter, faster.

Some very helpful places to start include search engines and general directories, travel directories, booking sites, and travel guides. You'll find just about all the tools you need for finding good ideas and estimating costs, as well as links to other sites that can help you plan every detail of your trip. This chapter deals with using directories and tapping into the resources you'll find on the high-traffic booking sites. After all, even if you decide not to buy online, you can still take advantage of all the legwork that's been done to pull together the lists of good Web sites and links to online traveler's resources.

Who's on First??

As the Web continues to evolve, new terms crop up and old terms get fuzzy. What you thought was a search engine turns out also to be a directory, a travel channel, a booking site, an e-zine and... so don't get too hung up on terms.

Try these distinctions for help. A *directory* is essentially a listing of links to other Web sites. A *search anything* is a site where you can use keywords to locate Web sites. A *booking site* lets you compare rates and reserve and purchase travel services and goods. And *travel guides* provide extensive information on destinations and travel itineraries. An *online travel service* puts it all together in an effort to build an audience that it can sell to travel marketers.

Ladies and Gentlemen, Start Your Search Engines!

Search engines offer a lot more than keyword searching. Most have nicely organized categories, or *directories*, you can click through to narrow your search. Yahoo! pioneered this approach. It's a directory with a search function, meaning it searches sites that it has previewed and filed into categories. It then spiders the Web looking for links to documents containing your keywords. But within each Yahoo! category, you'll find a listing of links. So, from Yahoo!, you can click on **Recreation**, then **Travel**, and then **Directory** to get to a page of travel directories that can help you start planning.

It goes without saying that there are directories and search sites besides Yahoo! that bring together the resources of the Web and put them into easy-to-use categories. In fact, there are plenty of sites that do this. I refer to Yahoo! throughout this book, though, because it's one of my personal favorite online directories, and it's also one of the most popular sites on the Web.

Yahoo! also offers a second travel link at the top of its home page that takes you to its version of an online travel service. This is not a links-only directory, but offers other services, including reservation and booking tools.

Other search engines offer similar features. I like the Excite travel page (**www.excite.com/travel**). It is easy to read and well organized, with a nice balance of text- and graphics-based links. There is a directory section, a tools section, news section, destination links, and a featured link to Preview Travel, an online travel service and booking site.

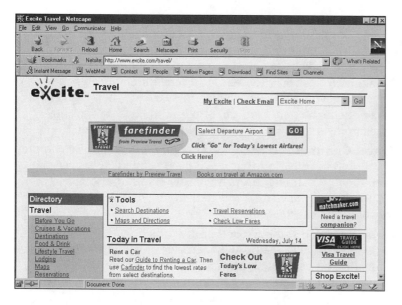

The Excite travel page provides a host of options for getting travel ideas and information. From here, you can click to travel guides, booking sites, and other resources.

Simply put, using the travel directory feature of a search engine is a great step toward traveling smarter online. Here's how it helped in a recent search I tried. First, I did a keyword search for pubs in Ireland. My results? Nearly 300,000 matches to scroll through! Then I tried the Yahoo! directory approach, and in just a few clicks, I found The Brazen Head, Dublin's oldest pub, as well as a whole host of other choices for sampling a pint.

Here's a list of some other travel directories worth checking out:

➤ **Netscape Travel Channel** (**www.home.netscape.com/travel**) The result of Netscape and Travelocity's partnership to bring together all kinds of traveler resources, plus lots and lots of links for shopping for travel gear, books, videos, discounts, and restaurants.

➤ **HotBot** (**directory.hotbot.com/Recreation/Travel**) If you're looking for a specific kind of travel activity, this is a great place to begin your search. For starters, you'll find information and links to sites on railroads, honeymoons, special-needs travel, singles travel, solo travel, ecotourism, and adventure travel.

Also, HotBot links you to Lonely Planet destination guides and several newsgroups. Another plus is the list of recommended sites to help you find the best and most helpful travel sites.

➤ **Looksmart** (www.looksmart.com) Not as comprehensive as some of the other well-known search engines, but it offers several features that make it unique. It is one of the best places to look if you're trying to plan a vacation that's out of the ordinary. The activities section gives you links for festivals, wining and dining, and outdoor recreation. Also, it begins with a list of activities that you might not normally find, such as diving through shipwrecks or searching ancient cities.

➤ **Snap** (www.snap.com) Looks similar to many other search engines, but when you start searching with it, you'll find that this one has some great online articles and links to help you make your travel plans. One of the best parts of this site is the travel planner. It lets you choose from several different categories, such as family travel, honeymoon, B&Bs, and business travel. Then it gives you great tips and links to help you plan. You can also link to Preview Travel to make all your travel arrangements through the online booking system.

➤ **Webcrawler Travel Channel** (www.Webcrawler.com/travel) A really comprehensive site. You can find information that you'll need before you go, get maps and weather reports, and book travel through Preview Travel. It also gives the coolest place on earth for each day and a top 10 list of travel bonuses, such as how to maximize your frequent flyer miles.

➤ **AOL Travel** (www.aol.com) This online community, which you reach by going to and typing the keyword TRAVEL, is for AOL members only, but if you belong, you can find information on car rentals, airlines, hotel rooms, and more. You'll also find tips and resources for family travel, choosing the right cruise, where to get discounts and deals, how to participate in online travel forums, and lots more to help you become a smarter traveler. You'll also be eligible for travel discounts, just because you're a member of AOL.

Be Selective: Use Travel Directories

Travel directories are refined directories that sift out nontravel Web sites and focus only on categorizing and providing links to travel-related information. Many also provide travel features, articles, and tools. Probably the best possible starting point if you're just beginning to explore destinations and the costs of your dream trip, travel directories can point you in the right direction and help you navigate much more quickly to content you can use.

Each travel directory has its own way of organizing things, but all directories use categories to take you from general to specific information, working down through a hierarchy of information and links, to the nuts and bolts of planning—to where you want to go, what you want to see, and how you can get there.

They also point to more specific lifestyle- or destination-based directories—such as the Great Outdoor Recreation Pages at **www.gorp.com**—which you can bookmark to visit for additional research later.

Now That's *What I Call a Travel Directory!*

My mom told me never to play favorites, but I've got to draw the line somewhere when it comes to reviewing the best of the best travel resource Web sites. Actually, though, the sites listed here are here for a reason: They're darned good starting points. Why should you wander around the Web looking for quality Web sites when you can start at a travel directory that does all the dirty work for you? So here's a list of my favorites:

➤ **Fodor's Travel Resource Center (www.fodors.com/resource)** A site to behold. I'll admit readily that a majopr reason I like this site so much is its simplicity.

It's clean and crisp, just like my starched linen tablecloth (not). It's a thorough collection of travelers' resources and links, plus it includes objective reviews of travel Web sites and online travel tools, without being too cheesy or hard-hitting "salesy." Plus, it's compliments of the good folks at Fodor's, one of the most popular and critically acclaimed travel guide publishers on the planet. I refer to this site throughout the book, so just go ahead and add it to your Favorites or Bookmarks list.

➤ **Kasbah Travel Search Engine (www.kasbah.com)** Calls itself the world's largest travel search engine and features an index of more than 100,000 "hand-picked" travel sites. That's a lot of hands, huh? It's well-designed and easy to follow, with categories including Reservations, Activity Travel, Travel From, Travel Essentials, Travel Toolbox, and Global News. There are lots of handy tools and info, such as ATM locators, health information, travel magazines, and loads of destination links. This site is a must-see for anyone planning a trip in the United States or abroad.

➤ **Planet Rider (www.planetrider.com)** Catalogs the "best" five percent of travel sites on the Web. It also offers links to planning tools, including The Weather Channel, maps, a currency converter, bargains, travel stores, and more. Site descriptions and ratings make your trip to Planet Rider well worth the visit.

Kasbah caters to your "inner explorer." Comprehensive categories, a searchable index of worldwide destinations, travel features, and tools provide a grand tour of high-quality travel information and resources.

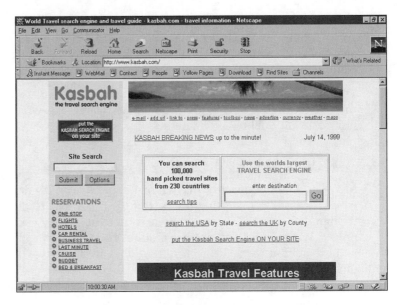

Good Design Makes the Difference

Why do some Web sites feel so good and others just don't? Good visual design combined with smart programming helps—like what you see at Planet Rider (`www.planetrider.com`). This very well-designed site not only looks and feels good to the eye, it's easy to navigate and uses clear language, bold graphics, and programming features that put you at ease and in control. Planet Rider uses simple terms such as Destinations, Landscapes, and Activities. Also, it includes a brief comment or review of every site it lists. Finally, it uses a ratings system based on the quality of information and ease of use of each site.

All these features help when you're trying to choose a site. Another Planet Rider feature I like is the way it always launches a new browser window when you link to a new page. This means that you never leave Planet Rider when you link to a site from its directory, so you don't get lost as you explore the Web. Don't miss this site. The only thing you'll question is why there aren't more like this!

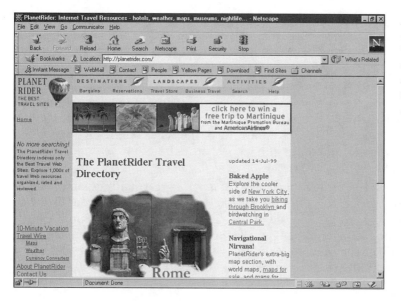

Planet Rider (www.planetrider.com) will redefine what you expect from a Web site. Smart and good looking, this site should be on your list of favorites.

➤ **Rec.Travel Library** (`www.travel-library.com`) A directory of personal travelogues and worldwide travel and tourism information. You'll find some offbeat
bits here, like the CIA World Factbook, as well as general travel tips and reference information.

Still want more? There are some other good travel directories worth checking out.
Here's a short list of other sites you should check out if you're looking for an ideal
jumping-off point for your travel planning adventures:

➤ **Cybertrip** (`www.cybertrip.com`) Full of useful information to help you plan
your trip. You can link to Travel Now (`www.travelnow.com`) to book your air, car,
or hotel reservations. And be sure to check out the Travel Kit. It's got the
goods—from world time zones to exchange rates to travel agents—to make
travel planning a little easier.

➤ **The Virtual Tourist** (`www.vtourist.com`) Has an extensive list of links in the
Travellers' Tools section, and is still growing. (I know that feeling.) You can also
get connected with other travelers through the site's message boards and travel
chat rooms.

➤ **Travelsites** (`www.travelsites.com`) Helps you figure out where to go, how to
get there, and where to stay in its three main sections, which give you links to
tourism offices, airlines, car rental agencies, and hotels. The I need a Vacation
section offers package tour opportunities and lists of travel agents by interest to
help you find the vacation that's perfect for you.

➤ **Travel Source** (`www.travelsource.com`) has plenty o' links to help you find
exactly the vacation site you've been looking for. If you're a disabled traveler, or
if you're looking for sea kayaking trips, this place has links for all types of travel
activities and traveler lifestyles.

➤ **Travel Links (www.travellinks.com)** Simple to use. All you have to do is click on **Search** and either enter what you're looking for or choose a category. There's minimal advertising or other distractions to keep you from the travel information you're looking for. Also, if you want the convenience of having travel information brought to you, you can sign up for an email newsletter.

➤ **TRAVEL.com (www.travel.com)** Operated by travel agents and powered by the Internet Travel Network. You can book travel plans or shop for travel gear at this nicely compiled Web site. The newest feature of the site is online message boards that let you post questions and get responses from travelers and travel agents around the world.

➤ **Group Travel Network (www.grouptravel.net)** A great starting point if you have ideas about organizing a trip for a special-interest group, like your bicycling club that wants to go to the Tour de France, and then bike all over Europe. Just contact these good folks, and they'll make the customized arrangements for the whole lot of ya. The site offers an extensive list of destination links, traveler tools, and other online travel resources.

Who Says You Can't Have It All?

Why not plan and book your trip at the same time? That's what some very savvy sites are all set to do for you. What started as booking sites for travel agents has morphed into portals/channels/online planning services and multipurpose sites that allow real-time booking. Expedia, Microsoft's entrant and the largest travel Web site online, and Travelocity, fall into this category. They have pulled together a host of vital travel resources to provide a one-stop online experience for planning and purchasing travel services. They're not the only online booking sites, but for purposes of discussion, what you'll find at these sites is generally what you'll find at other booking sites. (Of course, all apologies to the other sites not discussed here. Don't worry, though. I'll talk about more booking sites throughout the book.)

Okay, so you've landed at a major online booking site. Don't know where to go? No problem. Try the destination guide. Don't know how to get there? Relax. You can book your plane, train, or automobile on the spot, along with a room that fits your budget and your taste. Need a map? Okay. Need an itinerary? You bet. Need to keep track of your frequent flyer miles? Want to compare schedules or prices? This is the place. The wealth of services on today's fastest-growing travel sites is impressive, extremely cool, and convenient. In fact, you can't help but like the one-stop approach of these sites.

Finding the major one-stop sites is relatively easy because they're all looking for you! But the simplest method would be to start from your favorite search engine or directory and click **Travel**. You'll probably find yourself smack dab in the middle of Travelocity or another major booking site, or at least you'll be staring at a banner ad prompting you to click through to the site, which is no surprise in this highly networked and co-sponsored online arena.

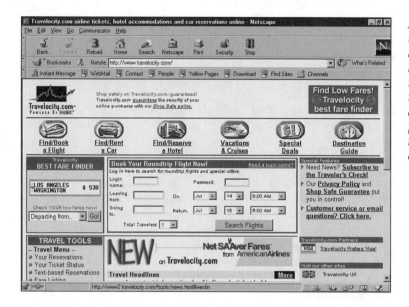

At Travelocity (www.travelocity.com), a one-stop planning and booking site, information is well organized and easy to find. I like the searchable flight index and best-fare finder, services that many multipurpose sites offer.

You'll find a lot of the same features at these big booking sites. The differences you'll find are how good the graphics and multimedia features are and how information-rich the site really is. Does it include unusual destinations? Is the information interesting and helpful, or is it superficial and little more than a link to a packaged deal? And how commercialized is the site? Again, this comes down to substance. Some sites I've visited have the feel of a discount store. Many cross-promote related goods and services, usually as features or links. Commercialization adds a lot of convenience to a site, but it also means your choices may be limited to special promotions and bundled travel services. It also means a lot of banner ads, which you may have figured out by now I'm not too fond of.

Try to exercise some caution. If you're just beginning to explore the possibilities, you should probably look further than a one-stop site. Go to Kasbah or another travel directory and check out the fares listed on airline and rail Web sites, too. It's a good idea to take your time and do your homework before you start paying for the details of your trip.

Travelocity Packs a Punch

Travelocity (**www.travelocity.com**) lists schedules for more than 700 airlines and has reservations capabilities for more than 420 airlines, 37,000 hotels, and more than 50 car rental companies—the most on the Web. Launched in March 1996, the site pioneered online bookings and continues to provide reservations capabilities for 95 percent of all airline seats sold.

Other travel tools available at Travelocity are destination guides to more than 275 countries, courtesy of Lonely Planet guidebooks and World Travel Guide. For those who want to get away from all the tourist traps and really see the country, Lonely Planet can help you find out-of-the-way places and attractions that most travelers never see. You can also access interactive street maps and door-to-door directions from MapQuest and weather forecasts for more than 700 cities from Weather Services Corporation.

If you're traveling overseas, you can find passport and visa information, a listing of world holidays, duty-free guidelines, currency/credit, and travel health information. The international business traveler can access a comprehensive database of essential business practices, such as banking hours, etiquette, making appointments, negotiating, and entertaining.

Looking for an art exhibit, a concert, or a local festival? Travelocity's up-to-date listing of events and activities will give you plenty of options on staying entertained.

Expedia Shoots and Scores

Expedia (**www.expedia.com**) has been billed as a "mall for vacation ideas" that offers one-stop shopping for vacation packages, cruises, resorts, and travel merchandise. Expedia is the largest online travel service today, with a one-week sales record that topped $16 million. That's the power of Microsoft and the extensive network of co-sponsors and promoters who are tapping into Expedia's popularity. The site is huge, almost too huge to move through quickly, with a service listing that includes Do Your Taxes, Buy Books, and Buy Videos. Still, there's no arguing that it's an excellent resource for travel planning.

Expedia's primary service categories are titled Travel Agent, Deals, Places to Go, Magazine, Maps, Find, and Help. On the home page, you get a whole bunch of other services, including Destination Info, Vacation Shopping, Highlights, Other Travel Planning Tools, Featured Hotels, and Featured Travel Provider (featured provider=advertiser?). You can also email postcards to your friends, manage your frequent flyer miles, and review travel advisories from the State Department. But deals are probably what Expedia does best.

Have I Got a Deal for You

Go to the Special Deals section of Expedia, and you'll find a quick and easy matrix of travel packages to a wide range of destinations. Specials are grouped by Best Deals, Sunny, Weekend, Family, and Activities, and are offered directly by travel suppliers. Each vacation description includes a one-paragraph summary, a link to detailed descriptions and supplier Web sites, the trip duration, a link to any special terms and conditions, the purchase expiration date, and simple graphic icons that sum up what you get in the package. Prices are all per person. As always, make sure you check out the terms and conditions before you bite!

Expedia's Special Deals section is the simplest way to find a great package deal fast. But don't assume that these are the best deals available. Do some comparison shopping, and call your favorite travel agent before you make a purchase.

Preview Travel Is Worth the Trip

Another one-stop online service that lets you plan, price, and book your excursion, Preview Travel (**www.previewtravel.com**) is well organized with convenient Web site features that make it worth a return trip. Services include online destination guides from Fodor's; hotel, air, and car reservation services that access the same computer database used by travel agents; and vacation and cruise shopping of more than 1,000 packages. Other resources and sections include Farefinder, Carfinder, Business Travel, Exclusive Offers, Travel Store, Travel Newswire, and Applause. The Fodor's guides are great, providing practical information and insider tips on local sites.

One of my favorite features is the Island Finder within the Fodor's guides. Just type in the kind of vacation or resort you are looking for, based on the kind of natural surroundings you prefer; activities and features such as diving, snorkeling, sailing, good roads, historic sites, and nightlife; and your general price range, and let Fodor's find your perfect island. You'll end up with a list of possibilities and links to detailed destination guides, complete with tips on how to save on travel there and the island's daily weather forecast.

Can't Get Enough One-Stop Shopping?

Here are some other similar one-stop shopping sites you may want to check out:

➤ **The Trip** (**www.thetrip.com**) Lets you find a flight, rent a car, or book a hotel room like most sites of its kind. It also offers a feature that will help those of you spontaneous travelers who are looking for a vacation at the last minute: Just sign up for the Impulse Trip email newsletter to be notified of special deals.

➤ **Internet Travel Network** (www.itn.net) Powers many of the smaller travel reservation sites and has an easy-to-use search function to find the perfect flight, hotel room, or car rental. Also, the site provides several helpful features, like the Low Fare Ticker, which is a running list of low fares and discount deals. Other travel resources include time across the world, driving directions, and real-time flight arrival and departure tracking.

➤ **Leisure Planet** (www.leisureplanet.com) Connects you to sites that let you find a flight, book a hotel room, rent a car, choose a cruise, or find a travel agent. Leisure Planet does its own searching for flights and hotels, but it also connects you to sites where you can book other items, such as cruises.

➤ **LeisureWeb** (www.leisureWeb.com) Lets you search through vacation promotions and destinations and make your reservations online, too. It also gives a featured vacation for a specific destination (for example, Disney's Fort Wilderness Resort).

➤ **TravelNow** (www.travelnow.com) Simply has you choose airline, car rental, or hotel, and then begins the search and reservation process. This site is strictly devoted to finding reservations and doesn't offer any articles or information. Something this site does have, however, is a group section. If you and your group will number more than 20 people or require more than 10 rooms, you can fill out a form, and the TravelNow experts will help you make all the reservations. Most sites do not have this feature, requiring you to make room or flight reservations one at a time.

➤ **Global Online Travel** (www.got.com) Not only creates instant car, hotel room, or flight reservations for you and tells you about hot deals, but it also gives you tips on finding the best deal on flights, like staying overnight on Saturday or flying out on a Tuesday.

Whatever Floats Your Boat, There's a Directory for You

If your idea of a dream vacation has more to do with what you can do than with where you go, lots of options and helpful directories await you online. Many specialized directories on the Web can link you to travel options based on your favorite activities and interests. How about a tour of golf courses in Scotland? Or a family ski vacation? Educational trips are another choice, as are singles trips, seniors trips, and special-needs packages. You can find most of these sources through a travel directory like Kasbah or Planet Rider. Or you can look under Lifestyle Travel at a search engine travel directory.

All these sites are good references for finding travel options that fit your lifestyle:

➤ **The Great Outdoor Recreation Pages** (www.gorp.com) The most complete source of outdoor travel and recreation information I've found on the Web. It has links that will help you plan your trip, find activities and attractions, and locate special-interest vacation packages. If your travel plans involve the great outdoors, you can bet you'll find plenty of information at this site.

➤ **The Family Travel Files** (`www.thefamilytravelfiles.com`) A family travel site that provides a travel directory, an e-zine, links, and resources. This isn't the most complete site, but you can find informative and interesting articles on very specific locations.

➤ **The Family Adventure Travel Directory** (`www.familyadventuretravel.com`) Searchable several different ways. You can look for a specific travel agency or company, a location, or an activity. This is an awesome site to locate unusual travel activities and locations, so if you are looking for dog sledding in Alaska or gorilla trekking in the Congo, this is a great site for you.

➤ **Family Travel Guides** (`www.familytravelguides.com`) Lets you search for family-friendly lodging and special family deals. It also gives tips from travel experts on how to survive a family vacation. You can also check out great recipes for kid-pleasing snacks to make the car ride just a little easier.

➤ **Yahoo! Senior Guide** (`seniors.yahoo.com`) Information on senior discounts and vacation packages. Also, you can check out the Top Picks section to find out about some of the best vacations for seniors. If you want to find out what other people think, you can use the message board to ask questions or to simply read about other seniors' vacations.

➤ **Senior Circle** (`www.seniorcircle.com`) Offers a complete online travel-planning service for seniors. It's an authorized affiliate of Travelocity where seniors can find bargains, seasonal destinations, armchair traveling, tickets, reservations, tours, and links to other travel sites.

➤ **Connecting: Solo Travel Network** (`www.cstn.org`) Designed to make traveling solo safer. You can learn about special trips for solo travelers, tips, FAQs, and travel tales. The site can also help you find destinations and companies that are singles-friendly and tells you how to join the Solo Travel Network to connect with other solo travelers.

➤ **Solotraveller** (`www.solotraveller.com`) Wants you to sign up and become part of its online community. You'll be able to search through and find partners for you vacation plans. Or check out the message boards for valuable information about traveling alone, like solo dining.

➤ **Access-Able Travel Source** (`www.access-able.com`) Can connect you with just about any information you might need to know about disabled-friendly travel agents and tours. Also, it offers a monthly newsletter with up-to-date travel information for disabled travelers. One of the best features is the message board, where travelers and travel agents ask and respond to questions by sharing their own experiences. If you need to find a hotel in Germany with a roll-in shower or a rental car agency in California with a wheelchair-accessible van, this is the place to go.

➤ **Global Access** (`www.geocities.com/Paris/1502`) Provides tips and resources for disabled travelers, along with reader input and travel tales, travel books, and links to sites that provide a wide range of information for people seeking special-needs travel options.

The Least You Need to Know

➤ You can find a wealth of travel resources by using search engines.

➤ Travel directories are a great place to start planning your trip.

➤ One-stop-shopping sites provide directory-type features plus e-commerce options.

➤ Start your planning at travel directories for all kinds of lifestyles, like families, seniors, singles, and adventurists.

THIS WAY AND YOU'LL FIND WHAT YOU SEEK...

Chapter 8

Using Destination Guides to Research and Plan Your Trip

In This Chapter

➤ Going online to gather destination, entertainment, and dining information

➤ Creating custom miniguides for your city or country, and learning how to download maps

➤ Ordering brochures and literature from travel bureaus and visitor centers

I have a terrible habit of accumulating guidebooks and road maps for even the shortest day trips or vacations. Most of the books are long outdated, and I have a glove compartment full of maps I bought to find hotels in various towns I stayed for just one night. Now, in the grand scheme of things, a glove compartment full of useless maps is not one of life's major problems, but it is clearly an unnecessary one. If only I had planned ahead and checked out online destination guides before I left, I wouldn't have this accumulation of useless maps and books, nor would I have wasted money on them.

Online destination guides are available for every major city and country in the world, and they're much more helpful than your basic road maps. They are even more manageable than some guidebooks. When you find the site of your dreams, you can search for specific locations, get current weather information, find the type of restaurant you're looking for, book a hotel room, read a list of notable tourist attractions worth checking out, discover upcoming events, or locate movie theaters and other sources of entertainment. These sites are useful if you're visiting a city for the first time or the 50th. They can also be handy if you're moving there permanently.

Finding City and Country Guides to Find Your Way Around

City and country travel guides are easy to use, when you find them. There are literally thousands of city and country guides on the Web—major cities like London, Paris, and New York each have dozens of city guides, some official, others put together by travel agencies or businesses that want your travel dollars. The best way to find the online city or country guide you're looking for is to type the name of the location into your favorite search engine. Some search engines, however, work better than others. Both Yahoo! and Snap have their own city guides, which in turn link you to specific sites related to the city. AltaVista, Lycos, and HotBot first give you a list of sites relevant to the geographic area, and you can find the city guides within that list (Lycos, however, does have its own maps).

Yahoo!'s Get Local sites, like this one for Dallas/ Fort Worth, Texas, help you find information for specific cities.

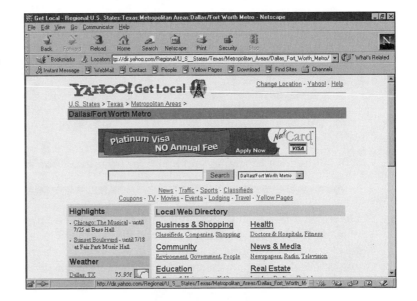

Some of the most useful city sites are sponsored by tourism offices, local newspapers, and chambers of commerce that want to promote local businesses. This can work to your advantage—keep an eye out for Web-only deals offered by some of the advertisers on these sites. In particular, hotels offer online discounts at many of these sites.

An Internet Miracle

In the June 27, 1999 Travel section of the *New York Times*, Nicholas D. Kristof, *Times* Tokyo bureau chief, describes a minor miracle he discovered while searching through Tokyo city guides on the Web: "A hotel room in Tokyo for $21? It seems incredible, but the Hotel New Koyo charges just 2,500 yen for its smallest single rooms, including service charge and tax. In a city where a fine melon can cost more than $100, that is an extraordinary find, and I turned it up through a Web site called Planet Tokyo at `www.pandemic.com/tokyo`." Kristof confirmed the price with the hotel, but he does not give any indication exactly how small the rooms are. (For pictures of the rooms and facilities, check out the hotel's English-language Web site at `www.tctv.ne.jp/members/new-koyo`. The rooms actually aren't much smaller than my college dorm room.)

Top Worldwide City Guides

If you don't want to fish around with a search engine for the site you need, you can try one or more of the many sites that contain worldwide travel guides and links. There are far too many sites to list here, but the following are a few of the best places to start your search for travel information in the United States and abroad. Just click around these sites to see what they have to offer:

➤ **Travel Notes** (`www.travelnotes.org`) One of the most comprehensive, interesting, and informative travel Web sites available. I like Travel Notes because it is a nonprofit Web site—they are trying to inform you rather than sell you stuff. This means that in addition to offering their own useful and extensive travel guides, they also include links to many other travel guide sites, along with objective reviews of many print and online travel guides.

➤ **Expedia World Guide** (`expedia.msn.com/wg`) In addition to providing extensive cultural information and travel advice, the individual country guides also contain maps and outside links to other travel guides.

Chattin' Up a Storm

Most travel Web sites, like the ones listed in this section, contain pages in which you can converse and share information with other travelers with similar interests. These chat rooms or communities are organized by destination as well as lifestyle, hobbies, and other interests. About.com features one of the most extensive lists of these pages in the TalkAbout chat rooms, so check out `www.about.com` first to see if you can find a room that reflects your own interests.

➤ **About.com (`home.about.com/travel`)** Check out GuideSites, which covers international travel destinations and features articles about different attractions and activities. Here, you get everything you would expect from a travel guide, plus some extras. One of the nice things about About.com is the comprehensive cultural information it includes in GuideSites. You can also sign up for email newsletters that will update you with recent news and travel tips on your destination. And join in the TalkAbout chat rooms for help from other travelers who have been or are going to the same place.

➤ **World Wide Travel Source (`www.wwtravelsource.com`)** Contains a large number of categories, covering almost any kind of information you could be looking for. On the search page, you can look for sites by continent, country, or city. The site also contains an alphabetical list of worldwide travel guides and directories on the Web. Although the list of links to both internal and external sites is not as extensive as the ones at Travel Notes or Expedia, the information provided is specific and concise.

➤ **Open World City Guides (`www.worldexecutive.com`)** Although this site mainly features worldwide hotel discounts for business travelers, the city guides offer just the basic information for anyone overwhelmed by the other, larger sites. This site doesn't list every city, and its maps are not very detailed, but it does give some useful help, such as directions from the airport to downtown, tipping hints, Internet access locations, and basic business decorum. If you get tired of surfing around Expedia or About.com, you might want to come here for the essentials.

➤ **CitySearch (`www.citysearch.com`)** If you want a site that gives specific city information, check out this site. CitySearch has its own pages on most major U.S. cities, plus cities in Sweden, Denmark, and Australia. CitySearch provides the best examples of what city guides can offer. You can zoom in and move around on the interactive city maps (provided by MapQuest) to find the location you want, or you can type in your starting and ending points for door-to-door directions. You can also get your local hotel, restaurant, and entertainment information here.

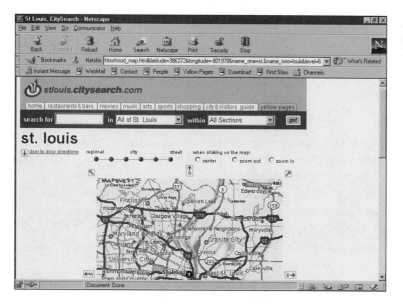

An example of CitySearch's interactive maps, this one is for St. Louis.

The Top Travel Guidebooks Go Electronic

Most companies that publish travel guides also have their own Web sites. Although the purpose of these sites is mainly to sell books, the sites themselves also contain abbreviated versions of the print guides that can help you in your travel planning. Plus, if you like what you see, you can go ahead and order the book. If you've relied on guide books in the past to plan your trip, you've heard these names before. If you like what you saw in print, take a look at the Web sites for the electrified version of these popular destination guides.

➤ **Lonely Planet** www.lonelyplanet.com

➤ **Let's Go** www.letsgo.com

➤ **Rough Guides** travel.roughguides.com

➤ **Fodor's** www.fodors.com

➤ **Frommer's** www.frommers.com

Some of the best features to look for in a destination guide site are the maps available to users. Some sites offer only one map that shows the general area of a city or region, along with popular places of interest. More advanced sites, like CitySearch, give users interactive maps that can be searched for specific locations or manipulated to show different views of an area. Most importantly, these maps can be printed, so you don't have to buy a new road map for every city you visit. Even better, these maps are essentially created by you to show the places you want to see. After you've used the site to find a hotel and restaurant that suits you, you can locate your choices on the map. I've used these maps for both day trips to nearby cities and for longer vacations.

Tired of Tourist Traps?

A frequent complaint travelers make about guidebooks—and the same could be said about popular travel Web sites—is that the places they recommend for eating, sightseeing, and entertainment end up being the most popular places tourists go on vacation. Especially if you're on an international vacation, you may want to avoid other tourists and discover your own places. That can often be much more rewarding. Of course, keeping a guidebook as a safety net can come in handy after you've been wandering around for hours and still haven't found a place to eat or sleep.

He's a Real Nowhere Man, Living in a Nowhere Land...

The Knowhere Guide at www.knowhere.co.uk/index.html is one of the most unique travel guides available on the Web. Designed for travelers in their teens to mid-20s, this travel guide for England is organized by town and region. The town guides contain lists of record shops, music and clothing stores, cinemas, arts and crafts, games, skateboarding and biking shops and spots, comic shops, cafés, restaurants and pubs, street entertainers, and even local celebrities. This unconventional site is not for everyone, but it is an excellent and unique site for its audience. Such specialty sites are useful for vacationers seeking offbeat travel information. Most of the major international travel sites, especially Travel Notes, have links to unique sites like this.

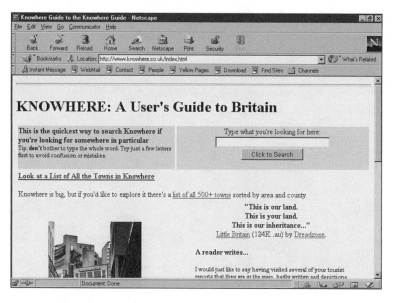

The Knowhere Guide is designed specifically for young adults traveling to England.

Creating Your Own Custom Miniguides

When shopping for guidebooks, I often find myself buying more than one for the same destination. One guide might offer glossy color pictures and easy-to-follow maps, and another may have more extensive hotel, food, and entertainment listings, but with grainy black-and-white pictures and low-quality maps. If one of the books does not offer all, or even most, of the features I need, I usually end up buying both. Then, in a year or two, the information becomes outdated, and I end up buying more books for the next vacation.

Fodor's Travel Online at **www.fodors.com** has one solution to this travel conundrum: custom miniguides. Here's how they work. You first get to choose from a list of 99 cities worldwide, plus a list of general information categories: hotels, dining, recommendations, and essential information. From here you click to a screen that allows you to pick more specific categories to create your own miniguide. These categories include locations within the city, price ranges, hotel facilities, cuisine, transportation, and many other basic travel facts. You can also check the **Our Choices** box to get a list of Fodor's recommendations. After you've checked all the boxes you want, you can click the **Create My Miniguide** button at the bottom of the page and wait for the site to do its work.

As an experiment, I created two separate miniguides: one for London, England, and one for Baltimore, Maryland. For both, I picked all the general categories. In the price ranges for hotels, I wanted to be economical, so I picked the "under $115" category for Baltimore and, splurging a little more for the international trip, I picked both "£80–£130" and "under £80." In Baltimore, only two hotels came up at under $115, but one was a hotel that Fodor's recommends. The site allowed me to select different districts of London, which the Baltimore section did not allow, so I was somewhat selective here, picking locations that I knew were close to places I wanted to visit. I still found 16 hotels in my price range, and the information about the hotels was objective, with descriptions highlighting the pros and cons of many of these lodgings.

The Fodor's Travel Online site allows you to create your own miniguide for one of 99 international cities.

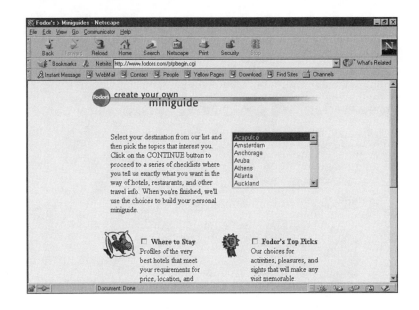

With the dining, I was a bit more selective. If I'm going to London, I only want to try traditional British food (as dangerous as that may be). I also want to check out more traditional pubs and restaurants, rather than fancier establishments, so I limited my price range to under £35. I received 39 restaurant and pub choices, many of which were recommended by Fodor's. With Baltimore, I chose the whole price range, but I limited the cuisine to American, Continental, Italian, and Seafood. Here, 14 restaurants showed up, from "jacket and tie required" to 24-hour diners. In all the restaurant listings, the menu descriptions were mouthwatering. Here's one for Bertha's in Baltimore: "On the main menu, the ballyhooed mussels are the outstanding item. They come steamed, with a choice of eight butter-based sauces such as a garlic sauce with capers, or—in late summer through fall—a basil-pesto sauce made with homegrown basil."

The rest of the information is extensive and basic, much of what you would get in any good online travel guide. The miniguides are written for international travelers, however, so much of the driving and cultural information in the Baltimore guide, like driving on the right side of the road, turning right on red lights, and so on, is not all that useful to American travelers. However, the costs for parking, taxis, buses, and so on can help you figure out your budget. Finally, each guide lists descriptions for top picks of the best things to see and do.

What makes this guide especially useful is that all your essential travel information is concentrated into one short text. You can bookmark your miniguide, or you can print it to take along on your trip.

Although your custom miniguide may not be the only guidebook you need, it can help you filter out the information you don't need in a guidebook, giving a distilled list of essential information. There are no maps or pictures here, though, so this service won't completely replace Fodor's or other companies' guidebooks.

Welcome to Our Town, Any Town

On any road trip throughout the United States, you will come across visitor information centers and kiosks just off the interstate or at rest areas. Here, you can load up on free maps and brochures for local attractions. Most states and major cities now have their own tourism Web sites: Just type in the name of the state plus **tourism** into your favorite search engine. Also, metropolitan convention and visitors' bureaus have their own informative Web sites. At these sites, you can check out links the same way you would the rack of brochures. You can also order tourism information through the good old-fashioned mail.

Please Send Me a Glossy Brochure...and Some Coupons

Most tourism sites have email forms for you to fill out if you want more information. Some allow you to choose what kind of info you want, and others simply put you on a mailing list (an email list, a regular mailing list, or both). If, however, you only want specific information, and you don't want to be inundated with electronic and paper mailings, you might want to contact the local visitors' bureau or department of tourism directly. Their Web sites will usually have contact information either on the bottom of the home page or on a separate contact page. Look for an email address, and then send a polite, short message listing the information you want. If they have the information available electronically, they may send it to you as an email attachment, often as a PDF file. (Whoa, horsey. I'm about to tell you what to do when that happens.)

Holy Tumblers! It's the Adobe Acrobat Reader!

Often, maps and other travel information are available on a Web site or via email as downloadable PDF files, which you can read using Adobe Acrobat Reader software. The Adobe Web site (**www.adobe.com/prodindex/acrobat/readstep.html**) describes Adobe Acrobat Reader as "free, and freely distributable software that lets you view and print portable document format (PDF) files." The portable document format allows you to read downloaded documents exactly as they originally appeared in print, with the same graphics, formatting, and fonts, even if your word processing program doesn't support that particular graphic, format, or font. According to Adobe, "PDF has become an Internet standard for electronic distribution that faithfully preserves the look and feel of the original document complete with fonts, colors, images, and layout." This is particularly useful for travel planning because it allows you to download maps and texts without having to worry about your computer "misreading" or distorting these documents.

Downloading Adobe Acrobat Reader is free, and the instructions on the Adobe Web site are easy to follow. From the list provided, simply click the platform or operating system you use on your computer. (Acrobat is available for both Mac and PC.) Then choose the application you are most interested in using (this information is to give Adobe statistical information and won't affect the software you're downloading).

Also, type in your email address for the purpose of registering the software. Finally, review the memory capacity of the program and make sure that your computer has enough available memory to support it. If your computer's memory is okay, then click the **Download** button. The download could take some time, so be prepared to wait.

With Acrobat installed on your computer, it'll be a cakewalk when it comes time to download maps, travel guides, government documents, and other texts that can help you plan your vacation. And since most of this information is free, it's worth spending the time to have this handy tool available.

The Adobe Acrobat Reader download page features easy instructions for installing the software on your computer.

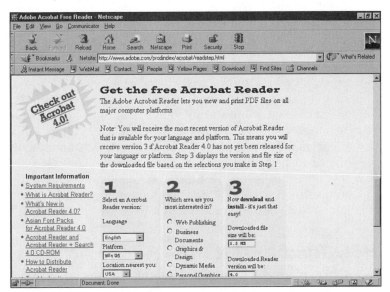

The Least You Need to Know

➤ City and country guides on the Web provide information on dining, lodging, entertainment, and other services. They also may contain maps, directions, special offers, and coupons that can make your travel easier and more enjoyable. The best way to find these guides is through a search engine.

➤ You can use Fodor's Travel Online to create a custom miniguide for your next vacation.

➤ You can use email to contact the department of tourism in the area you plan to visit for travel information and special offers.

➤ You can download PDF files containing useful travel information by using Adobe Acrobat Reader, which is available free on the Web.

Chapter 9

Taking Care of Business Travel

In This Chapter

➤ Tapping into online business travel resources

➤ Using online services to track frequent flyer miles and other travel discount programs

➤ Finding software, hardware, and other tools for staying connected on the road

➤ Going online to gather information for international business travel—foreign customs, etiquette, and languages

Thanks to the Internet and the Web, you'll find an endless supply of online resources and tools to save time and money when making your business travel plans. Travel and entertainment often can be a big hunk of a business's annual expenses, and with the world of e-commerce bringing markets closer together, the business travel market is expected to grow exponentially over the next few years. So while more and more businesses turn to the online world to make their travel arrangements, online resources and travel tools are cropping up to give you more control when making your travel arrangements.

How much business travel you do each year will dictate how you use online travel planning systems to save time and money, as well as how you use the Internet to stay connected when you're on the road. Keep in mind that these days, your business associates and customers expect to be able to communicate with you no matter where in the world you are, so you need to look at hardware options to find the machine that's right for you. You also need to look at Internet access options, as you don't want to have to dial a long-distance number to get a connection.

This chapter goes over the basics on online business traveler resources and how to tap into online flight mile trackers, find hotels that have Internet access, and use your laptop to make the most of your time away from the home office. And although you'll find much of the same information and resources to help you with lodging and transportation issues in the next few chapters, this chapter focuses on the many Web sites dedicated exclusively to the business traveler. Chapter 22, "Staying Connected: Plug In and Log On from the Road," also discusses staying connected on the road, so if you don't find what you're looking for here, give that chapter a once-over.

Web Sites Especially for the Independent Business Traveler

If you're a do-it-yourself business traveler, one Web site may be able to meet all your travel planning needs. At one of the most popular business travel Web sites, Biztravel (**www.biztravel.com**), you can book airline flights, rental cars, and hotel rooms. Or you can use the exclusive Automated Upgrader to increase your chance of a successful move to first class. You can even view all your flight options according to your personalized travel preferences and get last-minute travel assistance 24 hours per day from Biztravel's customer service center. You can even track your frequent flyer account balances, or have a free paging service alert you to flight departure gates and times. You can get notifications of last-minute changes, or drag and drop your travel itinerary into your desktop calendar software or handheld organizer. Best yet, the services are free! If you sign up as a member of Biztravel, be sure to have all your frequent flyer and travel discount program information with you when you go to register. After you've added all your information, you'll be amazed at how much time and money you can save when planning business trips.

Don't Miss Michael Steinberg!

For news, reviews, tips, and links for the business traveler, don't miss Michael Steinberg's Business Traveler Info Network, at **www.ultranet.com/~mes/biztrav.htm**. This thorough and easy-to-navigate business traveler's resource has links to airlines, car rental agencies, hotels, international travel information, weather forecasts, city-specific information, information for PalmPilot users, and links to freeware, shareware, and demoware of the latest, most popular software. Mr. Steinberg's Web site even has travel technology product reviews and an archive of links to online news reports on business travel. You can join the mailing list for news and reports, or email Mr. Steinberg with questions, tips, or comments.

PC Magazine's Road Warrior, at **www.zdnet.com/pcmag/special/roadwarrior/open.htm**, is a great starting place for business travelers. You can use it to get the scoop on organizing your life before you travel and to gather the information you'll need on the road. The Road Warrior guide has a traveler's checklist, laptop and notepad accessories you'll need before you go, travel tips for connecting on the road, top Web sites for business travelers, online services, AOL access numbers, technical support and top notebook vendors, and the Road Warrior's Little Black Book. You get lists of toll-free numbers and Web addresses to major airlines, hotels, car rental agencies, and major credit card companies in case your credit card is lost or stolen. Need to know long-distance access numbers or how to contact major overnight delivery services? Just print out the Little Black Book before you hit the road, and you're off and ready to go.

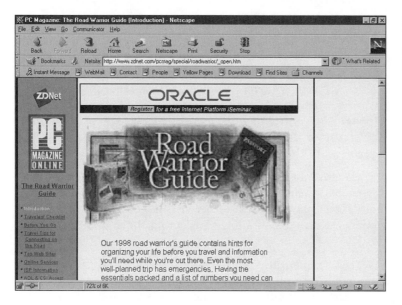

PC Magazine's Road Warrior helps you get organized for taking business on the road.

Businessmeetings.com, at **www.businessmeetings.com**, is an online search and reservation tool that helps you locate meeting venues in your destination of choice. Just complete a quick and easy online form and email your request for a quote. A meeting planning travel advisor will call you back to complete your arrangements. You'll also find a list of more than 6,000 links to business-specific press sites, useful travel and tourist information, and international travel tips.

Frequent Flyer Programs Can Mean Frequent Headaches

Ever get a headache trying to figure out all that frequent traveler information? And have you ever wondered if you're really getting what you earned, or if there are additional advantages and programs you just don't know about? Well, the Web has come to your rescue.

Gettin' Your Business Publications Online

You can keep up with current events on the road by going online to visit *Wall Street Journal* (**www.wsj.com**), *USA Today* (**www.usatoday.com/life/travel/ business/ltb000.htm**), or CNN (**www.cnn.com**). In fact, most media, including TV, radio, newspapers, and magazines, are available online. For a complete list of online news sources, visit Yahoo!'s News and Media directory at **dir.yahoo.com/News_and_Media/**.

Go to Internet Travel Network Business Travel Resources, at **www.itn.net**, and click the **MileageMiner** link, under the Travel Resources heading. The MileageMiner program is designed to help you take control of your frequent flyer programs all at one convenient location. You can store all your mileage accounts, track points, manage your accounts, and keep abreast of the best places and deals going for your mileage.

The personalized reports are also updated daily on the secure MaxMiles Web site, so you can have access to your personalized report any time you need it. Promotional offers included a six-month free trial period, but otherwise, use of the service runs about $2.95 per month or $29.95 a year—not bad considering the amount of time and money you can save.

At **www.frequenttraveler.com**, frequent flyer guru Randy Peterson gives the lowdown on the current 10 best programs in travel and offers his opinion on other air travel issues. You can also get the latest information on partnerships between hotels and airlines or airlines that swap miles with each other by reading the Program, Partners, and Rumors report. The international desk has frequent travel news from around the globe.

Get a Head Start on Impressing Your Clients

Throughout this book, you'll find online resources for gathering destination and other travel information, so if your business travels are taking you to an unfamiliar city, or entertaining clients is on your list of things to do, go online before you leave. You can preview attractions and activities, make dinner reservations, purchase tickets, or get maps to help you get around town. Take a few minutes to go online and see how these traveler resources can help save time and money on your next trip.

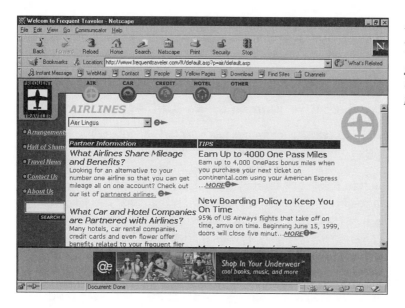

Randy Peterson's Frequent Traveler, at www. frequenttraveler.com, gives the scoop on the latest frequent travel programs.

For city information, a good place to start for major U.S. cities and a handful of international destinations is CitySearch, at **www.citysearch.com**. If you can't find the city you're traveling to, don't panic. You can locate official convention and tourism bureau Web sites for almost any city and country in the world at the Tourism Offices World Directory (**www.towd.com**). And if nothing else, you can usually locate regional information, starting with any search engine. Being prepared with city information also lets your client know you mean serious business, so take advantage of the abundance of free online information.

To learn more about going online to download maps or create point-to-point driving directions, see Chapter 4, "Traveler's Online Resources 101," and Chapter 12, "Trains and Buses." Otherwise, you can visit the popular map site MapQuest, at **www.mapquest.com**.

If you need to locate world bank and world holiday information, visit World Holidays at **www.worldholidays.com**. France pretty much shuts down in the month of August, so be sure to do your homework when making your international business travel plans. Be sure to go online so you know when and when not to try and set up a meeting with your international clientele. Doing a little bit of homework also demonstrates that you've taken an interest in your client's culture and society, which is an inexpensive way to pay a compliment to your international customers.

These Executive Women Mean Business

The Journeywoman Web site (**www.journeywoman.com**) offers this interesting tidbit of information: According to a recent study at Penn State University, by the year 2000, women will account for 50 percent of all North American business travelers. Journeywoman responds to this information by providing tips and advice for women business travelers from tried and true executive women on the road. The Ms. Biz section of the site has travel safety tips, business etiquette tips, solo dining advice, and lots of other practical advice for business women takin' the show on the road. You can check out recent articles at **journeywoman.com/msbiz/msbiz.html**.

Another Web site to check out is the Executive Woman's Travel Network from Delta Air Lines and American Express at **www.delta-air.com/womenexecs** for tips on making your business trips easier, safer, and more productive, plus exclusive airfare and partner offers. Get valuable travel tips and information, like coping with jet lag or proper business etiquette in Chile. Or visit the City Profiles section for information on popular business travel destinations.

Journeywoman is an e-zine specializing in women's leisure and business travel.

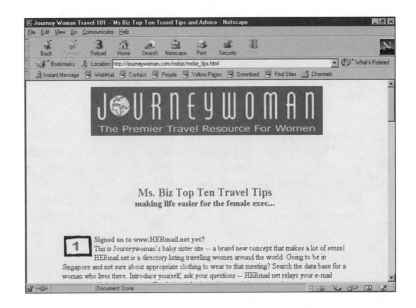

Out of the Office Doesn't Mean Out of Reach

These days, at the very least, business travelers need access to their email to stay in touch on the road and to cost-effectively communicate important information with the home office and customers. And with some recent advances in telecommunication systems and the Internet, you can download faxes, calendars and daily planners, correspondence, reports, and important up-to-the-minute information. If you're going international, though, you need to do some pretravel research to make sure you have the correct electrical equipment and modem—because foreign phone lines and electrical systems can ruin your laptop. Before you hit the ground in Belgium and plug into the hotel phone connection, you need to be sure you have the correct adapter and accessories.

Sometimes you just have to show up for a meeting and you don't need to take a laptop or handheld PC—just a pager and a calling card. But what if you're on an extended trip and you need to stay productive in nonmeeting hours or have work to do afterhours to prepare for the next day? Sometimes you need to make special arrangements to be sure you can access the information you need, without spending a fortune on long-distance bills. One place to start when looking for hotels with Internet access is Internet Hotels, at **www.internethotels.net**, for a short list of U.S. and international hotels that offer online hookups. You should also check with the hotel itself to find out what kind of business traveler facilities and services it offers.

Another option is to look into wireless connections. A good place to start your shopping is Mobile Planet, at **www.mplanet.com**, an online catalog featuring items for the business person on the go. The major phone companies, too, like Sprint and AT&T, have special programs for businesses requiring wireless or universal Internet access.

Getting Business Travel Product Reviews Online

Sure, there are lots of ways to stay connected on the road, but most likely you're going to need a laptop, notepad, or personal digital assistant (PDA) like a PalmPilot to retrieve information from the homebase and stay productive and reachable around the clock. (For more information on PDAs, see Chapter 22, "Staying Connected: Plug In and Log On from the Road.") I'm not in a position to recommend one system or brand over another without first knowing what your needs are. But lucky for you, there are plenty of people who will tell you what you need and why you need it.

A good place to start for product reviews is *PC Magazine*'s Small Business Buying Guides at **www.zdnet.com/smallbusiness/filters/buying_guide/pdas/** for the low-down on all your business travel techno needs. Another guide is Product Review Net, at **www.productreviewnet.com**. From the home page, just type in the keyword of the item you're interested in buying, and you'll get both editorial and enduser reviews. Otherwise, consult with a reputable computer hardware specialist, or pick up a copy of *The Complete Idiot's Guide to PCs* for the lowdown on laptops, handhelds, and other computer devices that are designed for mobile users and business travelers.

I like CNET's product review site, too. You get down-to-earth reviews, input from real users, rating systems, price comparisons, and recommendations from CNET's editors. Check them out at **www.computers.com**.

What About Unified Messaging Services?

Online unified messaging services aren't free, but there is no such thing as a free fax or voicemail message, is there? In any case, when it comes to convenience, unified messaging systems may be the best way to go to keep up with faxes, email, and voicemail. But what is unified messaging? It's a complete solution for managing your communications from anywhere in the world where you have access to a computer or telephone. One of these services, JFAX.COM Unified Messaging (**www.jfax.com**) brings all your voice messages, faxes, and email messages to a single place—your email inbox. With unified messaging, you get a personal phone number in your destination city, and when a fax or voice message arrives, it's converted into an email message and sent to your inbox. If you're at your computer, simply click to view your faxes or listen to your voicemail messages. If you're away from your computer, dial a toll-free number to check your voice, fax, and email.

On the average and at the time of this writing, using a unified messaging service includes a one-time service activation fee, usually around $10 or $15, plus a monthly service fee, usually around $10 or $15. If you use a toll-free number to access your email inbox by phone, you'll be charged for each additional minute, usually around a quarter or so. If you use JFAX.COM to send faxes anywhere in the continental United States, you'll be charged about a nickel per fax page. International prices may vary. For local service in Japan, there is a one-time service activation fee of about $30 and a monthly service fee in the $20 to $25 range.

The Least You Need to Know

➤ Business travelers can use online reservation and frequent traveler tracking systems to manage their own business travel.

➤ You can easily locate city information, print maps, and get business traveler tips online.

➤ You can use email, unified messaging services, and other online business traveler services to stay connected when you're on the road.

Chapter 10

Air Travel

In This Chapter

➤ Deciding which type of air travel Web site to use

➤ Going online to learn the secrets of the airline industry

➤ Getting tips and advice from other travelers and air travel experts

➤ Finding out what the major one-stop travel shopping sites have to offer

➤ Finding discount airfare and Internet-only bargains

If I had a nickel for every time someone asked me, "Which Web site should I use to get the best deal on airfare?" I'd be close to retirement. In fact, if that's a burning question in your mind right now, go ahead and send me a nickel...or more, if you're so inclined. Besides buying directly from an air carrier, you can make use of the hugely popular fare comparison sites like Travelocity, Expedia, Internet Travel Network (also known as GetThere.com), and Preview Travel to locate the best deals on airfare. In fact, you can hardly ignore these sites when you go online to plan a trip. The key thing to remember, though, when you start checking out fare-compare and airline corporate Web sites is that they essentially all draw on the same source for travel rates and schedules—the same global distribution systems that travel agencies use.

Don't Duplicate Your Efforts

There are only a handful of these travel information systems, like Sabre, Worldspan, Amadeus, and Galileo, and they're used by all the travel service providers to make travel information accessible to consumers and travel agencies. So remember that you're probably going to get the same information at one booking site that you'll find at another—and that includes what you'll find at the airline's site or the fare-compare sites. It's the same information!

The real difference between the various sites is the way the discount rates are handled, how easy it is to find reduced fare information, and the types of features the site has to handle multidestination itineraries. For now, think about what kind of traveler you are and create a profile for yourself. That will determine what kind of information you need, how often you need it, and what's most important to you as a travel planner. Is it price? quick access to travel resources and tools? one-stop shopping? online customer support? site security and privacy? Remember, though, an easy way to save time online is to make use of sites like Fodor's that have pulled together links and other resource sites for you.

The first question to ask yourself is: Are you going to buy online, or are you just researching options and rates? If you're looking and not booking, you can find a fare quote online and then have your travel agent check out the rates and book the flight for you. (In fact, at Internet Travel Network, you can book your ticket online and pick it up at your travel agency.) If you're buying online, you benefit from the luxury of the fare-compare features that instantly get rates from as many airlines as you want, and you also have access to Internet-only bargains. Plus, using the Web to compare rates sure beats calling around to five or six different airlines and talking to a representative at each.

The second question to ask is: How much do you travel? If you travel by plane more than three times per year and select your air carrier based on price alone, you should probably choose one multipurpose booking site, register as a member, and take advantage of the various tools and tracking services available to help you find the best deal. If you're a frequent flyer, you should use a site that lets you search based on flight rewards and gives you the tools you need to maximize your frequent flyer miles. If you get one vacation a year and don't travel by plane very much at all, you could go either way...directly to the airline if you know about a special deal or price, or log on to one of the fare-compare sites. It's up to you.

116

What Is Electronic Ticketing and How Does It Work?

You can go online to find answers to this question, and many of life's other mysteries. The Electronic Ticketing site (`www.iata.org/eticket/links.htm`) lists several informational sites on electronic ticketing. You can find out what others think, and learn which airlines are using electronic ticketing. You can gather tips for using ticketless travel or learn about one company that's working with self-service ticketing and check-in. At Travelocity (`www2.travelocity.com/custsvc/e_tkt.html`) you can find out about the electronic ticketing process and why you should choose electronic booking, when you will be billed, how to change reservations with an e-reservation, how to travel without a paper ticket, and how to pre-reserve a seat.

Are you a flexible or impulse traveler? Can you fly out on a moment's notice for a four-day weekend in Vegas? Then find an online booking site that has a special category for impulse travel and last-minute bargains. If not, you probably don't need to worry about weekly low fare notifications sent out by the airlines or a discount virtual travel agent. Or what if your air travel itinerary is somewhat complicated—say you're flying to one city, driving to the next, then flying back to the original destination and returning by plane to your city of origin? Ouch, now my head hurts. Better use a booking site that can handle multiple destinations. Or what if you're a business traveler and you're on the road maybe as much as eight or a dozen times each year? That's some serious frequent flyer miles you've racked up, so you may want to look at a site like Biztravel (`www.biztravel.com`) for your online booking needs.

That's a lot to think about, but the good news is that the online booking sites have already asked those questions, too, and have put together systems to meet the needs of any kind of traveler. The sites reviewed in this chapter represent the best of the best, and I can't recommend one over the other, as I haven't found any huge differences between them. As a general rule of thumb, you'll find similar features and the same rate and schedule information at each site. You just have to test drive each one and figure out which one you like the best.

There's some pretty fierce competition in the travel industry. And it's not just between the air carriers. The fare-compare and low-fare Web sites want your business, too, as much as everyone else. As a traveler, what you can expect out of this competition are great rates, superb online customer service, and quick and easy access to all the tools and information you need to plan your trip. And remember, the sites are after your business, so what's good today will be even better tomorrow, as the battle to win your business rages on.

Bookmark Fodor's Resource Center at www.fodors.com/ resource/airtravel to start your online air travel planning or shopping. With links to airline Web sites and online booking sites, you're just a click away from becoming your own travel agent.

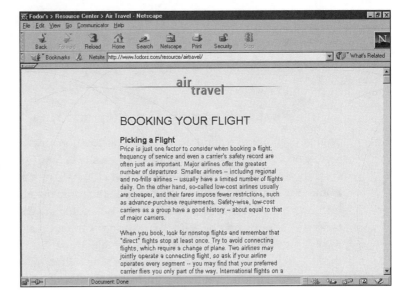

Some Sites to Get You Started

Curious about how the air travel industry works? Ever wonder how rates are determined and why it costs more to fly one way than round trip? You can go online to meet and learn from air travel experts and get the inside scoop on the mysteries of the air travel industry. Be sure to read up on the differences between domestic and international airfare pricing structures and regulations—it's interesting stuff!

Strangeways, Here We Come

Ever wonder about the aircraft you're flying on? Who made it and where did it come from? Strangeways Airport Transport Guide, at **www.strangeways.com**, has information on airports, aircrafts, and airlines, plus a directory of airport Web sites. If you're flying in a particular region, just click on the image map, and you'll be linked with the airlines that serve the area. Then click on over to the airline of your choice.

If you're the curious type and want to learn more, check out the following sites for the down and dirty of the air travel industry:

➤ **Moon Publications Practical Nomad**
(`www.moon.com/practical_nomad/pnexcerptsmyths.html`) The publisher of *Road Trip USA* and other great travel books offers advice and information for air passengers and travelers in general. Check out the Myths About Airline Fares and Routes for advice and explanations on the myths and mysteries of air travel, like why it's costly to purchase an open-ended ticket. The Practical Nomad also says tickets are not always cheaper at the last minute, because if you plan ahead you can normally get a better deal. Any myths you may have believed about air travel will be shattered! This is an essential starting point, too, if you're looking into international air travel.

➤ **The Ticked-Off Tourist** (`www.ticked.com`) A thing or two to say about the air travel industry, like "Senior Tourists Ignored," a feature article on how the online booking and fare-compare sites don't always help seniors find out about senior discounts. Even though senior discounts are often available, many of the search functions don't have a place to indicate whether you qualify for such a discount.

➤ **Passenger Rights.com** (`www.passengerrights.com`) Airline passengers have rights? Yes, but you've gotta fight...for your right...to fly-ay (apologies to the Beastie Boys). Even if you don't get your way, it at least gives you a forum to vent your frustration and share your air travel horror stories with other passengers. You'll be shocked at some of the things that take place on airplanes and in gate terminals. If you have a complaint to register, you can do it through this site.

➤ **Consumer Reports Online** (`www.consumerreports.org`) Click **Categories**, **Leisure**, and then **Reports** to learn about how the airline industry is affecting travel agents. Are they losing commission and being squeezed out of the process? Is it cutting down the number of options that the travelers have? Get the answers to these and other air travel questions. Looking for the inside scoop on other reports on travel, scams, and other topics of interest to travel consumers? Check out the first and most referenced consumer protection organization this side of the Rio Grande. You can access many of the reports for free, or you can get an online subscription to *Consumer Reports* for a low monthly fee.

➤ **The Air Traveler's Handbook**
(`www.cs.cmu.edu/afs/cs.cmu.edu/user/mkant/Public/Travel/airfare.html`)
The FAQs posting from the **rec.travel.air** newsgroup, courtesy of Mark Kantrowitz of Carnegie Mellon University's computer science department. The site includes information and links on airlines, charter flights, frequent flyer programs, airports, online reservation systems, and more. It's a good starting point if you have questions about air travel or need a starting place to learn about the travel industry. It includes lots of non-air travel links, too.

➤ **Fodor's Resource Center** (`www.fodors.com/resource/airtravel`) One of the best sites for travel information on the Web. You can find a listing of all major airlines in the United States and abroad, and you can preview aircraft layouts. You can also find out about airline safety, locate places to book online, book charter flights, find consolidators, find couriers, learn how to cut costs, find discount passes, get information on check-in and boarding, learn more about how to enjoy your flight, and dig up contact information on where to complain about service.

➤ **Airlines of the Web (`www.flyaow.com`)** Dedicated to online information and reservation systems. One nice feature about this site is that you can become a registered user, or enter the site as a guest and never log on. Features include a low-fare ticker, toll-free airline numbers, cyberfare specials, cargo airlines, medical transports, airport codes, air tips, aircraft specs, and virtual airlines.

➤ **Aviation Internet Resources (`www.air-online.com`)** Several databases you can search for airline, aircraft, and airport information. You can also talk about the airline industry in the airline newsgroup, or check out aviation news resources.

Airline Directories

Sometimes the easiest way to buy airline tickets online is to go straight to the source. All the major airlines have virtual ticket booths where you can get schedule and rate information, and of course book the flight using a credit card. You can also sign up for email notification of special deals and end-of-the-week discounts. This is especially valuable if you live in or near a hub city. But you need to read the fine print. As usual, special deals come with strings attached and often have blackout dates or require Saturday stays. Before you commit your money, spend some time reading the restrictions and guidelines posted on each site. Of course, it's easy to locate toll-free numbers for assistance if you can't find the information you're looking for or need help making your reservation.

Major North American Carriers

If you're a loyal flyer on a major North American carrier, or you simply want to collect fare information or book a flight, you'll find most of the following sites have easy-to-use navigation and other helpful information to help you book your flight, whether you do so online or work with your travel agent:

➤ **Alaska Air**   `www.alaskaair.com`

➤ **Aloha Air**   `www.alohaair.com`

➤ **America West**   `www.americawest.com`

➤ **American Airlines**   `www.aa.com`

➤ **American Trans Air**   `www.ata.com`

➤ **Continental Airlines**   `www.continental.com`

➤ **Delta Air Lines**   `www.delta-air.com`

➤ **Hawaiian Air**   `www.hawaiianair.com`

➤ **Northwest Airlines** `www.nwa.com`

➤ **Reno Air** `www.renoair.com`

➤ **Southwest Airlines** `www.iflyswa.com`

➤ **TWA** `www.twa.com`

➤ **United Airlines** `www.ual.com`

➤ **US Airways** `www.usair.com`

➤ **Vanguard** `www.flyvanguard.com`

➤ **World Airways** `www.worldair.com`

International Airlines

Don't worry. Just because you're flying Japan Air Lines doesn't mean you can't log on to an English version of the Web site. For fare and schedule information and to book your flight, most of the following major international carriers offer online ordering and customer support:

➤ **Aer Lingus** `www.aerlingus.ie`

➤ **Aerflot** `www.aerflot.org`

➤ **Aero Costa Rica** `www.centralamerica.com/cr/tran/aero.htm`

➤ **AeroMexico** `www.aeromexico.com`

➤ **Air Canada** `www.aircanada.ca`

➤ **Air China** `www.airchina.com.cn`

➤ **Air France** `www.airfrance.fr`

➤ **Air New Zealand** `www.airnz.com`

➤ **Air UK** `www.klmuk.com/main/home/index.asp`

➤ **Alitalia** `www.alitalia.it`

➤ **Austrian** `www.aua.co.ata/aua`

➤ **British Airways** `www.british-airways.com`

➤ **Canadian Airlines** `www.cdnair.ca`

➤ **Cathay Pacific** `www.cathaypacific-air.com`

➤ **Cayman Airways** `www.caymanairways.com`

➤ **China Air** `www.china-airlines.com`

➤ **Cubana** `www.cubaweb.cu/cubana`

➤ **El Al (Israel)** `www.elal.co.il`

➤ **Finnair** `www.finnair.fi`

➤ **Gulf Air** `www.gulfairco.com`

➤ **Iberia** `www.iberia.com/home.html`

➤ **Icelandair** www.icelandair.is/interpro/icelandair/ipbwi2.nsf/pages/front
➤ **ILAN Chile** www.lanchile.com
➤ **Japan Airlines** www.japanair.com
➤ **Korean Air** www.koreanair.com
➤ **Kuwait Airways** www.travelfirst.com/sub/kuwaitair.html
➤ **Lufthansa** www.lufthansa.com
➤ **Malaysia Air** www.malaysiaair.com
➤ **Mexicana** www.mexicana.com
➤ **Philippine Airlines** www.philippineair.com
➤ **Polynesian Airlines** www.polynesianairlines.co.nz
➤ **Qantas** www.qantas.com.au
➤ **Royal Jordanian** www.rja.com.jo
➤ **Scandinavian Airlines System** www.sas.se
➤ **Singapore Airlines** www.singaporeair.com
➤ **South African Airways** www.saa.co.za/saa
➤ **Spanair** www.spanair.com
➤ **Swissair** www.swissair.ch
➤ **TAM Airlines** www.tam_airlines.com.br
➤ **Thai Airways International** www.thaiair.com
➤ **TransBrasil** www.transbrasil.com.br
➤ **Turkish Airlines** www.iminet.com/sms/Turkish
➤ **Virgin Atlantic** www.fly.virgin.com/atlantic
➤ **Virgin Express** www.virgin-exp.com

One-Stop-Shopping Sites

Thanks to the online information network—that thing we know and love as the Web—it's never been easier to compare airfares, research schedule information, and even get Internet-only discounts. The multipurpose booking sites, or fare-compare or one-stop shopping sites, are certainly tapping into the sales potential of the Web, and have created and developed Web sites that are easy to use and can help save you time and money when purchasing your airfare online.

1travel.com

www.1travel.com is jam-packed with free information about saving on travel expenses. No wonder it's gotten so many awards and accolades. Using this airline savings toolkit, you'll find features like airline news, ask the expert, alternative airports, drive-and-fly guide, low-fare airline directory, pricing strategies, and a flight check to find out if a flight is on time. You'll also find extensive links for travel activities, destination guides, lodging information, weather, yellow pages, currency exchange, and maps. You can also sign up for low-fare notification.

Travel Now

www.travelnow.com lets you book international and domestic airfare simply by entering your departure and arrival cities and dates. In the International Fare section, you begin by choosing dates and whether you depart from the United States. Then you choose your departure city and arrival city, and voilà!—it finds the lowest fare. Just for fun, I did a fare search from Indianapolis to Paris, traveling January 5 to January 25. The lowest price I found was $839 on United Airlines. Then I used the same itinerary plans in the Domestic Airfare section, but had the use of more filtering criteria to customize more aspects of my trip. I also got to choose how I wanted the entries displayed and my choices for times and airlines. The flights I found going through the Domestic Airfare section were between $650 and $720. Go figure.

Internet Travel Network

Way back in 1995 Internet Travel Network (www.itn.net or www.getthere.com) launched the very first online real-time reservation system for use by consumers. Although the Sabre system was accessible via the Web to travel agencies, ITN pioneered what we know today as consumer-oriented online booking sites. Now known as GetThere.com (you can still locate the site at www.itn.net), Internet Travel Network has an easy registration process, making it good for first-time users. You can book online for airlines, hotels, car rentals, and cruises. One nice feature is that you don't have to wait until you're ready to enter your credit card number to get to the secure part of the site. Doesn't that make you feel good?

One feature this site has that many others don't is the multicity search. If you're planning a trip that takes you through several countries or cities and you plan on getting around by plane, this is the perfect site. You can also combine air and car travel and create an air/road trip itinerary. This site is especially helpful if you're taking a world or European tour. The Internet Travel Network system powers other popular travel sites, such as The Trip, Flifo, CNN's Interactive Travel tool, and TravelWeb, so you can use a number of sites (I like The Trip myself) to get the same rate and schedule information.

Travelocity

Travelocity (www.travelocity.com) has several useful features when it comes to making airline reservations and for locating deals and discounts. Fare Watcher is a unique email fare notification service that monitors up to five different flights and alerts you if the fare changes significantly. My buddy Tricia got an email yesterday alerting her that a flight to Cancun had dropped $280 below the price she indicated she was willing to pay, and then today, she got another email saying the fare had risen $300. Moral of the story? If you find a good deal, book it, Dan-o.

➤ Travelocity's Flight Paging features gives you updates on important flight information, via your alphanumeric pager. For departure/arrival information, you find out the current status of a flight with real-time departure and arrival information direct from the Sabre system.

➤ The Travel News section has the latest on fares sales and other news from the world of travel.

➤ You can create a profile that tells Travelocity your preferences in seating, payment, delivery address, and personal information.

➤ The Best Fare Finder allows you to find low fares in the United States, Canada, the U.S. Virgin Islands, and Puerto Rico if you're flexible with when you are flying. There are normally restrictions on the time of day and day of week you can fly, but the Best Fare Finder gives you the cheapest flight. You can also search by destination and travel date. This will not give you the lowest flight to the destination, but it will produce the lowest fare for the chosen day.

➤ You can find the status of a reservation by going to the main travel menu and choosing **Retrieve Existing Reservations**. Ticketing and delivery information is displayed if your ticket has been printed.

Previewing Seating Plans at Travelocity

Travelocity and most other online booking sites have travel seat maps available for most of the major airlines. When booking your flight, you can see which seats are open and where they are. This is a nice feature if you like sitting in a particular part of the airplane.

Microsoft Expedia

Microsoft once again takes the cake in terms of popularity and revenue with this hugely popular online booking tool. Ranked the number-one travel site at `www.100hot.com`, you'll run into Expedia just about anywhere you go online. From the mighty Fare Wizard to the Fare Tracker email low fare notification, Expedia has plenty of features to make your online airfare shopping a breeze. Here's a quick overview of the features you'll find at Expedia:

➤ You can use the Lowest Fare Finder by typing in your departure and arrival cities. Restrictions on when you can fly might apply, so make sure you read all the rules.

➤ In the Fare Wizard you enter the city of departure, destination, dates, and number of people traveling (up to six) and their ages. Then you can choose whether it is more important to depart at the times you listed or to get the cheapest fare. It will then generate a list of fares. Next choose **Choose and Continue**, and you will get a detailed description of the flight you chose (miles traveled, flight time, meal, airplane, cost with taxes).

➤ Get specific flight information by entering an airline, a travel date, and a flight number.

➤ Sign up for Fare Tracker, an email newsletter, and find out about low fares. You can specify up to three trips to track. You will receive an email update on the best fares every week.

➤ Become a member of MaxMiles MileageMiner. For about $30 a year, you can check the current status of your frequent flyer program miles, view detailed records of your travels, verify missing credits, find out how to get more miles, and watch for upcoming expirations. If you order three tickets from Expedia in one calendar year, Expedia will pay the membership fee.

My Momma Told Me, You Better Shop Around

A good number of the online booking sites let your hold your airfare search results for about an hour, giving you time to check out other possibilities before you book your flight. Although you aren't technically reserving the seat, you can save your results in the system while you shop around. Remember, though, the rate you're quoted can change quickly, so you have to pay to lock in the price.

Preview Travel

The highlight of Preview Travel (**www.previewtravel.com**) is a feature you won't find on any of the other booking sites. Preview Travel's Farefinder collects fare information based on the airport of departure. It lists schedules and prices for every flight leaving a particular airport and lets you get fare information without also having to enter a destination or even a particular travel date. You can look for low fares up to three months in advance, and get information about current prices compared to a three-month average so that you can easily locate rates that drop five percent below the three-month average.

When you select hotel, air, and car reservations, you have to log in to the system. After you've registered (and as long as your browser is set to accept cookies), each time you return to the site, you're greeted personally and are able to access your travel preferences, information, and itinerary profiles and reports. Then you can choose which option—air, hotel, or car—you would like to get information about and make reservations for. You can also modify your profile, sign up for an email newsletter, and more.

Stand-outs at Preview Travel include the FareAlert notification service and thorough destination guides, courtesy of Fodor's. Some other highlights you'll find at Preview Travel include:

➤ The FareAlert service notifies you via email if the fare you want to pay is found, and gives the details on the restrictions and requirements.

➤ The Travel Sorter gives you one-stop shopping for all your travel needs.

➤ The Travel Newswire offers special travel deals and industry news. The two featured fares for Friday, July 16, were $99 cross-country fares and $39 America West fares.

➤ Destination Guides by Fodor's travel writers lets you research your trip to more than 200 U.S. and international destinations.

➤ At Vacation and Cruise Packages, you can search either by destination or by interest. Also, you can choose the vacation finder option and pick a search function. There is also a section with reviews from other travelers.

➤ Under Great Summer Deals (or other seasonal offerings depending on the time of year you're traveling) you can get special offers that are only good for a limited time.

➤ The Car Finder and Fare Finder give you up-to-the-minute listings of the cheapest fares and car rentals.

➤ The Business Travel Center tells you about special corporate deals and frequent flyer and traveler information.

➤ To make this site more accessible and easier to use, the Site Shortcuts feature lets you access any part of the site from any other. The categories you can access are reservations, destination guides, vacations and cruises, fare finder, car finder, business travel, travel newswire, tips and advice, travel store, map center, weather center, video gallery, currency converter, site overview, and about us.

The Trip

www.trip.com is powered by Internet Travel Network. Known on Trip.com as IntelliTrip, this reservation and fare-tracking system is the same thing you'll find at other online travel ticket sites like Web Flyer (**www.webflyer.com**)—but I really like the look and feel of this site. Another highlight of The Trip is the FlightTracker feature, which allows you to track, in real-time, the arrival and departure of a given flight. Say your mom is due in on the 3:00 from Tampa. You can check the arrival time and gate to make sure her flight is on time. And if the flight is running behind schedule, you can be notified via email when it lands. Cool.

The Guides and Tools section has several categories for you to explore: destination guides, maps, airport guides, currency converter, world clock, per diems, international holidays, fare aware, and flight alert. The newsstand also gives you a wide selection of information. You can find out more about deals, headlines, top story, plugged in, road warrior, on your side, ask randy, frequent flyers, and trip talk.

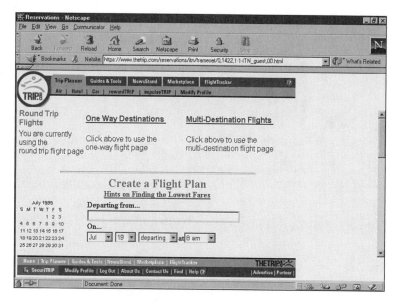

The Trip's airfare search features let you search for fares based on frequent flyer rewards, best price, or multicity destinations.

Internet Bargain-Hunting for Travel

How easy is it to find Internet-only discounts? If you know where to look, it's quite easy. In fact, you don't even have to go out looking. Besides going out and looking for discounts on airfare, you can have them come to you through low-fare notification through your email (but we'll talk more about that later).

Learn2 Shop for Bargain Airfares (`www.learn2.com/browse/tra.html`) tells you what you need to know to find a reduced fare. Learn what a courier company is, how to consult consolidators, where to find charters, how to use your modem, how to research rebaters and travel agents, and how to call airlines directly. This is a good beginning tutorial for bargain hunters.

Another good place to get your feet wet with finding special discounts for online shoppers is Epicurious Travel's "Airfare Bargains on the Net" primer, complete with links, descriptions, and tips on finding good deals on air travel. You'll find this information at `www.travel.epicurious.com/travel/c_planning/02_airfares/intro.html`.

Most online booking sites have special Internet-only fares and claim that the price quoted is only guaranteed when you book through their Web site, although I've been quoted the same rate by calling a toll-free number or by looking at other airfare discount sites. But as long as you get a good deal, who cares?

Learn2 teaches you how to find the best deals on air travel, from calling consolidators to putting your modem to work. This is one of my all-around favorite sources of information.

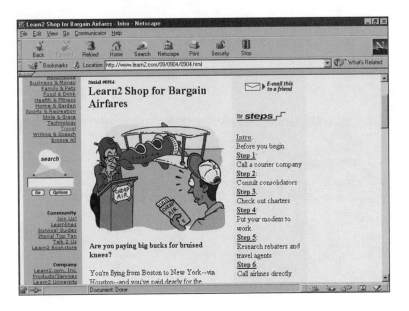

As of this writing, the following major airlines offer such discounts through their sites:

➤ **American Airlines** `www.aa.com`

➤ **American Trans Air** `www.ata.com`

➤ **America West** `www.americawest.com`

➤ **British Airways** `www.british-airways.com`

➤ **Continental Airlines** `www.continental.com`

➤ **Delta Air Lines** `www.delta-air.com`

➤ **Northwest Airlines** `www.nwa.com`

➤ **Southwest Airlines** `www.iflyswa.com`

➤ **Swissair** `www.swissair.com`

➤ **TWA** `www.twa.com`

➤ **United Airlines** `www.ual.com`

➤ **US Airways** `www.usair.com`

Reduced Fare Notification Services

Go to Epicurious Travel's Discount Travel section online (at `www.travel.epicurious.com/travel/c_planning/02_airfares/intro.html`) and kill all your birds with one stone at the All-in-One Signup. On this page Epicurious has generously and thoughtfully assembled the signup forms for all seven (Air Canada, American, Cathay Pacific, Continental, Icelandair, Southwest, and US Airways) of the bargain-fare notification programs they review. These forms go straight to each airline's computers. To unsubscribe or to report problems, you must contact the airlines directly.

Fare Mail (**www.mytravelguide.com/tools/faremail.asp**) also helps you find low fares. You have to enter your name and password, and then fill in a form with more information. Fare Mail will then send you an email to notify you when the fares to the destinations you have chosen drop. You can then go to **www.mytravelguide.com** to purchase a ticket online. To sign up for the service, enter your home airport, email address, destination information, how many times you want to be notified, and for how long (you can make it automatically stop in three weeks, for example, if you just want to try it out).

Smarter Living (**www.smarterliving.com**) is a free online consumer community dedicated to helping people save time and money. Smarter Living sends its members weekly email newsletters detailing last-minute Internet deals and the latest travel promotions. Why go looking when Smarter Living will deliver the latest information on 20 airlines, all to your email inbox for free? It also has a growing travel resource section that includes guides and travel tools. Plus, members are eligible for special discounts on hotel rooms, airfare, and car rentals. You can't book through this site, but you can easily link to the travel providers' online systems or find toll-free numbers to make reservations.

The following major airlines offer fare notification emails, but once again, be sure to read the rest of the chapter, as I'll give you some pointers on finding discount airfare at other types of travel sites:

➤ **American Trans Air**   www.ata.com

➤ **British Airways**   www.british-airways.com

➤ **Delta Air Lines**   www.delta-air.com

➤ **Northwest Airlines**   www.nwa.com

➤ **Southwest**   www.iflyswa.com

➤ **Trans World Airlines**   www.twa.com

➤ **US Airways**   www.usair.com

Consolidator Fares

Consolidators buy big blocks of tickets from airlines well in advance of the flight to get discounts from the carrier—the airline would rather know the tickets are sold, rather than risk being stuck with a bunch of unsold seats. So the discount gets passed along to you, if you know where to shop. Listed here are some of the more popular discount airfare sites. Be sure to read the fine print so you understand the rules of the game before you spend time shopping for deals. Some sites require you to give your credit card information just to become a member (to discourage casual shoppers from tying up the Web site), so if you're not comfortable with one consolidator's shopping policy, move on to the next:

➤ **Cheap Tickets Online** (**www.cheaptickets.com**) Requires immediate online registration with a credit card number to enter the site, but the online discount ticketing agency does have exclusive deals with major air carriers, so if price truly is your main concern, it's worth a look. The search process can be tedious, especially for an occasional user. After you enter your travel information, you get results from each airline, and then you have to sort through those results to check availability and flight times. Another bummer is that if you don't purchase a ticket within your first five logons, your account is suspended for about two weeks. Although I did find some of the lowest rates here, I just wasn't wild about the interface and the no-buy, no-look policy. The credit-card-first policy is to discourage the casual shopper from getting in the way of serious shoppers. After you're registered, though, it's just seven clicks to a really good deal on airfare.

➤ **Up and Away** (`www.upandaway.com`) A consolidator that gets reduced rates from the airlines and then sells them at prices that beat the best fares available directly from the airlines.

➤ **Best Fares** (`www.bestfares.com`) A consolidator that tells you hidden travel deals, air travel bargains, weekly Net specials, and more. You can also find out about deals by signing up for the email newsletter.

➤ **Going Places** (`www.pbs.org/wnet/goingplaces2/expert-q4-week2.html`) Has an Ask the Travel Expert section, with travel experts to answer your travel-related questions. Go online to PBS to learn about air consolidators—what they are and how they can be beneficial. This site also recommends consolidators that you should check out.

Using Online Airfare Auction Sites

Don't want to pay full price for your airfare? No problem. How much would you like to pay? Just name your price at an online auction site, and see if your price is matched. The sites differ slightly in how they work, but they're easy to use and you'll find plenty of help on getting your feet wet. Some of the sites even have practice auctions where you can test the waters before you enter the real bidding game. A word to the wise—be sure to read the FAQs and the fine print before you use the sites. Some require credit card information upfront to use the system, and others automatically bill you if your price is matched:

➤ **Travel Bids** (`www.travelbids.com`) A reverse online auction. You enter in your name, address, credit card number, a one-line description of your travel needs (like leisure or business), a full description of your travel needs, the number of passengers, and how long you give the agents to respond. Then your vacation is bid on by several different travel agencies, and you get to pick the best trip. A $5 fee is included in this process. You can even check out some of the deals that other people have gotten.

➤ **Priceline** (`www.priceline.com`) This site lets you name your price for home mortgages, credit cards, airline tickets, and hotel rooms. You can fill out a request with where you want to go, the dates you want to travel, and the price you want to pay. The best way to get a low price is to find out what the going price is on the market, and then bid 25 to 30 percent below that. If you enter an unreasonable bid, you just won't get any takers. Remember that after you submit a request and your price is matched, tickets are automatically issued. Also, all tickets purchased through Priceline are nonrefundable, nonchangeable, and non-endorsable. You also can't select a specific airline, and you can only submit one request per trip. By requesting a ticket from Priceline, you agree to depart between 6 a.m. and 10 p.m., make up to one stop each way, and not to use any frequent flyer miles or upgrades. A lot of rules, huh? Something about the home mortgage services seems a little funny to me. I've heard stories about people getting incredibly good deals through Priceline.com, but I've also read some not-so-flattering reports. I'd say exercise some caution, but check it out if you're curious about this new way to buy travel.

➤ **Onsale.com** (`www.onsale.com/category/air_travel.htm`) Gives a list of airfares available to bid on. There are also "QBs," or quick buys, but you don't have to bid on these: The quantity of QBs is limited, and the price is only open for a certain amount of time.

➤ **Bid 4 Travel** (`www.bid4travel.com`) Also has auctions for different travel-related items. You can bid for cruises, sailing charters, hotels, air, and so on. The site has a list of hot deals so you can see what is currently happening at the site. Also, you get to see the restrictions for each auction. At this writing, there are no airline fares up for auction, but there are several hotel rooms, especially in Orlando, Florida.

➤ **eBay** (`www.ebay.com`) I feel safest using eBay online auctions because of its online escrow system. Your travel dollars are safe, shopping at this hugely popular online auction house. Although you'll find more travel packages than just airfare for sale, it's worth a look around. Again, I'd exercise caution with online auctions and "discount sites" in general, and whatever you do, *read the fine print*. If the site offers an escrow service to hold your cash until the goods are delivered, it's worth the small fee to have a little peace of mind.

➤ **Amazon.com** (`www.amazon.com`) Another reputable source for good deals and plenty of options. An easy-to-use system, the World's largest bookstore is perhaps the pinnacle of electronic commerce sites.

Air Courier Flights

A courier flight is a discounted method of traveling internationally, oftentimes up to 50 percent the regular airfare. A courier company purchases a regular ticket on a major airline and then offers a split fare arrangement—you pay them 50 percent or less of what they paid and get the seat and the carry-on luggage allowance. The courier company gets the check-in luggage allowance. You simply act as the courier, or warm body, as international regulations require that check-in luggage be accompanied by a passenger. It's also a customs regulation that passenger luggage can only gain immediate customs clearance if the passenger is present. So in exchange for accompanying a letter, package or check-in luggage, courier flights can mean big savings. Usually on the return trip, you don't have to worry with courier duties.

Often you can earn frequent flyer miles on these overseas excursions, but be sure to check with the courier company. Generally, courier flights can be booked from one day to three months in advance, but last-minute deals go on special two weeks before departure, sometimes as much as 60 to 80 percent off the regular price. When you have flown with a courier company several times, you are eligible for their standby list (ability to leave at a minute's notice). People who fly standby usually fly for free. Read more about courier travel at these informative sites:

➤ **Courier Travel (www.couriertravel.org)** Lets you search for discount international airfare by destination, departure city, or last-minute deals. To become a courier, you have to join the club for about $40 per year, or $55 for couples or companions. That's not bad in light of the savings potential. The site also has a FAQs section and a thorough explanation of how courier travel works, so if you're just curious, check it out.

➤ **Courier Travel Flight News (www.beatthemonkey.com/travel)** A site where you can order a list of courier companies for about $6, which isn't too bad considering you could save big bucks on airfare. You can purchase flights for much less by doing this, and you can even make ticket plans several months in advance.

➤ **Courier Flight Airfares and Details (www.adventure1.com/chplist.htm)** Gives a list of flights that typically need couriers, how much they typically cost, and how long you have to stay at the destination. Flights originate in the United States and go all over the world. To access the courier information, you then have to purchase a book with all the contact information.

Flexible Traveler? Check Out Airhitch

Airhitch (**www.airhitch.org**) lets you fly across the Atlantic for under $500 roundtrip. Basically, the system is similar to flying stand-by. It was created for the free-spirited, independent traveler.

Tracking Your Frequent Flyer Miles with the Greatest of Ease

Although some of the one-stop booking sites—like The Trip (**www.trip.com**)—let you search for airfare based on the rewards and frequent flyer programs, other Web sites are dedicated to helping you get the most out of your frequent flyer rewards. If you travel often, you should take a peek at these sites:

➤ **MaxMiles MileMiner (www.maxmiles.com)** For about $30 per year, you can make use of this online frequent flyer tracking service that helps you manage your reward programs to make sure you're getting what's coming to you and how to get even more rewards for your flight miles. A partner of Expedia's travel service, you'll find this service featured on Expedia's Web site as well.

➤ **AirEase (airease.net)** Software that can be downloaded free to track your frequent flyer miles. It comes equipped with information on most major airlines, hotels, and car rental agencies. You just have to download the software and create a personal profile. You can also post or read messages about the software, or receive email notices on updates to the program.

Just for International Travelers

There's a big difference between international air travel pricing and that of domestic airfares. Important distinctions affect how you should shop around for discounts on international travel. For a complete explanation of how international airfares differ from domestic pricing structures, be sure to read through Travel Library's "FAQs: Consolidators, BucketShops, and Discounted International Airline Tickets," at **www.travel-library.com/air-travel/consolidators.html#5**, courtesy of travel agent Edward Hasbrouck. Mr. Hasbrouck says there's no point in going to United States–based online booking sites like Expedia or Travelocity to do your international airfare shopping, but you should check out travel agents, consolidators, and specialists in finding deals on international travel. You can get a start at these helpful online resources:

➤ **European Travel Network (www.etn.nl/)** Allows you to look for the hottest deals in international travel. Find low fares, cheap cruises, low-cost car rentals, and more. Also, you can sign up to win free trips. This site can also connect you to travel chat and other interesting features.

➤ **Air Supply (www.air-supply.com)** A travel agency specializing in international travel. You can find the going rate on international airfares and send in a fare request to find the best rate.

➤ **FAQs on Air Consolidators and International Ticket Discounters (www.travel-library.com/air-travel/consolidators.html)** A travel library entry about how to get the best deals on international airfares.

You Can Pick Your Friends, and You Can Pick Your Seat...

But you can't pick your friend's seat. According to Trip.com's Travel guides and strategies page (www.**securitrip.com**), this is what they had to say about the best row to sit in on the plane; of course, this guide refers to coach class seating, not business or first class:

To sum up the good advice you'll find in the "Guides and Strategies" section, these are some things you should look for when picking your seat, based on what's important to you as a flyer:

1. **First on, first off**   If you want to make a mad dash for the exit door once the plane lands, get a seat close to the front of the plane. Even if you're flying with a carrier like Southwest that doesn't have reserved seating, getting to the airport about an hour before your flight increases your chances of getting the seat you want.

2. **Fresh air**   The second-hand smoke issue applies only on international flights, but obviously if you have an aversion to cigarette smoke, you'll want to pick a seat in the no-smoking section. The circulation of fresh air moves from the front of the plane to the rear, so unless the smoking section is in the front, a seat in the first third of the plane is better.

3. **Smooth or crunchy?**   I'm not talking peanut butter here. A wing seat offers the smoothest ride, while the seats in the back are usually the bumpiest. Another reason to get to the airport early.

4. **Onboard entertainment**   Unless those inflight magazines can hold your attention for the duration of the flight, you may want to catch a flick en route, so be sure to steer clear of galley areas, as you won't be able to see a thing, and get a seat about three rows back from the screen for optimal viewing.

5. **Lazy boy**   I just took a flight with a companion who chose the no-recline row. Granted, we were close to the front, but we sat in an upright position the whole way. The rows at the very back of the plane and the rows in front of the emergency exits usually don't offer room to recline.

6. **Setting up camp**   Want some room to spread out? If the flight's not sold out, sometimes the rows at the rear of the plane and near seats blocked out for flight attendants are open territory for stretching out or spreading out.

7. **Long legs?**   I'm no Amazon queen, but even people of average stature have trouble finding seats with enough leg room. If you're long and lanky, leg room is a serious concern, and there are seats that offer more room than others, but of course, there are strings attached. The main entrance area seats have more leg room, but toilets or galleys can mean an increase in traffic. The bulkhead has lower traffic, but no under seat storage, and often times nearby seats are occupied by moms and babies. The emergency exit rows have more leg room, no moms and kids, and under-seat storage. You'll be called on to perform emergency duties if the need arises, but how often does that happen?

8. **Other special considerations**   If you're non-ambulatory, special seating is available, but make sure it's close to handicap-accessible toilets. Bulkhead seats are ideal for parents traveling with kids. And if it's simply peace and quiet you're looking for, a seat farther away from the galley and toilet areas offers the least distraction.

Thanks to The Trip (`www.trip.com`) for these handy tips in selecting airplane seats!

The Least You Need to Know

➤ Many airlines and online travel agents offer Internet-only discounts and travel deals.

➤ You can buy directly from airlines or use fare-compare sites to get the best deal and make quick and easy reservations.

➤ You can go online to find airfare consolidators and other discount airfare brokers.

➤ You can bid on airfare and travel packages at online auction sites.

➤ You can learn about the secrets of the airline industry, get tips and advice from air travel experts, and learn how to fly like a pro.

Chapter 11

Takin' It to the Streets: Traveling by Car, RV, or Motorcycle

In This Chapter

➤ Finding roadside attractions and oddities on the not-so-beaten path

➤ Finding your way with interactive atlases and maps—for free

➤ Finding RV travel resources and park directories and connecting with like-minded road warriors

➤ Avoid traffic headaches by getting reports on traffic, road conditions, and construction zones

➤ Locating information and safety tips for international road travel

I've been there, and you *can* get there from here. But how many times have you been on the road and stopped to ask directions to get an answer like this: "Take a left at the first railroad crossing. You'll pass about five or six houses, go under the bridge, and take a left when you come to a fork in the road. Head away from town, and keep your eyes peeled for a big, brown cow. It's pretty much a straight shot after the cow, but if you pass the little white chapel with the red door, you've gone too far."

Nothing can be more frustrating than getting lost on the road, especially if you have a car full of people thinking to themselves, "Should've gotten a map," or "Should've gotten better directions while we had the chance." Hopefully thoughts won't turn to "Should've stayed home." Well, the Web has plenty of road travel resources available for free to anyone needing door-to-door or city-to-city directions, insider information on roadside attractions, daily construction warnings, speed trap reports, weather conditions, or a guide to off-the-beaten path restaurants and shops. Even if you're a wanderer on the road less traveled and don't mind getting lost, there are plenty of oddities and bizarre roadside attractions that you'll be happy to discover.

Finding Online Road Trip Guides

There's the road trip and then there's traveling by car. If you're trying to get there fast or looking to get a slice of Americana life on the road, this chapter's for you. I've compiled a list of road travel sites that feature the various styles of road travel— including cars, RVs, motorcycles, and road tripping—as well as interesting roadside attractions.

Although many of the popular travel sites like Travelocity and Expedia offer road trip guides, those sites are more oriented to air travel, hotel and vacation packages, and road travel on major freeways. To find specific road travel information, I'd recommend starting at a search engine or directory. Or get started at one of these road travel resource sites, and soon you'll be on your way to getting ready to take it on the road.

To find these tips and guides, I once again started with my trusty Web directory. Yahoo! (**www.yahoo.com/recreation/travel/automotive**) has a directory of sites covering car rental information, driving directions, highways and roads, recreational vehicles, roadside attractions, scenic highways and byways, traffic and road conditions, and vanning. The following are some of my favorites:

➤ **Moon Books Road Trip USA (www.moon.com/road_trip/index.html)** has the most extensive list of road trip links I've come across. It's an online extension of one of the most popular road travel books, *Road Trips USA*, and if you don't go anywhere else to research your road trip, you'd better stop here. Interactive driving tours along more than 30,000 miles of classic blacktop include point-by-point descriptions that cover kitschy oddities, local history, apple-pie diners, and more, distributed over 10 yards of clickable image maps. The travel links include guides to old roads, travelogues, byways, highways, and "mobilia." You can also order your own copy of *Road Trip USA*—recommended reading for any road tripper—directly from the publisher.

➤ **The Great Outdoor Recreation Pages** (**www.gorp.com/gorp/activity/byway/byway.htm**) has lots of links to national scenic biways and other recreational drives, and also features driving activities and attractions, listed by region.

➤ **Roadside America (www.roadsideamerica.com)** The authors of *Roadside America* magazine put together an equally entertaining Web site. It's a hilarious, strange, and wacky guide to offbeat road travel and roadside attractions. I'd like to meet those folks some day. Perhaps I'll run into them in Muncie, Indiana, when I go to check out the World's Largest Collection of Mason Jars. Or maybe at the pet cemetery in Terre Haute, Indiana, when I go to pay my respects to Stiffy Green the bulldog.

The Online Guide to Road Food (Not Road Kill)

A must-see site for planning your road trip or driving adventure, Eat Here (www.eathere.com) points you in the direction of old-fashioned good food and cheap eats. Eat Here is the original online dining guide to more than 550 popular roadside diners and road food restaurants in the United States and Canada, and includes authentic recipes, budget vacation-planning links, books, cookbooks, and videos. Click the **Road Signs** page and explore goofy signs (like "Eat Here. Get Gas") spotted in roadside eateries and along the highways and byways. And if you have stories to share or diner recommendations, the site has interactive forms where you can type in and post your tale of road food adventures.

There's No Such Thing As a Free Trip...

They say the road to Hell is paved with good intentions. So make it a point if you're traveling across an unfamiliar route or to a never-visited destination to go online and create point-by-point driving directions, print out maps, order atlases, or get traffic and road condition reports.

There are a number of route-planning programs online, including Mapquest (www.mapquest.com), Mapblast (www.mapblast.com), Maps On Us (www.mapsonus.com), and DeLorme (www.delorme.com). The features of these mapping systems are fairly similar and they're all user friendly, so see which one you like best. Upon entering the mapping sites, you'll be asked where you're coming from and where you're headed. And because many of the mapping sites are sponsored or supported by hotels and other lodging facilities, you'll also have the option to include places to stay along your route. You can even ask for restaurant stops, ATM locations, gas stations, national parks, and historic landmarks. You can also request directions that take you along scenic routes, direct routes, or major interstate routes.

So for my trip out west, I created a guide at Free Trip (www.freetrip.com) going from Lafayette, Indiana (you're probably wondering why I would want to leave Lafayette), to San Francisco, California, with a preference of scenic routes, including en route facilities for B&Bs, ATMs, and national parks. After I entered my information, an online itinerary was created in less than a minute. I also had the option to have an email version of the itinerary sent to my inbox, although I'd recommend just printing out the online version of your route planner, since the email itinerary contains essentially the same information that you see onscreen.

Traveling on Busy I-95? Need Exit Information?

The *Online I-95 Exit Information Guide* is the Internet version of a travel book containing food, gas, lodging, camping, shopping, and road side information along I-95, the busiest interstate in the nation. The online site at `www.usastar.com/i95/` `homepage.htm` also contains the latest road construction reports and weather information, a guide to the best gas prices, and an I-95 travelers' forum.

Route-planning tools offer point-to-point directions and include en route information like lodging, rest stops, and attractions.

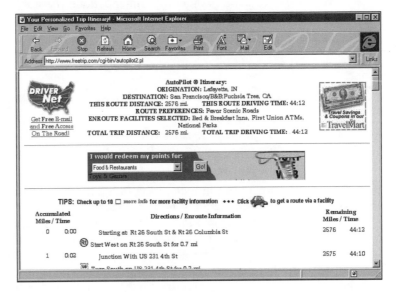

Then I prepared a second itinerary for the next leg of my trip, from San Francisco to Astoria, Oregon, and went through the same filtering options to select what en route services and attractions I wanted included in my customized itinerary.

What's with All the Construction?

For traveler's tales of life on the road, newsgroups are a good place to fish for bits of advice, post questions, and get answers to some of life's deepest questions. The `misc.transport.road` site is where travelers, like Bruce, can ask questions and get helpful answers:

Question: *What is the story with the construction on U.S. 6 where it crosses the NY Thruway, near Harriman (Interchange 16)? They did a nice job of connecting it to NY 17 (the future I-86), but what now? Is it being widened all the way to the Bear Mountain Bridge?*

—Bruce K.

Answer: *Because of crossover accidents coming down the mountain, we're adding a median barrier. It was decided to connect the acceleration lane for the ramp from Rte 17/Averill Ave to the climbing lane, to provide a constant cross section, rather than dropping the right lane, then adding a right lane on the far side of the bridge. It's only going up the mountain to just west of Rte 293.*

—Jim M.

Locating Traffic Reports, Road Conditions, and Maps

Although rush-hour traffic jams and hectic weekend and holiday travel often result in horrible driving experiences in major metropolitan areas, a traffic delay any time during your road trip travels can really ruin your day, and sometimes your whole vacation. And although it's impossible to predict traffic problems caused by accidents or other unplanned events like loose livestock on the freeway, avoiding major construction zones or planning ahead to take detours can save you a lot of time and frustration.

Learning to Control Road Rage

Thanks to the good folks at AAA for providing an Adobe Acrobat PDF brochure called "Road Rage: How to Avoid Aggressive Driving." You can download the brochure from `http://www.aaafts.org/Text/roadrage.pdf` and print it out right from the Web. To get your free Adobe Acrobat Reader and directions on how to install this useful plug–in, visit `www.adobe.com/prodindex/acrobat/readstep.html`. Adobe's Acrobat Reader works on all operating systems and browsers.

Did you print out the AAA road rage brochure I told you about earlier? After you read this tale of traffic horror, you might want to bring it along for the ride, because it's best to be prepared for life's little surprises…like sink holes. On a family trip to Florida when I was a kid, both southbound lanes of the interstate caved in (literally); there was no way around the massive hole in the road, and no exit ramp for miles in either direction to detour traffic. Besides having to sit between my brothers, who refused to acknowledge the "no legs or arms in my zone" boundaries that I had established early on in the trip, the car's air conditioner rolled over and died. And there we sat, for six miserable hours, like sardines, with no air conditioning.

Now, sink holes aren't as common as road construction. If you plan ahead and scout out traffic reports and road conditions before you go, you can either plan an alternate route or alter your schedule to pass through at a time when traffic flow is least likely to be heavy.

Here's a list of sites you can check with before you set out on your journey to get up-to-the-minute information to help avoid foreseeable traffic problems:

➤ **Metro Networks (`www.metronetworks.com/transportation.html`)** Provides traffic (Metro Traffic Control) and local news, sports, weather, and other information to more than 1,800 radio stations and 100 television stations in more than 70 markets in the United States. Included on their site is a list of travel and transportation links to state department of transportation Web sites, major metropolitan traffic report sites, and other travel links.

➤ **Federal Highway Administration (`www.fhwa.dot.gov/trafficinfo/index.htm`)** Lists current national traffic and road closure information. Since the information is broken down by state, if you're travels take you across state lines, search for regional information under any of the states you're traveling through. For example, there's a Gary-Chicago-Milwaukee traffic site dedicated to travel through "Da Region."

➤ **Traffic Spy (www.trafficspy.com)** A good source for traffic and roadwork information sites. The folks who put together the travel Web site directory on the Traffic Spy site say they "spied on a zillion highway-traffic related sites." From that research and with ongoing updates, Traffic Spy provides visitors with travel information at home and away. You'll also find a city and state directory of traffic reports, as well as roadwork and travel information. Many major metropolitan city sites have real-time traffic reports, some even live cams.

➤ **The Web Speed Trap Registry (www.speedtrap.com)** Has a thorough listing of known speed traps by state and highway, and tips on what to do if old smokey nabs any of you leadfoots out there. The site even has reports of foreign speed traps.

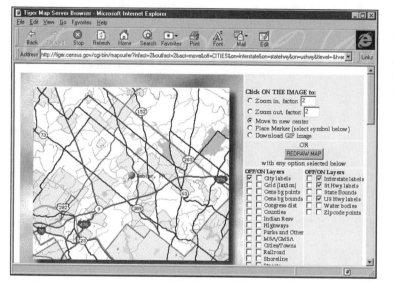

The Speed Trap network at www.speedtrap.com links you to speed trap zones across the United States and some foreign countries.

Getting Ready for Narrow, Overseas Roads and High-Energy Adventures

If you're headed overseas and plan on getting around in a rental car, there are a few things you should know before you get behind the wrong-sided wheel of a car. I'll talk more about overseas driving in Chapter 13, "Getting Around," but there are a few sites you can check out if you do plan on driving on your international adventure:

➤ **The Travlang Company (www.travlang.com)** Has information for European and other international road travel to help you learn about road signs and conventions, traffic codes, traffic-related vocabulary, and general rules of thumb for safe travel.

➤ **At Europe by Car (www.europebycar.com)** Apply for an international driving permit and find information on road safety, as well as car rental and leasing options. (I'll talk more about that in Chapter 13.)

➤ **The Association for Safe International Road Travel** (www.asirt.org) A nonprofit organization that promotes road travel safety through advocacy and education. The Road Travel Reports contain information on road conditions, driver behaviors, seasonal hazards, city, rural, and interstate traffic. The site also lists the most dangerous roads in more than 60 countries around the world.

Wanna Be Recognized Around the World?

When traveling overseas, it's a good idea to carry an international driving permit (IDP), even if you don't plan to drive. If you need to communicate with foreign authorities, this form of identification is more widely recognized than others forms. Valid in over 150 countries, the permit contains your name, photo, and driver information, translated into 10 languages. If you belong to an auto club, you can usually apply for your IDP at the office and sometimes online. You can also download an application at DLC Driverlicense.com (www.driverlicense.com) and send it in with the necessary documentation, or visit one of their offices.

Reviewing Safe Driving Tips at Consumer Reports Online

A good number of the reviews and reports at Consumer Reports Online (www.consumerreports.org) are free for the taking, but you can also subscribe to the online version of this popular magazine for a very low monthly fee. Of special interest to travelers, though, is the report at www.consumerreports.org/Special/Samples/Reports/9806driv.htm, where you'll find many important tips and more. The following are some of the tips that happen to be my pet peeves, but the site's list is much more extensive, so be sure to check it out:

➤ Go with the flow of traffic.

➤ Signal your intention!

➤ Stay off the car phone while you drive!

➤ Stay out of the left lane unless you're passing (a law in many states).

➤ Buckle up.

➤ Be nice and let other drivers merge.

RV and Camping Info

RVs are truly a family travel and camping vehicle for all seasons. But RVs aren't just for camping. With all the comforts of home, these versatile vehicles are a fun way to enjoy life on the open road. These homes on wheels are gaining in popularity every year, and they take travelers to national parks, sporting events, cycling adventures, and other fun-filled road trip destinations.

From RV newsgroups to forums and message boards, you'll find lots of RV information online, including buyer's guides, tips for rookie RVers, newsletters, RV show dates, and much more. Here are some good places to start looking for RV info online:

➤ **GoRVing** (www.gorving.com) Lots and lots of links to help the recreation vehicle traveler take the trip of a lifetime. The site offers tips for traveling with kids and pets, plus a directory of RV campgrounds and parks across the United States.

➤ **U.S. National Forest Campground Guide** (www.gorp.com/dow) Fred and Suzi Dow began surveying and publishing information on campgrounds in the U.S. National Forests in the summer of 1996 and have gathered an extensive pool of campground information and pictures.

➤ **U.S. Army Corps of Engineers Recreation Facilities** (www.gorp.com/gorp/resource/us_nra/ace/acemain.htm) The Army Corps of Engineers provides more than 30 percent of the recreational opportunities on federal lands. You can find some ideal camping spots, listed by region.

Another RV resource listed at this site is "RVers Have Many Sources of Information," by Chuck Woodbury (www.gorp.com/gorp/activity/rv/outwest2.htm). Check out Chuck's article, which lists organizations and paper media–based sources of information for RV enthusiasts and first-time RVers.

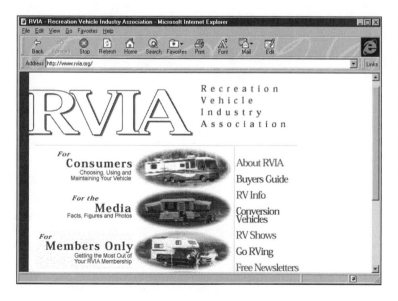

The Recreation Vehicle Industry Association (www.rvia.org) has lots of useful information for both experienced and rookie RVers. Link to the GoRVing Web site from the Rookies RVers button, or get the scoop on the latest models of RVs if you're looking to buy.

Easy Riders Take to the Road

If your passion for road travel involves two wheels instead of four or more, you'll still find plenty of tips, resources, and motorcycle sites on the Web:

➤ **The Motorcycle Vacation Guide** (`www.mcguide.com`) Offers an operator's guide, a vacation archive, a message board, articles, and links to trip planning services.

➤ **Road Riders** (`www.roadriders.com`) An extensive list of touring information and site links, including campground information, motorcycle rentals, worldwide travel tips and guides, and a rider's message board.

➤ **Road Trip Travelogue** (`www.road-trip.net`) A motorcycler's travelogue with daily updates from the road.

➤ **Bikermania** (`www.bikermania.com`) Features motorcyclists' rights, clubs and organizations, and links to information on restoration services, riding apparel, bike safety, classifieds, and off-road resources.

The Least You Need to Know

➤ You can find off-the-beaten path roadside oddities and attractions at road tripping sites.

➤ You can create customized point-to-point driving directions and lodging guides online and print out maps to take on the road.

➤ Up-to-the-minute traffic and road condition reports are available online.

➤ RV and motorcycle travelers will find plenty of forums, message boards, and links to guide you to useful online sources for road travel information.

Chapter 12

Trains and Buses

In This Chapter

➤ All aboard for train and bus travel

➤ Save time and money going online to find schedules, fare information, special offers, and multi-city pass information

➤ Take the scenic route and preview the scenery online

➤ Go online to gather schedule and route information if you're traveling internationally by bus, train, or subway

If you travel by train or bus, you know how nice it is to sit back, relax, and enjoy the ride. And for people who just don't like to fly or drive long distances, bus and train travel are good options for getting to your vacation destination. Travel by train or bus can often be more affordable and offer more flexibility than flying, and major carriers like Greyhound, McCafferty's Express Coaches, Eurail, Interrail, and Amtrak offer student, child, family, and senior discounts, as well as seasonal travel passes for multi-destination travel.

You can go online to buy train and bus passes, compare costs, check schedules, get fare information, and preview destinations. If you're traveling internationally, the Web is an excellent place to check Eurail and Interrail information and get the inside scoop on the best (and cheapest) way to travel. You'll even find information on group and theme travel, such as sporting events, shopping, holiday, historical, dining trips, and lots of other special-interest tours.

Finding Schedules and Fare Information

The Amtrak (**www.amtrak.com**) and Greyhound (**www.greyhound.com**) Web sites have up-to-the-minute schedules and fare information, and up-to-date information on special offers and seasonal promotions. I haven't come across any low-fare notification services or online auctions for finding cheap bus and train tickets, but who knows…the Web is still young. You can sign up for a Rail Mail notification at **www.amtrak.com**, and Amtrak will send you updates on special offers, theme travel, and other excursions on the Amtrak Northeast line (and possibly other lines in the future). On the Web, you'll find plenty of travel agents that specialize in train and bus travel. They have the latest scoop on good deals, so if you're new to train or bus travel, it might be a good idea to check with an agent.

Train, Train, Let's Go Away

The good folks at Amtrak said it best: "What's the attraction of train travel? It's the scenery." Think about it. You rarely see Amtrak trains chugging along next to you on interstates or highways. That's because the tracks run along scenic routes, along vistas and rivers, 'round mountains and through valleys. Well, you'll have to check the route you're taking to get the details on scenic attractions, but the point is, it's a nice, relaxing way to travel.

So whether you're taking a train to get from point A to point B, or to check out the sights between the two points, you'll find all the information you need when you visit the Amtrak Web site. For tips and advice on planning scenic rail travels or for a glimpse at sample itineraries from experienced rail travelers who recommend routes based on the time of year you're traveling and what time of day you're passing through, these itineraries are specific to the Northwest, Southwest, and Northeast scenic triangles. After all, you don't want to be traveling through the Great Plains during the day and through the Rocky Mountains in the middle of the night. (If you're like me, on the other hand, you feel that mountain passages are best left to the darkness.)

The Amtrak Web site (**www.amtrak.com**) has gone through some major improvements over the past few years. What once was a not-so-user-friendly site is now a rail traveler's dream. At the Amtrak Web site, you can connect with travel agents specializing in Amtrak travel, purchase passes and tickets, get up-to-the-minute rate and schedule information, use the station locator search feature, preview routes, watch video clips of some of the routes, and find links to lots of Amtrak-related sites, as well as some "unofficial" Amtrak Web sites and other rail-related sites.

Getting the Most for Your Railway Money

Just because they like you, Amtrak sells Rail SALE tickets exclusively through its online reservation system at **reservations.amtrak.com**. These Rail SALE fares offer substantial discounts—up to 70 and 80 percent off the regular fare—on one-way travel to certain destinations. Sure, you might have to leave the terminal at 6:00 a.m., and you have to be willing to use your credit card online to make the purchase, but it's a good deal if you're looking to save on transportation costs.

If you're interested in one of these Rail SALE tickets, be sure to read the restrictions because these tickets are nonrefundable, and you can't exchange them, use them with any other offer, and so on. You most definitely can't get these great deals through a travel agent or an Amtrak ticket clerk. So get your credit card ready and check Rail SALE fares for your destination of choice! If you need tips for ordering tickets online, check out Chapter 6, "Before You Buy...Protecting Yourself Online."

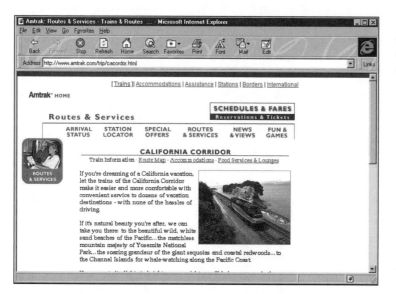

You can visit Amtrak online to check arrival status, use the station locator, or order tickets.

Here are some other train travel sites for checking schedules and fare information, as well as finding other general information on train travel in North America:

➤ **Rail Travel Information** (`www.res.bbsrc.ac.uk/plantpath/Railway/`) is maintained by Mike Adams, a U.K.-based railway enthusiast. This page contains links to useful U.S. and international rail travel resources: schedules, maps, route planning tools, and so on. These sources are generally in English, and some are maintained by enthusiasts, so you'll want to contact the railway for official details. Mike makes it easy by listing URLs for most of the major rail lines, and provides other useful travel links. This is a must-see site if you're traveling by train.

➤ **Fodor's Resource Center** (`www.fodors.com/resource/traintravel`) Fodor's is on of my favorite all-around traveler resource sites on the Web. The Train Travel Resource Center includes United States, Canada, and international rail travel information and lots of links to other train travel sites.

➤ **Train VIA Rail Canada** (`www.viarail.ca`) Canada's rail system Web site, featuring fares and schedule information, special offers and packages, a preview of Canada's major destinations, and much more, all in English and French.

➤ **Train Web** (`www.trainweb.com`) A comprehensive guide to rail travel Web sites, including private railcars, rail traveler reports, books to enhance your Amtrak and VIA travel experience, and more.

Finding Train Touring Routes

Once again, my trusty buddy Yahoo! has helped me find train touring routes for the United States and international destinations. To get this type of information, go to `www.yahoo.com`, click **Travel** (under the Recreation and Sports header) and **Train Travel**. This category is broken down into Companies, Railroad Museums, Tourist Trains, Train Hopping, Web Directories, and Usenet.

If you use another search engine, look for similar category breakdowns, or just use the keywords **train AND tours** and include a region or destination like **southwest** or **California** if you want to pinpoint your information more quickly.

In Yahoo!, the Usenet link will take you to various train newsgroups, but when I visited, the topics being discussed were along the lines of model trains and other train enthusiast interests than about travel. There are other travel newsgroups at `www.deja.com` you can visit if you have specific questions about scenic train travel. See Chapter 5, "Online Travel Communities 101," for the scoop on using newsgroups.

You can also use a search engine to find a number of amateur and commercial sites with scenic train touring route information, a couple of which are listed here:

➤ **RailServe** (`www.railserve.com`) One of the most comprehensive railroad site directories on the Web. Not only does it provide passenger and urban transit rail information, but it also provides all kinds of mouth-watering information for model train and railroad enthusiasts. Besides the impressive list of rail sites you'll find (more than 3,000 of 'em) the RailServe Web site features a forum, a chat room, and a search feature. The chat and forum are geared toward non-passenger travel, but you never know what you'll find in a chat room or forum. The most amazing thing about this award-winning site is that it was started in 1996 by a 13-year-old boy named Christopher Muller.

➤ **Great Train Escapes (`www.greattrainescapes.com`)** Offers three magnificent rail and land journeys, which highlight the most beautiful regions in the United States and Mexico. You can travel by deluxe train and motorcoach during the daylight hours and spend nights in hotels. At the site, you can send in a reservation request form for a tour operator to call you back. As always, make sure to read the fine print on deposits, refunds, cancellations, and so on.

➤ **Orient Express (`www.orient-expresstrains.com/index.html`)** Offers high-style train travel through exotic routes in southeast Asia, as well as Europe and Australia. Use the site's Travel Planner to find the route, schedule, and itinerary of your choice, and even make your reservation online. You can also preview some photos of the compartment and scenery along your route.

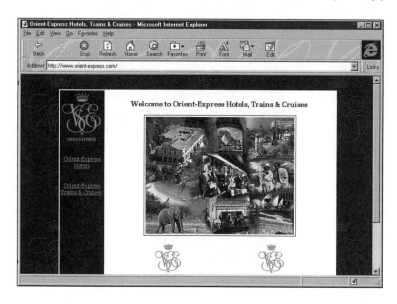

The Orient-Express Web site features train and cruise specials, complete with routes, regularly updated special offers, and links. You can preview dining menus, train and ship layouts, and scenic route photography, and you can complete an online booking form.

Some of these rail information sites and sites like them are "unofficial," so before setting in stone any plans to visit, call ahead to train museums or railroad attractions to verify information. (You'll notice, too, that some of the scenic rail tours are offered through tour operators and travel agencies—not completely do-it-yourself, but you wanted to find out about scenic train routes, so there you have it.)

Special Information for European Travelers

I've said before if you can find a Web site that's gone to all the trouble of researching and gathering links to related Web sites, you should take full advantage of someone else's efforts. And on that note, here's a big, fat thanks to Rick Steves' Web team for building a one-stop European rail travel information site (**www.ricksteves.com**), complete with message boards, Eurail and Interrail train information, links, resources, tips, advice…just about everything you ever wanted to know about train travel in Europe.

Rick is an expert on European travel and has pulled together some very helpful and informative Web sites to help you plan your European vacation. One of Rick's areas of expertise is rail travel, so be sure to visit his site to save time when you go online to research your European rail travel options.

Travelers Speak Their Minds on the Top European Scenic Train Routes

Wanna hear what real travelers have to say about the best and most beautiful scenic train routes in Europe? Take a look through travelers' postings at Rick Steves' official Web site (**www.ricksteves.com/graffiti/graffiti50.html**). Read postings like this, from Jeff K. of Park City, Utah: "One that I will always remember is the trip from Brigto Locarno, Switzerland, via Italy. You change from the Brig–Milan train in Domodossola to a narrow gauge local. It winds through the steep, narrow valleys, stopping frequently. The views are of old stone houses, small vineyards, and tiny villages perched on steep hillsides, accessible only by footpath. Truly a stunning step into the past!"

Locating Eurail Guides and Information

Rail travel in Europe is one of the most popular and affordable ways to travel from point to point or with a focus on just a few countries. You can also get passes for touring within select countries. And because the options are so varied, you're sure to find plenty of Web sites dealing with European rail travel. You can even order your Eurail passes online and get schedule and route information, so all aboard for Eurail travel site searching!

A good first stop in your search for Eurail and other European rail transport system information is Rick Steves' "Guide to European Railpasses" (**www.ricksteves.com/rail/ 99intro.htm**), which can help decide which pass you need. In fact, you'll learn just about everything you need to know about European rail travel. But if it's more information you crave, there are some other information-packed Web sites out there:

➤ Great Britain and Ireland aren't part of the Eurail system, but you can get a Britrail pass for travel there. You can visit **www.britrail.com** for complete information on fares and schedules.

➤ Eurostar's Chunnel, the high-speed passenger train that crosses the English Channel through a tunnel, takes you between London and Paris, and other key stops like Brussels and Euro Disney, along the way. You can get Chunnel schedules and pass information at **www.eurostar.com**.

➤ At Rail Europe's one-stop European vacation Web site (**www.raileurope.com**) you can get detailed fare and schedule information and purchase tickets (up to 60 days from the day you want to travel), plus book flights and reserve hotel rooms. This is a complete guide to all of Europe's various rail systems, including links, information national railways, and online timetables and travel planners. You can also visit the European National Railways and Timetables at **mercurio.iet.unipi.it/misc/timetabl.html**.

Get a Free 1999 Guide to European Railpasses

Leave it to Rick Steves, backdoor travel guru and host of the PBS "Travels in Europe with Rick Steves" series. Rick's kind enough to provide a free, online rail travel guide at **www.ricksteves.com/rail/** to help you make sense of the overwhelming options of European rail travel. You can also request a printed version of the guide by filling out an online request form.

Besides the railpass guide, you'll find loads and loads of travel tips, country guides, and the Graffiti Wall message board, which offers tips and advice from real-world travelers. If you're looking for guided tours based on Rick's backdoor philosophy, you can get that information at the Web site, too. It's a great resource for advice on point-to-point train tickets and car rentals.

To Reserve or Not to Reserve

Should you make reservations for rail travel in Europe? Rick Steves doesn't think so. Reservations, which carry a price tag, are required for some high-speed rails, longer routes, and first-class seats, but generally speaking, unless the schedule is marked with an *R*, reservations aren't required and usually aren't necessary. Unless you're traveling during a high-traffic holiday period, you can probably skip the reservations. Seat reservations, which cost from $3 to $10, can be made as far as two months in advance and up to a few hours in advance. You can get refundable reservations in Europe at train stations or travel agencies.

You can get expert advice on European rail travel at the Rick Steves Web site.

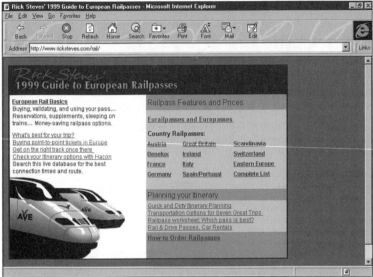

Would you feel better if you had reservations? For peace of mind, after you've purchased a railpass, you can call RailEurope at (800-438-7245) or the issuing company (check the upper-right corner of your pass) to make reservations. Reservations made in the United States cost $11 per seat, and cannot be changed or refunded, so you better not get off schedule on your European adventure! Definitely pay a visit to **www.ricksteves.com/rail/** to get tips and advice on traveling Europe by rail.

> ### From Trains to Ferries
>
> Sometimes your point-to-point travels require you to take a ferry from one shore to the next. For a complete guide to worldwide ferry systems, be sure to visit Dan Youra's Youra Studios International Ferry Listing at **www.youra.com/ferry/ intlferries.html**. Another worthy stopping point for ferry information is the Ferry Center at **www.ferrycenter.se**, a Swedish site devoted to ferry and waterway transportation systems throughout Europe.

Get on the Bus, Gus

I don't remember much about the trip, but as a young girl about 9 or 10 years old, my older sister and I traveled by bus to visit our aunt, Sister Pat the Nun ("The Good Sister"). Mom plopped us on the Greyhound, and off we went on an unsupervised adventure that took us about 70 miles from home. Over the course of the two-hour bus ride, I stole and hid a man's cowboy boots, consumed an entire bag of orange marshmallow circus peanuts, and shot spitballs at the old lady across the aisle. It was a young traveler's paradise.

Travel by bus sure can be fun, and it can be affordable. In fact, Greyhound has special discounts just for kids (under 12), but they must be accompanied by an adult. (I'd like to think I'm personally responsible for that policy.) In any case, if you don't like to fly or don't want to drive, bus travel may be the way to go. Offering service to and from 2,600 cities nationwide and 18,000 daily departures, Greyhound is the ticket. The Greyhound Web site, at **www.greyhound.com**, features fares and schedule information, service information, discount ticket information, and online ticket ordering.

There are other regional bus systems, like Peter Pan Bus Lines and Atlantic Express. You can also charter a bus for group travel, but I'll talk more about that in Chapter 18, "Custom Group Tours." For more information on charter buses, visit 4Charters at **www.4charter.com/main.shtml** or Fodor's Resource Center at **www.fodors.com/ resource/bustravel**. At these sites you can find information and links to bus routes and service in Asia, Australia and the Pacific, Europe, Latin America, the United States, and Canada. The good folks at Fodor's also provide discount pass information and tips, as well as links to bus pass retailers for Europe, the United States, Canada, and Australia and the Pacific. This site is one of the best on the Web, no matter how you plan to get where you're going.

You can purchase tickets and special passes at the Greyhound Web site— and you can check schedules and route information.

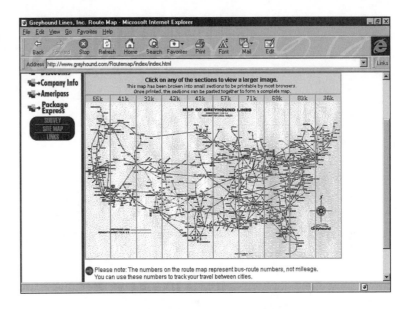

And of course there are the ever-popular tourist mobiles—sightseeing tour buses, like Grayline (**www.grayline.com**) buses, which serve more than 200 worldwide tourist destinations. But I'll talk more about those in the next chapter and in Part 3, "Cruises, Package Tours, Group Travel, and Custom Group Tours."

The Least You Need to Know

➤ You can locate domestic and international bus and train schedules and rates online, and buy tickets and passes through the carriers' secure Web sites.

➤ You can research and preview scenic train touring routes online.

➤ You can go online to find schedules, maps, and fare information for European rail systems.

➤ You can buy rail passes for Eurail and Interrail and get help on choosing the pass that's right for you and your budget.

Chapter 13

Getting Around

In This Chapter

➤ Locating car rental agencies and getting the best deals and rates

➤ Reserving a car online and where to find consumer tips on getting the best deal

➤ Finding international car rental information

➤ Locating U.S. and international subway and rail transit information and safety tips

➤ Sightseeing by foot on guided walking tours

➤ Renting motorcycles or bikes to get around or check out the scenery

---

After you get to your destination, you can use a number of modes of transportation to actually see the sights: your feet, a bike, a train or subway, a rental car, inline skates, a motorcycle, or even a trolley. You might even be able to think of a couple other ways to get around, and chances are, you can find the information you need about your preferred mode of locomotion on the Internet.

Rental cars are the preferred method of getting around most places because of the flexibility and freedom they offer, but before the wonderful world of the Internet came along, it was kind of a pain to rent a car. You had to make numerous calls using toll-free numbers, wait patiently for a customer service rep to give you the latest rates and deals, and then call back the other places to see if they'd match the competitor's offer. Then you had to wonder if what one company called a midsize sedan was not really just a nice way of saying :"It's not a Yugo; therefore, it's a midsize." Without a uniform system for classifying car sizes and categories, you really just never knew what you'd get unless you asked for a car model by name. Well, those days of car rental frustration are over, thanks to online reservation systems that let you preview fleets or choose the exact make and model of choice.

And if renting a car is not your preferred method of getting around your vacation destination, finding public transportation information online or renting a bike or motorcycle is as easy as pie, too. This chapter gives you the lowdown on comparing prices, getting rental information, and reserving a car or any other type of transportation you choose.

Don't Worry, Honey—It's a Rental

If you've been to any of the one-stop-shopping travel sites like Expedia or Travelocity, you've probably noticed that besides plane tickets and hotel rooms, you can also use the online booking system to rent a car. But if you want to do more extensive comparison shopping, you should go to the Web sites for the major car rental agencies, as well as look into regional guides to find local rental agencies. Even though it's hard for the little guys to compete, you just never know what you might find.

You'll also find some helpful consumer tips and information on renting cars, plus things you should know about rental insurance, international rental information, and general safe driving tips.

You Want Me to Buy Another Book?

Even though you can find information on car rentals online and make your reservations online, I'm going to go ahead and recommend an invaluable tool that every traveler should get to help sort through the mumbo jumbo of car rental rates, insurance, and all the ins and outs of renting a car. This book is worth the $8.99 investment (I actually found it online for $7.29!) to help make sense of all your travel expenses. Pick up a copy of *Consumer Reports Best Travel Deals* for the skinny on renting cars and just about all your other travel needs, too. You can order the guide online at **www.amazon.com** and **www.barnesandnoble.com**, or pick it up at a real bookstore.

Trust me, you should get one of these books! You'll save time and money in the long run, and you'll feel better knowing you went straight to the source for making the best buying decision when it comes to your travel purchases.

Here are some good starting points for locating car rental agencies online and for making your reservations through secure online reservation systems (if you need a little help with making online credit card transactions, you might want to take a quick peek back at Chapter 6, " Before You Buy…Protecting Yourself Online"):

➤ **BreezeNet's Guide to Airport Rental Cars (www.bnm.com)** One of my favorite places to go when I'm looking for car rental information. In fact, Yahoo! rated it one of the Top 50 Most Useful Sites on the Internet. Quite an accomplishment, really, considering that there are millions of Web sites out there. Anyway, what I really like about this site, besides the links to more than 90 online car rental reservations systems, including international rentals, is that you'll find just about everything you ever wanted to know about renting cars. A Rental Tips section covers drop-off charges, making advance reservations, Internet discounts, how the same company can quote different rates on the same day, rental insurance, weekly rates versus daily rates, minimum age policies, special services you probably don't know about, and generally everything and then some on the business of renting cars. It's an excellent starting point for your rental car shopping.

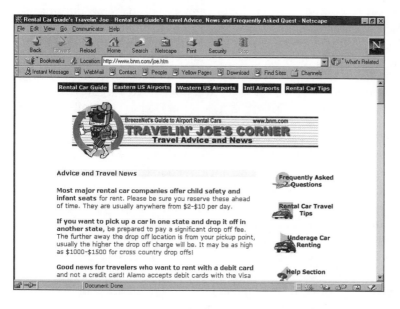

BreezeNet's Guide to Airport Rental Cars has a rental tips section that's a must-read before you rent a car, even if you're not getting a car at the airport.

➤ **Fodor's Car Rental Resource (www.fodors.com/resource/carrental)** Provides information on rental agencies, rental insurance, and links to the top agencies. You'll also find tips on how to save money by choosing an agency that includes shuttle service from the airport to your pick-up point. You'll also get the rundown on rental car requirements in the United States.

➤ **Yahoo!** (www.yahoo.com) You can start your search by going to this site and then clicking **Business and Economy**, **Companies**, **Automotive**, and **Rentals**. You can also start at Yahoo! to find local agencies in the region you're visiting or travel agents in the city or country you're going to. Just locate the regional guide and use **car AND rentals** as your keywords.

➤ **The Travel Library** (www.travel-library.com) Has a neat directory of what side of the road drivers use in countries around the world. You'll also get helpful hints on road safety and general travel information.

Comparing Rates to Find the Best Deal

Don't ask me how or why, but car rental rates are among the more complicated things about making travel plans. I have yet to come across a reasonable explanation of the method behind the madness of getting a good deal (and knowing it's a good deal) when renting cars. The best all-around Web site for comparing rates will give you options beyond the top four or five agencies, plus tips on where to find Internet-only discounts. Here are some of the best car rental rate comparison Web sites:

➤ **Internet Travel Network** (www.itn.net) Lets you compare rates from the largest number of rental agencies. When you arrive at the home page, click the **Rent a Car** icon, and you'll be taken to an online rate comparison form, where you select the pick-up and drop-off dates, as well as the size, make, and model of car you're looking for. From www.itn.net you can check rates for your destination and round-trip travel times at Able, Ace, Advantage, Airport Rent-a-Car, Alamo, Americar, Avis, Budget, Der Tours, Discount, Dollar, Eurodollar, Europcar, Enterprise, Hertz, Holiday Rent-A-Car, Midway, Montgomery Ward, National, Payless, Practical, Rent Rite, Rent-A-Wreck, Savmor, Sears, Thrifty, U-Save, U.S. Rent-A-Car, and Value. Whew! I told you this site had the most agencies to choose from! You can have your results sorted by price, vendor, car type, unlimited mileage, car make and model, and whether the car is on or off the terminal.

➤ **The Trip** (www.trip.com) Provides only rate information for Ace, Alamo, and Dollar. An up-and-comer in the one-stop travel shopping Web site family, this site gives you the same rate information as the other Web sites listed here, just not as much variety in rental agencies.

➤ **Travelocity** (www.travelocity.com) Has a decent representation of car rental agencies, and lets you search by pick-up and drop-off dates for your destination. Results are returned in order of price, best prices first.

➤ **Expedia** (www.expedia.com) Compared rates for seven of the major car rental agencies, although I had to dig to get to other agents besides Dollar, National, and Avis.

Reserve a Car or Get a Rate Quote with the Click of a Mouse

All the major car rental agencies, as well as a good number of local independents, have Web sites you can visit to get rate and availability information before booking your reservation online. Most of the sites have special discounts available only to online customers. And of course, using the Web to gather information and reserve your car sure can save time.

Don't waste another minute on hold waiting for a customer service rep to give you a quote. Go straight to the source and let your mouse do the walking.

➤ **Alamo Rent a Car (www.goalamo.com)** Lets you preview rates, make or modify a reservation online, and includes the Alamo Rental Guide with tips on understanding your rental agreement, what your rental protection options are, safety tips, and what extras you can get with your car, like car seats, cell phones, or ski racks.

➤ **Avis (www.avis.com)** Has an online reservation and rate request system, plus a handy-dandy destination guide complete with recommendations for scenic road tripping in and around major destination cities.

➤ **Budget Rent-A-Car (www.drivebudget.com/home.html)** Offers an "altered ego" quiz you can take to find out what kind of car you really wish you were driving. It's a reminder that you don't have to be on vacation to have fun in a rental!

➤ **Dollar Rent-A-Car (www.dollar.com)** Provides a printable coupon you can bring along to the airport for a free one-class upgrade.

➤ **Enterprise (www.pickenterprise.com)** Offers a preview of its fleet to help you pick a vehicle. A new online reservation system lets you reserve a rental, or you can use the office locator to find an agent in your area.

➤ **Hertz (www.hertz.com)** Worldwide Location Section lets you search for rentals, download interactive maps, and get driving directions to the nearest Hertz office. Get rate information, make or change reservations, and get the inside scoop on Internet-only bargains.

➤ **National Car Rental (www.nationalcar.com)** Features an easy-to-use rate quote and reservation system, and has special online discounts and promotions.

➤ **Thrifty (www.thrifty.com)** Has an online system for reservations, cancellations, modifications, or rate quote requests.

European and International Car Rental Web Sites

Touring international destinations offer several options for the traveler, including driving and taking trains and planes. Depending on your budget and your comfort level with driving on unfamiliar, sometimes narrow roadways, renting a car offers more flexibility, and sometimes even the relative cost can be more affordable than that of train travel.

Can You Rent a Car with Cash?

Not having a credit card is a major pain when you go to rent a car...most rental companies won't rent to you unless you have one. The key is to look for independent agencies that will take a cash payment, along with your purchase of car rental insurance. A list of airports where cash rentals are available can be found on BreezeNet's car rental guide (**www.bnm.com/cash.htm**). You'll find links with contact information so you can call ahead to confirm the availability of cash rentals and get the skinny on requirements and deposits.

To get a flavor of international car rental agencies and what you need to know before you make a reservation, the sites listed in this section will give you an idea of rates, rules, safety issues, and availability.

➤ **Kemwel Holiday Autos** (**www.kemwel.com**) Offers bottom-of-the-barrel rates for Israel and Western and Eastern Europe. If you're looking for international car rental information, it's a good place to start.

Kemwel Holiday Autos is one of the best international car rental agencies for rates, selection, and service, according to Arthur Frommer's Budget Travel Magazine.

➤ **Europe by Car** (www.europebycar.com) Offers excellent rates for rentals in Europe. It's a member of the European Automobile Association, sister AAA. You can also get a copy of an application for an international drivers permit at this site, which you'll need if you plan on doing the driving.

➤ **Auto Europe** (www.autoeurope.com) Provides the straight dope on seating, luggage space, and photos of cars to help you choose a car model that's right for you and your passengers. Book online, and keep your eyes peeled for hot deals and special prices.

➤ **Europe for Visitors Net Links** (www.goeurope.miningco.com/msub-auto.htm) About.com's Europe for Visitors section has lots of useful links for European car and rail travel. You'll find links to Online Travel Corp.'s tips on renting and driving a car in Europe, general comments on the European traffic code, foreign speed traps, and other travel information.

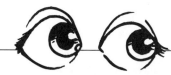

A European Traveler's Dream Web Site

About.com features a European map and geography section at `geography.miningco.com/mbody.htm?PID=2820&COB=home`, with links to European country and regional Web sites. You'll find the lowdown on time zone changes, climate and weather reports, maps, tourist information, and more than 170 articles relating to European travel.

Finding Your Way on Rail Systems and Subways

Taking a train, subway, or other rail transit system is an exciting way to get around town. Before you hop on, though, you can go online to find maps, routes, fare information, safety tips, and other transit system information for your destination city or country.

Subway Safety Check

Subways have a bad reputation, and sometimes rightfully so: They're the underground, the dark side, the belly of the city. On the lighter side, though, subways can often be the cheapest, fastest, and most interesting way to get around town. In some cities, it's the only reasonable way to get around, so you need to be aware of some basic safety precautions when going underground. Eurotrip.com's Scary Train page (`www.eurotrip.com/Preparation_and_Packing/Scary_Trains/index.html`) shares advice from other travelers and offers tips on being a safe and smart traveler on the world's subway systems.

Here's a list of sites to get you started on your rail and subway travel research and planning. The sites contain lots of helpful advice and many of them have maps, schedules, and other tips to help you make your way around town:

➤ **Subway Navigator** (`www.ratp.fr/index.eng.html`) An award-winning Web site based in France (don't worry—it has an English version of the site at Subway Navigator). You can get subway maps and information for subway systems in most international cities. You begin by choosing the city you're traveling in. If you know the departure and arrival stations, you can enter those. If you don't, you can consult the list of stations to find a station name. You can also use the map to orient yourself to map point-to-point rail routes, and you'll get arrival times, stop times, and information on which lines to take. You can even print a subway map and bring it along for the ride. If you have a color printer, you'll be able to print out the exact same maps you'll find in the subway station!

➤ **Subway Page** (`www.reed.edu/~reyn/transport.html`) Has printable maps for every subway system imaginable. You'll find links to world subway and other transportation information resources, plus a site menu featuring city subway maps; map collections of other transit systems; subway route navigation aids; city and area transit guides; metro area tram, bus, light rail, and rail system maps; individual, institutional, and corporate transit pages; general transit resources; books, bibliographies, and special items of interest; images relating to subways and urban transit; museums, historical displays, and clubs.

➤ **Rick Steves' Guide to European Railpasses** (`www.ricksteves.com/rail/`) Gives you the basics on riding the rail and tells you what's best for your trip, how to buy point-to-point tickets in Europe, how to find the right track once you're there, and helps you check your itinerary options. You can find out about features and prices in different countries, and even order your rail passes online.

➤ **Rail Connection** (`www.railconnection.com`) Has the tools and information you need to plan your European trip, complete with transit system maps and planning tips and tools. To view and download the transit maps, you'll need Adobe Acrobat Reader. There are links and directions on how to do this on the Rail Connection Web site, but if you need more help, take a short trip back to Chapter 2, "Browsers 101."

➤ **Rail Europe** (`www.raileurope.com/us/rail/fares_schedules/index.htm`) You can find point-to-point rail tickets. Choose two cities, such as Liverpool and London, the day of travel (say January 15), and currency (say US $). A list of fares and schedules will be created for you, including the travel time (three hours, for our imaginary trip), the cost for each kind of fare (that is, first or second class—$114 and $87 for us), and the distance traveled (285 miles in our case). Then you can choose what time you want to leave and order online. Note that the information you get is only for one-way tickets, but the return fares can also be purchased online.

➤ **Rail Travel Information** (`www.res.bbsrc.ac.uk/plantpath/Railway`) Tons of rail travel information and links. You'll find links to rail transit systems for Europe, North America, Asia, and more. You can learn about long-distance travel as well as metro travel. The site also gives reviews of each Web site featured on the links page.

➤ **NYCSubway.org** (`www.nycsubway.org/transitmaps`) You can find directions and print out subway transit maps for the United States and international cities.

Take a Rail and Car Combo Trip in Europe

For information on combining rail and car travel in Europe, visit `www.raileurope.com/us/rail/rail_drive/index.htm`. You can take the train for longer distances, spend the night in a hotel or take a sleeper train, and then spend the next day exploring in your rental car. BritRail Pass 'n Drive includes rail and road travel throughout England, Scotland, and Wales. EurailDrive Pass gives you train and car travel in the 17 Eurail countries. Europass Drive takes you through five Europass countries. France Rail 'n Drive Pass, Italy Rail 'n Drive Pass, Scanrail 'n Drive Pass (Scandinavia), and Spain Rail 'n Drive include a nice mix of rail and road travel in each of these countries. You can also create your own route, choosing from a host of rail options and car rental cars through Avis or Hertz in almost any country.

Get Up Off Your Bum—Take a Tour on Foot

To find scenic walking tours in your destination of choice, start at CitySearch (**www.citysearch.com**) to find guided walking tours or walking and hiking trails. Just click the area you're visiting, find the search feature, and enter **walking tours** or **walking trails** as your keywords. You'll get links to the Web sites of the walking tour companies, plus a schedule of tour times, a map with directions to the tour starting point, and a list of restaurants within a certain radius of the starting point. If you're looking for walking or pedestrian trails, you can search for city park information to get maps and tips on taking the leisurely way around town.

You can also find regional information for your destination and use the same search criteria. Or go to the Yahoo! main page and type **walking AND tours AND New York**, and you'll get links to Web sites offering walking tours in your destination.

Here are some cool Web sites I found that offer a neat way to see different towns:

➤ **Cross Country International Walking Vacations** (**www.walkingvacations.com**) Offers cross-country walking tours in Ireland, Scotland, England, France, Spain, and Italy. You can't make reservations or payment online, but there is a toll-free number to call, plus lots of useful information and great photos of the areas you can tour on foot.

Cross Country International Walking Vacations offers scenic, guided walking vacations.

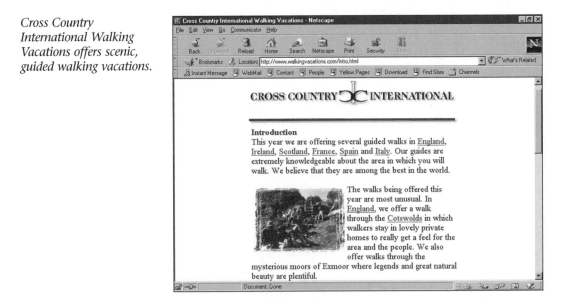

➤ **Victorian Home Walks** (**www.victorianwalk.com/**) Information on times and starting points for walking tours in San Francisco that take you off the beaten path to homes that are not normally shown. Information on the tour guide, cost, referrals, and more are available online.

➤ **Walk Softly Tours** (**www.walksoftlytours.com/**) Provides the nature side of walking tours. Read more about some of the previous tours, and also register online. This tour company claims to be one of the first ecotour companies in Arizona.

➤ **Downtown Los Angeles Walking Tour**
(**www.usc.edu/dept/geography/lawalk/dtb.html**) Get walking tour information for Los Angeles from the USC Geography Department. Print a map of a downtown LA walking tour or get information on taking self-guided tours to places like the Ronald Reagan State Building.

➤ **Wonderwalks** (**www.wonderwalks.com/**) Offers trips across the United States and Britain. You can find tour route information, schedules, and rates. If none of the trips meet your schedule or desired route, you can create a custom trip.

Common Sense Keeps You Out of Trouble

It almost goes without saying, but remember to exercise common sense when taking unguided walking tours or even if you're just going out for a walk in an unfamiliar neighborhood or town. If you decide to go for a stroll after dark especially, try and let someone know where you're going and what time you'll be back. A front desk clerk or concierge probably won't mind keeping an eye out for your return. And remember to take a box of popcorn to lay a trail so you don't get lost! If you do take a map, don't make it obvious to would-be crooks that you don't know where you're going.

Renting a Bicycle or Motorcycle

Depending on your destination, road and traffic conditions, and the distance between points of interest from your hotel or B&B, you might want to think about renting a bike or motorcycle to get around town. It's easy to find parking, you get in your daily exercise (well, with a bicycle anyway), and you don't have to worry about the hassles of renting a car or taking the subway. Even if it's only for a day or two, renting bikes and motorcycles is becoming increasingly popular, especially in international destinations.

The following sections list some Web sites to get you started. If you want to research more bicycle and motorcycle rental companies, just go to your favorite search engine and type in the keywords **bicycle AND rentals AND Ireland** or **motorcycle AND rental AND San Francisco** (or whatever your destination location).

Renting a Bicycle

I had the darndest time finding a bicycle rental directory, but if you use the search technique above, the odds are in your favor that you'll find a rental company in your destination of choice. Lots of the rental companies are tour companies, too, so if you want a guided bicycle tour, you're in luck. If you're just looking for a way to get around, take a look online at sites like these.

➤ **Blazing Saddles Bike Rentals (www.blazingsaddles.com)** In Seattle and San Francisco, you can find out about tours you can take in the area and pre-register for them. You can also schedule outings for a group. Contact information is provided at the site.

➤ **Cycles 4 Rent (www.cycles4rent.com)** Lets you rent a bike in either Santa Barbara or Ventura, California. Choose a location within those cities, and you can get rate information and choose one-, four-, or eight-hour rentals. You can also rent inline skates and bike accessories such as child carriers, bike trailers, or baskets. Every rental includes a helmet, lock, seatbelt, and pantleg bands.

➤ **Hellas Bike Travel (www.hellasbike.com)** Offers bike rentals and tours in Greece. For the independent biker type, you can hire bikes for short trips, equipped with a helmet, lock, repair set, and pump. For longer excursions, you can get luggage carriers, mudguards, and lights.

And a Few More Ways to Skin a Cat...

Your transportation options aren't limited to mechanical means or human power. What about horse power? Inline skates? Boats? Ferries? Depending on where you're headed and what's on your itinerary, these alternate forms of transport can add an interesting twist to your sightseeing adventures. I have a friend who rented a horse in England's Lake District and Wales, and another friend who makes it a point to take rides on more exotic modes of transport, like gondolas, camels, mules, and rickshaws. Hey, why not? You're on vacation!

Renting a Motorcycle

Whoa, easy rider. Looking for an exciting and hair-flapping way to get around your vacation spot? Maybe a motorcycle rental is a good way to go. Like bicycle rentals, you can take guided tours on your rented two-wheeler, or hit the open road on your own.

The sites listed here are specific to certain regions or cities, but just use your favorite search engine to locate motorcycle rental companies or tour operators in your destination. And remember to wear a helmet!

➤ **American Road Collection (www.budgetharleys.com)** Allows you to preview and rent Harleys. There are rental offices in Miami, Fort Lauderdale, West Palm Beach, Boston, and Martha's Vineyard. The site also provides information on Harley rallies across the United States.

➤ **Eagle Rider (www.eaglerider.com)** With locations in Los Angeles, San Francisco, San Diego, Phoenix, Chicago, Orlando, and Las Vegas, Eagle Rider provides motorcycle rental across the United States. Find out daily rates for different styles of motorcycles. Every rental includes a 24-hour rental period, unlimited mileage, basic liability insurance, DOT-approved helmet for driver and passenger, saddle bags, and all necessary locks. Reserve your hog online.

➤ **Bosenberg European Motorcycle Tours (www.bosenberg.com)** Offers individual and group motorcycle rentals in Europe, with routes in the Burgundy region and the Swiss Alps, the Classic Alps and the Dolomites, and the French and Swiss Alps.

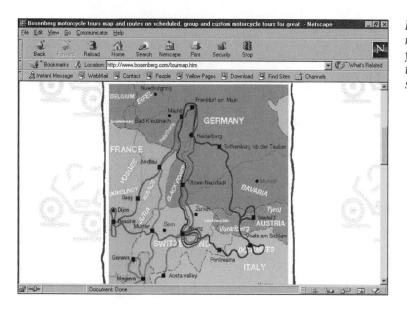

Bosenberg European motorcycle tours takes you on a variety of tours through the breathtaking, scenic Alps.

The Least You Need to Know

➤ You can compare rates and reserve rental cars online with easy-to-use rate comparison forms.

➤ You can find local rental agencies in your destination for cars, bicycles, motorcycles, and other transportation options.

➤ You can locate U.S. and international subway and rail transit tips, schedules, and rate information online.

➤ You can reserve and check prices on alternative ways to get around, like using inline skates, bikes, motorcycles, and your own feet.

Chapter 14

Hotel Guides and Booking Web Sites

In This Chapter

➤ Saving time and money using online hotel directories to research and contact hotels or hotel chains

➤ Finding and previewing your room and making reservations online

➤ Finding Internet-only deals and discount accommodations

➤ Using online travel auction Web sites to name your price

➤ Finding family-friendly hotels, honeymoon specials, and senior discounts in hotels around the world

---

Holy cow. There are lots of Web sites you can visit to locate hotels anywhere around the world. And because sleep is a big part of everyone's day (or night, in most cases), especially on a rest-and-relaxation vacation, taking the time to find the perfect place to lay your weary head at night is an important part of the trip-planning process. You may be looking for lodging based on a number of other criteria, like price, location, or amenities. When you go online to find a hotel, you'll be amazed at the wealth of information for booking your accommodations.

There's more than one way to skin a cat, even when it comes to finding hotel rooms. Whether you're searching for a particular hotel chain, comparing prices, looking for reduced rates, scouting out reviews of hotels, or going online to book the room yourself, this chapter will help you locate the various types of Web sites to help you book or reserve that room. There are hotel directories, and then there are online reservation sites. And then there are discount finders and virtual travel agencies that can help you find and book the hotel that's right for you.

If you're looking for specific information on non-hotel lodging, like B&Bs or vacation rental properties, turn to Chapter 15, "Alternative Lodging: B&Bs, Hostels, Furnished Rentals, and Campgrounds." You'll run across non-hotel lodgings in some of the Web sites in this chapter, too. So, if you're undecided about what kind of lodging you're looking for, read through this chapter and Chapter 15 to get a feel for where to begin your search for the perfect hotel, B&B, or home exchange.

Hotel Directories

Different hotels offer different features, some you may like and some you may not. But you certainly don't want to read through every hotel description to find exactly what you're looking for. Let the magic of the Web do it for you! That's why you went online in the first place…to gather as much information as possible in as short a time period as you can. For free.

Maybe you're a loyal traveler who only stays in Holiday Inns because you like the service and accommodations. Or maybe you get special prices at any Holiday Inn, or you belong to a travel discount club and you have to stay at a Holiday Inn to earn points. So, the obvious answer would be for you to find the Holiday Inn Web site, locate a hotel at your destination, and book the darned room. No problem. But what if you're going someplace and there just isn't a Holiday Inn, or simply no room at the Inn. What do you do? You have to find something else, obviously, and ideally you can get as good a discount at another hotel. Going online may be the way to go.

As usual, a good place to start if you're looking for a particular hotel or hotel chain is the Yahoo! directory or your favorite search engine. Just type in the name of the hotel and the city you're headed to.

Should you book a room directly with the hotel? Are there special offers for Internet shoppers only? Can you get more than just hotel availability and rate information at the hotel Web sites? What about maps and activity guides? It depends. For the most part, hotels publish rates based on availability and demand. Special deals are easiest to find for last-minute excursions or for off-season travel. But in areas where there are lots of hotels, you may have more bargaining power. In any case, it's easy to compare prices using the Web, or to get toll-free numbers to call and verify that you're getting the best possible deal.

Using Yahoo!'s Web Directory? What Does the @ Mean?

In Yahoo! category listings, if you see an at sign (@) next to a category—like **Hotels@**—that means the category has been cross-referenced so it can be located from various starting points. For example, in Yahoo!'s main page, you can enter the **Business and Economy** section, and click through to **Companies** and then **Travel and Lodging** to get a link to hotel directories. Or you can go to the Yahoo! main page, click **Travel**, **Lodging**, and **Hotels**, and then get the directories. You'll arrive at the same place...there's just more than one way to get there. And of course, you can always locate your category by using a keyword search at the main page of Yahoo!.

Booking Sites

You may have noticed if you visited any of the multipurpose travel Web sites, like Expedia, Travelocity, or Preview Travel, that you can book hotel rooms, reserve rental cars, or buy plane tickets online. These multipurpose sites can be used to handle all your travel planning, or only certain aspects of it. Here's a quick rundown on what hotel booking features you'll find at some of the major multipurpose travel booking sites. Most of the sites require you to register, which is a simple, painless process. And, if you book hotels online, you'll find down the road that taking a few minutes to register will allow you to use enhanced features, like itinerary trackers, mileage trackers, expense trackers, and other features available to members only:

➤ **Microsoft Expedia (www.expedia.com)** The Hotel Wizard at Expedia's multipurpose travel Web site searches a database of more than 40,000 worldwide lodgings. So to make it easier for you to find what you're looking for, you complete a form with easy-to-use pull-down menus to narrow the search results and filter out hotels that are out of your price range or otherwise don't meet your requirements. For example, you can narrow your search results by selecting hotels that belong to a certain chain. Or you can look for rooms that are accessible to the disabled and offer a free continental breakfast. Maybe you'll only stay at a hotel that allows smoking and has a fitness room. The Expedia Hotel Wizard also provides regional maps to help find the hotel, as well as links to destination guides.

➤ **Travelocity (www.travelocity.com)** The hotel finder at Travelocity is similar to Expedia's Hotel Wizard. You start your search by entering the name of the city you're visiting, the dates you need a room, the number of guests, and the number of rooms. From there, you can indicate more specific preferences to help narrow the playing field. Oddly enough, though, when it comes to indicating amenity preferences, like swimming pool, weight room, handicap accessible, you can only select one item as the ultimate preference. After your results are returned, you'll see symbols under each hotel listing that indicate what services and amenities are available. So, just choose the amenity that is the most important, and you can whittle down the results from there, and even find out about nearby restaurants, entertainment, directions, and other things you want to know before you make your reservation.

➤ **Preview Travel (www.previewtravel.com)** The nice thing about Preview Travel's hotel finder is the room availability link. After you've located your hotel, you can check its availability. With the other hotel finders, you have to go through several steps of the search process before you find out if the room is even available. Other features at Preview are the LowFare notification service, which sends out weekly email for the upcoming weekend's specials at hotels in destinations you've selected during the registration process. It'll track rates and specials for three months, and send you a nice little email letting you know when the rate has reached a certain point. There's no obligation to book, but if you're a spontaneous traveler, it's sometimes fun to find out on a Wednesday that your favorite city is yours for the taking when Friday rolls around.

Preview Travel has a special section to help you find discount hotels, courtesy of the Hotel Reservation Network.

Hotel Directories and Booking Sites

Besides the multipurpose travel sites, you'll find Web sites that are specific to booking hotels and other lodging accommodations. Some of them may provide links to other travel itinerary items, like airlines or car rentals, but the main focus is on booking hotel rooms. And that can be a plus, as the attention is given strictly to rooms. Although I haven't necessarily found differences in rates or availability using the multipurpose Web sites versus using booking sites, I have noticed that options outside hotel chains are fairly limited with multipurpose sites, and there are fewer options for discounts or special deals.

If your hotel preference is open and you know where you're going and how much you want to spend per night on lodging, start your search at one of these hotel directory sites, and if you find what you're looking for, you can even reserve your room online.

➤ **All-Hotels (www.all-hotels.com)** This award-winning site is hands down my favorite online independent hotel booking site. Not only does All-Hotels have one of the widest and most eclectic mixes of lodging options, the system is by far the easiest to use and provides the most information on hotel policies, amenities, and services. Recent Web site upgrades bring the total number of hotels, B&Bs, and other accommodations to a whopping 100,000 listings! And for the smaller independent hotels that can't offer online reservation systems, you're directly linked to the free services of an online travel agent that handles the reservations for you.

The Web site even includes special sections on discount hotels, B&Bs, and a luggage store. And unlike so many of the other hotel booking sites, this one offers international listings and has a currency converter link for easy rate conversions. The Traveler Feedback Form lets people just like you submit reviews of hotels so other travelers can make more informed decisions when choosing accommodations. And for all you one-stop-shoppers, you can connect to Travelocity's online air ticketing system, or to a car rental reservation system, to complete the rest of your travel purchases online. No wonder this Web site was ranked the number one independent hotel booking site in 1998!

➤ **The Hotel Guide (www.hotelguide.com)** How about a database of 60,000 hotels and lodgings around the world? Well, that's what you'll find at the Hotel Guide. You can start with a general search for all hotels in your destination, or skip to a detailed search to narrow results based on your requirements. Either way, you'll get an alphabetical listing of hotels, and from there, you get a quick preview of rates, a quality rating, and links to the hotel's Web site, if available. After you've located a hotel you're interested in, you can get information on amenities, activities, and nearby attractions. You can also purchase membership in the Hotel Guide for access to added features and discounts.

At All-Hotels.com you can use the Instant Reserve System to book hotel rooms at more than 70,000 hotels around the globe.

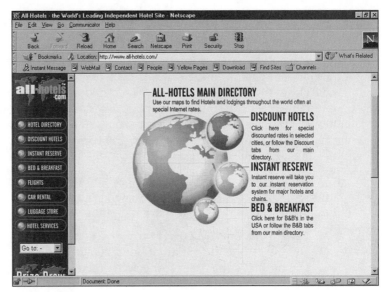

➤ **The Accommodation Search Engine** (www.ase.net) It's a directory. It's a search engine. It's a hotel guide. And it's all rolled into one, making it a good place to start your search for hotels, B&Bs, vacation rentals, villas, or just about any other lodging option. The Accommodation Search Engine searches more than 38,000 worldwide listings and lets you book either directly with the establishment or through the free online booking system, where available. Not all hotels are equipped to handle online reservations, so you may have to email the establishment to get rates and availability information. After you've selected your destination area, you can specify requirements such as price, type of lodging, facilities, and activities. You might find it a little hard to get around when you get into the actual hotel listings and descriptions, but in terms of the search and selection power, plus the huge number of listings, this Web site is a must-see.

➤ **Places to Stay** (www.placestostay.com) Places to Stay is a partner in the WorldRes program (a universal online hotel and accommodation reservation system, used on Web sites like Travelocity, Yahoo!, AOL, and many regional convention and tourism Web sites). It is an online reservation system that allows quick and easy access to a database of tens of thousands of properties around the world. You can get real-time rates and instant confirmation, and you can get in on hot deals and save with special offers, discounts, and packages available only to online customers.

➤ **AOL Travel's Hotel Center.** If you're a member of AOL, you can use the keyword **HOTEL** to get to the Traveler's Advantage feature, which links you to hotel listings and availability internationally, and also provides discounts on hotels, motels, and other lodgings. You can book online or use email to inquire about rates, services, or availability.

Discount Hotel Sites

Hotel chains often offer special clubs and discount programs to customers who book online or shop within a network of travel providers. For example, if you fly on certain airlines and stay at certain hotels, you get additional discounts off airfare and room rates. You can also get frequent guest points to be used for purchases, discount travel packages, and special services or offers. And although you may run across specials from time to time on hotel directories and booking sites, there are online reservation systems for hotels that specialize specifically in discount or budget hotels. So if you're looking to save a few bucks, take a look around. Some of the sites claim discounts up to 65 percent off the regular rate, but that makes you wonder sometimes if the regular rate isn't sky high to begin with. Anyway, if you watch your Ps and Qs, or refer to *Consumer Reports Best Travel Deals*, you'll get the skinny on finding discounts on hotels around the world.

These Web sites are worth checking out, but be sure to locate the cancellation policy information and deposit requirements to make sure the savings are worth the potential hassle:

➤ **1Travel's Hotel Wiz (www.hotelwiz.com)** For instant confirmation and online booking at more than 43,000 properties worldwide, take a tour through Hotel Wiz. If it's just discount hotels you're looking for, you can get up to 40 percent off at more than 15,000 participating discount hotels listed at Hotel Wiz. Brought to you by the good folks at 1Travel, the Hotel Wiz promises big discounts on hotels the world around. You can also post or read reviews of hotels, print maps of all U.S. hotels, and find out about last-minute deals. The site also has links to low airfares and car rental prices, so if discount travel is your bag, this is a site you may want to check out.

➤ **Hotel Discounts (www.hoteldiscounts.com)** Hotel Discounts boasts discounts on hotel rooms up to 65 percent off the regular rates. Although the search options are few, your results will include links to detailed information on current rates, quality ratings, maps, and photos of the interior and exterior of the hotel. This site helps you find discount hotels only in the most popular travel destinations, but if you're visiting one of the cities listed (from Amsterdam to Anaheim, or Florence to Fort Lauderdale, the list is always growing to cover every major American city and the top international destinations), you may just find a bargain of the century.

Travel Auctions: Name Your Price for Hotel Accommodations

Isn't the Web an amazing thing? You can visit an online travel auction site, post the price you want to pay on a hotel room (or an airplane ticket or a cruise or vacation package), and travel agencies bid to win your business. This section lists some of the most popular travel auction sites. If you decide to use an online travel auction site, take the time to read through the site's FAQs (frequently asked questions) section, and be sure you understand the terms of the agreement and how billing, payments, and cancellations or changes are handled.

One auction site in particular, Priceline.com, requires you to give your credit card information, and after you make an offer on a room and the price is matched, you have to make the purchase. Even if you can't use the reservation or if find the room someplace else cheaper, after you make an offer, you're obligated to buy. Personally, I think that's a bit of a risk to take if you're just doing it to see if you can get a good price, but if your travel plans are firm and you're looking for the cheapest rates possible, it's worth checking out. I've heard stories of unbelievably low rates, so if you're the gamblin' type, give it a whirl.

Spontaneous traveler? Gamblin' fool? Priceline is a travel auction site that lets you name your price. If an agent matches your price, the room is yours.

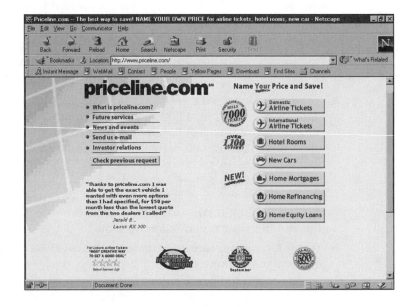

Here are some of the more popular online auction sites, most of which have step-by-step instructions on how to use the systems. And as always, be sure to read the fine print before you place a bid or give credit card information.

> ➤ **Travelfacts Auction (www.bid4travel.com)** For discounts on hotels in Europe, Canada, Mexico, the United States, the Caribbean, and Bermuda, the Travelfacts auction lets users bid on items offered by hotels and cruise lines. (This is like a regular auction, as opposed to a reverse auction, where the buyer posts a listing and has travel agents bid to match the offer.) You have to be a registered user to place a bid. When you find something you'd like to go for, you use an online form to enter a valid bid amount and the number of items you're bidding on. You can retract a bid only while an auction is active, and after an auction has

closed, there are no bid retractions allowed. Although you can't be forced to purchase items successfully bid on, if you back out on your bids a couple times, you could be barred from participating in future auctions. Be sure to read through the How It Works section before you register or make a bid.

➤ **Priceline.com** (`www.priceline.com`) To make your offer on a hotel room in the U.S. city you're visiting, go to the site and select the city, the dates of your stay, how many rooms you need, the quality level (1, 2, 3, 4, or 5 stars) of the hotel you'd like, and how much you want to pay per night. You confirm your request with a major credit card. Priceline.com then goes to work to find the best available hotel that will agree to your price. With Priceline.com Hotels, you'll stay in one of the major national brands or well-known independent properties, but you won't know which one until the purchase has been made. You'll have an answer to your request in one hour. If Priceline.com finds a hotel to match your bid, you'll immediately confirm your reservation and charge the complete amount,—including standard hotel taxes of up to 20 percent,—to your credit card. Then you'll get an email and printed confirmation of your reservation. All you need to do is show up on the first day of your reservation with your Priceline.com Hotel Confirmation Number and a credit card to cover any applicable local hotel taxes and any incidental charges like room service or phone calls. Beware, though. If you have any special needs or preferences, you're instructed to take care of those issues when you check into the hotel. And, the reservation is non-changeable, non-refundable, and non-negotiable.

Is the Advertised Rate Single or Double Occupancy?

Generally speaking, when you locate rate information for a hotel room, the rate is based on single occupancy. Say you find a hotel room in Chicago's Magnificent Mile for $129 a night. Not bad, except that when you go to make the reservation for you and your sweetie, you'll be asked how many guests are staying and suddenly the rate doubles, even if you're sleeping in the same bed. Why do they do that? Because they can. Most hotels don't charge extra for bed partners, but some even may impose a surcharge for single occupancy!

The Least You Need to Know

➤ You can preview hotels and get destination information or maps.

➤ You can locate hotels and lodging accommodations around the world and make reservations online or through email.

➤ You can find special discounts, last-minute deals, and Internet-only special prices for hotels and other lodgings.

➤ You can use online auctions to name the price you want to pay for a hotel room.

Chapter 15

Alternative Lodging: B&Bs, Hostels, Furnished Rentals, and Campgrounds

In This Chapter

➤ Locating, reserving, and finding special deals on B&Bs

➤ For the budget-conscious traveler, look into hostels using directories and online communities

➤ Arranging house swaps online using member databases

➤ Finding furnished houses, apartments, condos, and villas

➤ Previewing and reserving campgrounds and national parks

There are tens of thousands of hotels in the world, and it's usually pretty easy to find a room just about anywhere you go. But you may have a soft spot for the old-fashioned (and fashionable) B&B scene—there's something special about staying in a home away from home. If you're into furnished rentals or home exchanges, nonhotel lodging alternatives are a great way to cut down on dining expenses. And for the traveler who enjoys living in a community, meeting neighbors, and getting away from the proverbial beaten path and the common tourist traps, B&Bs and vacation rental properties offer a memorable and distinctive vacation experience.

For the young budget traveler, hostels offer an inexpensive place to stay and the opportunity to meet other travelers. Elderhostels are increasing in popularity, too, as senior travelers are discovering the advantages of staying at these facilities that offer more than just lodging. Elderhostels are designed to connect like-minded travelers and offer the chance to participate in educational travel experiences.

You outdoorsy types know Mother Nature makes a great hostess, so I've collected some campers' resources and directories of parks and campgrounds to help you plan your next outdoor adventure.

B&B Guides and Directories

Rise and shine! Your home-cooked breakfast awaits. There's nothing better than waking up in a big, comfy bed with the sun peeking in through the bedroom window. You can make the dream even better by getting snuggled up in bed inside a 15th-century castle turned B&B. Or maybe you and your sweetie decided to go for the homey atmosphere of a mountain-top B&B for your honeymoon instead of making the usual hotel accommodations. Well, sit down and enjoy the view, because if B&Bs are your thing, you're going to love what you find online.

Starting Your Search at the B&B Channel

A great place to start your online search for a B&B is the Bed and Breakfast Channel, at **www.bbchannel.com**. Here, you'll find profiles for more than 19,000 B&Bs in the United States and Canada, and 1,700 more throughout Europe, Central/South America, Asia and the Pacific, the Caribbean, the Middle East, and Africa. The great thing about the Bed and Breakfast Channel is that you can search for the perfect place using a variety of criteria. You can search by inns and B&Bs that offer online booking, or for B&Bs and inns that offer deals and promotions. You can search by name, amenity or feature, or members of various B&B or innkeeper associations. And of course, you can always search by region, with the interactive B&B locator.

The B&B Channel boasts a directory of more than 19,000 inns and B&Bs around the world.

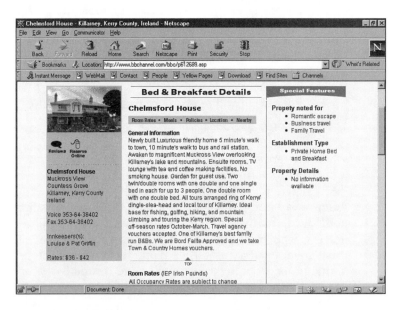

If you're searching by location, just click on the region you're visiting, and you'll get a drop-down list of the cities in the area with B&B listings. Select the city where you'd like to stay, and you'll get a listing of all B&Bs registered with the Bed and Breakfast

Channel. Depending on the type of listing the B&B has paid for, you'll get varying levels of information, in addition to addresses and phone numbers. Some listings include photos of the B&B interiors and grounds, reviews, and recommendations.

Another cool feature you'll find at the Bed and Breakfast Channel is the message board. Here, you'll find forums covering B&B issues and questions about inns and B&Bs all over the world. There's also a Special Topics forum that covers employment, announcements about B&Bs, help for aspiring innkeepers, events, famous B&Bs, and specialty B&Bs, which include inns and homes that cater to guests with pets, horses, or specific lifestyles.

The message board is accessible to guests, but you might as well register as a user. If you see a message you want to respond to, you'll have to be a member to post a reply, either directly to the message board or via email to the person who posted the message. Registering here is a quick and painless process. Simply choose a username and a password, answer a few basic questions, and you're on your way to becoming a member of the Bed and Breakfast Channel message board community. You can even elect to be notified, via email, of new postings to the board or to replies to your postings. There's a thorough and easy-to-understand help section that takes you through the technical stuff about the forums. If you read Chapter 5, "Online Travel Communities 101," you already understand the basics of how online communities work.

What's the Difference Between a B&B, a Country Inn, and a Homestay?

According to the B&B Encyclopedia at `homearts.com/affil/ahi/main/homesty.htm`, a *country inn* serves both breakfast and dinner and may have a restaurant associated with it. Although they're usually found along the East coast, a few country inns are in other regions of the United States. A *B&B's* primary focus is lodging, and as the name implies, breakfast is the only meal served and can be a full-course gourmet breakfast or a simple self-serve buffet. The innkeepers usually live on the premises. It can have from 3 to 20 rooms or more, but usually not more than 40, unless it's a historic property. Like many country inns, many B&Bs specialize in providing historic, romantic, or distinctive decor, often offering such niceties as canopied beds, fireplaces, and tea in the library. Many are decorated with antiques and other furnishings from family collections. A *homestay* is a room available in a private home. Homestays have one to three guest rooms. Because homestays are often operated as a hobby-type business and open and close frequently, only a very few unique properties are included in the B&B Encyclopedia publications and directories.

Here are some other B&B locator and booking sites you should check out:

➤ **Fodor's B&B Finder** (`www.fodors.com/resource/lodging/`) To get to this helpful site, you can enter the URL or go to `www.fodors.com` and click **Resource Center** and then **Lodging**. The B&B finder has reviews of more than 2,000 B&Bs in the United States, and includes illustrations, plus a regional overview and nearby sights, activities, and restaurants for each inn.

➤ **Professional Innkeepers Association of America** (`www.paii.org/directories.html`) Maintains a directory of directories of B&Bs around the world. All B&Bs you'll find listed here, of course, are members of the association.

➤ **HomeArts and American Historic Inns' B&B Encyclopedia** (`homearts.com:80/affil/ahi/main/ahihome.htm`) Lists more than 12,000 historic inns throughout the United States and Canada. You can search by state or region, and use location and amenity criteria to narrow your results. Want to be on a farm? Want to be near skiing? Want an inn with fewer than six rooms, and on the waterfront? No problem. The powerful search engine gives you lots of options to choose from.

➤ **Bed & Breakfast Online International (BBI)** (`www.bbinternational.com`) An electronic directory dedicated to B&B accommodations around the world. BBI is designed to do searches by country, region, and local area. You can also throw in your two cents' worth in the review and recommendations area.

Planning Ahead for the B&B of Your Choice

Because of the growing popularity of inns and B&Bs, you should start your search for the B&B of your choice at least three (preferably six) months before you plan to arrive, especially if you're traveling during peak travel season (May to October). If you're traveling during the off season, and not during the Christmas holidays, you'll probably have a wider selection, and you may even find deals or discounted rates. Be sure to check deposit requirements and cancellation policies when booking that far in advance.

Special Packages for Honeymooners, Families, and Seniors

If you plan on taking the kids along to a B&B, you need to ask specifically if kids are welcome. Many of the B&B whose listings I've run across simply do not welcome kids. If the B&B does allow children (or pets, for that matter), find out if there are activities for children either on the grounds or in the nearby community. For the scoop on family-friendly, senior-friendly, and romantic getaways, be sure to check out Lanier Travel Guides (`www.travelguides.com`). It was rated four stars by Yahoo! Internet Life for Best Bed and Breakfast Site. Or read the online B&B Gazette (`www.travelguides.com`), which gives information on romantic getaways and family and senior-friendly inns. For senior travel information, check out Yahoo! Senior Travel, at `http://senior.yahoo.com`, where you'll find B&B listings, tour packages, and lots of other senior-travel-related information.

Condos, Apartments, Villas, and Vacation Homes

Furnished rentals are a great lodging alternative to hotels if you want a vacation place that's roomy enough for the whole crew and comes with cooking facilities. Home exchange directories list rentals and homes for trade (which requires a bit of planning and coordination between the two parties), and services that search for a house or an apartment for you and handle the paperwork. Of course, fees apply, but sometimes you can save time going through a locator service. Otherwise, email exchange, online classifieds and bulletin boards, plus the handy-dandy member databases are useful tools when it comes time to locate a vacation rental. Yahoo! Travel also has a long list of rental properties. Go to the Lodging category, and you'll see a link to vacation properties. Or check out these sites for the scoop on local or international home rentals:

➤ **1001 Villa Holiday Lets and Rental Properties** (`www.1001-villa-holidaylets.com`) Search the database of thousands of rental properties worldwide. The Fast Search feature helps you find top golf and ski trip rental properties, or you can sign up to be notified via email of new listings or recommended properties.

➤ **Hideaways International** (`www.hideaways.com`) A fee-based vacation rental property locator service that lists villas, townhomes, apartments, flats, condos, and other furnished rentals in Africa, Canada, South and Central America, the United States, the Caribbean, and Europe. The membership fee is $129 (on special for $99 when I last visited the site, but price is subject to change) and includes guide books, newsletters (for printed materials, additional fees may apply for residents outside the United States), insider tips and advice, unlimited access to Hideaways' professional travel staff, and other members-only benefits and discounts. You can take a guest tour of the Web site to check out the types of properties listed, as well as get a feel for the price range you're dealing with. Each listing includes a description of the property and its surroundings, amenities, services, activities, and property ratings. You'll also get the inside scoop on whether the property is handicap accessible, whether clothing is optional (nudist-friendly B&Bs), whether children or pets are allowed, and what the minimum lengths of stay are.

AOL's Travel Channel classifieds include listings for vacation rental properties and home exchanges.

Trading Homes

A home exchange offers an added advantage—you've got someone watching over your home while you're away on holiday. You also save money on dining expenses and have a unique opportunity to see the town from a local's perspective. Here are a couple of cool Web sites that feature home exchange databases:

➤ **Trading Homes International (www.trading-homes.com)** By trading your home for your next vacation, not only can you save thousands of dollars on your trip, but you also get to experience a travel destination not as a tourist, but as a local. A one-year membership to Trading Homes International (usually around $65) provides you with printed directories or access to the password-protected online member database. Here you can search through member listings, featuring photos of member homes, as well as information about the city and surrounding areas, desired exchange dates, and all contact information. You can pick a city on the world map locator and browse through all the available member homes in that area, or sign up for automatic email notification of new postings in your desired location.

➤ **International Home Exchange Network (www.homexchange.com)** Lists home exchanges, hospitality exchanges, and vacation rental properties in the United States, Canada, and plenty of other international destinations. The Home Exchange Network also features travelogues, links to destination guides and transportation information, travel tips, and links to other travel-related Web sites. The site's design is a little lackluster, but, hey, the fewer images, the quicker the download time, right? Unless you want to preview photos of your potential property exchange or rental, this site should do the trick. You don't have to become a member to reply to postings either, which is good and bad. That means you're competing with lots of other travelers looking for home exchanges.

Using an Online Currency Converter for Turning International Lodging Rates into U.S. Dollars

Some of the prices of international hostel and alternate lodging properties are listed in non-U.S. dollar denominations. For a quick conversion to U.S. dollars, visit My Travel Guide at `www.mytravelguide.com` and find the **Tools** section. You should see a Currency Converter link. The converter is easy to use—just enter the amount and select to convert to U.S. dollars or from U.S. dollars to the foreign currency amount. And for tips on getting the most from changing currency, Rick Steves' Web site (`www.ricksteves.com/tips/moneytip.htm`) has an informative article with advice on what kind of currency to travel with, when you should convert to foreign currency, and how to get the best rates on conversion.

Hostels

Because nearly half of the 5,000 or so youth hostels in the world are members of Hostelling International, a nonprofit organization, you may be required to be a member of Hostelling International before you're allowed to check in. Some hostels allow you to join on the spot, but others do not, so be sure to join before you hit the road. You can join your national Youth Hostel Association as a member by contacting your national office or Worldwide Hostels (`www.iyhf.org/iyhf/world.html`) for details. Your national membership card is valid for local as well as international travel if your country is a full member of the International Youth Hostel Federation (IYHF).

For other guides to hostels, visit these Web sites:

➤ **Europeanhostels.com** (`www.europeanhostels.com`) A new list of youth hostels and cheap hotels in Europe. There are also links to other budget travel sites to find travel guides, tour books, and visitor suggestions.

➤ **Hostels.com** (`www.hostels.com`) Everything you need to know to go hostelling, like what a hostel is, who stays there, what you need to go hostelling, and much more. You can also check out the worldwide hostel database (which they claim is the most complete directory of hostels anywhere). You can get advice on budget travel from the experts or read postings from other travelers using the Web site's bulletin boards. You can find answers, make friends, or connect with travel companions. You can buy tickets, buy gear, and buy books for your trip. Hostels.com is one-stop shopping for the hostelling enthusiast. Be sure to check out the Features section, which includes Places and Tales—real stories from real travelers, just like you.

Youth Hostels Aren't Just for Youths, Ya Know

Did you know you don't have to be a student or even youthful to stay in a hostel? Granted, some hostels do have age restrictions, but most don't. If you're looking for a way to save on lodging, check out hostels in your destination of choice and find out if persons of any age are allowed to stay.

At Hostels.com, you can learn about hostels, search the hostel database, and find answers, friends, and travel partners in the bulletin board discussions.

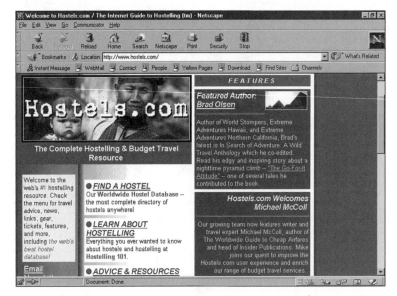

➤ **Europe's Famous 5 Hostels (www.hostelwatch.com)** Lists details for the top 10 (they expanded) hostels in Europe. You can print out a map of the hostel locations, swap information on the bulletin board, or get tips from other travelers.

➤ **Hostelling International—American Youth Hostels Organization (www.hiayh.org)** You can go to register as a member and even make hostel reservations at certain locations. Or you can just find out about the organization and its programs and local councils by taking a tour through the Web site. You'll also find links to other useful hostelling Web sites and general youth and budget travelers' resources.

Looking for Hostel Newsgroups?

You'll find plenty of hostel, budget, and backpacker newsgroups at the Deja.com newsgroup Web site. Either search by keyword **hostel** or go to the travel forum to find plenty of newsgroup discussions, tips, and advice from other hostel travelers. Some of the most active hostel newsgroups include `rec.travel.europe`, `rec.travel.budget.backpack`, `uk.rec.youth-hostel`, and `uk.rec.walking`. If you're looking for hostel information in a particular destination, just include the city or country name in your keyword search to find discussions and threads relating to your topic of interest.

Elderhostels

Elderhostel (`www.elderhostel.org`) is a nonprofit organization providing educational adventures all over the world to adults aged 55 and over. Program activities include life learning adventures such as exploring the wonders of the Grand Canyon or the Catskill Mountains. Applied arts and crafts programs, like making Shaker furniture or quilts, are integrated with field visits to museums, farms, or artist studios. Intensive study programs offer an in-depth educational experience, and intergenerational programs give you the chance to spend time with your favorite young person. Elderhostel programs accommodate special-needs travelers, and operate at hundreds of locations around the globe. You can go online to register for programs, get detailed information, and hear from other Elderhostel travelers.

Waking Up in the Great Outdoors

Finding information on campgrounds and parks is a cinch on the Web. I started my search at Yahoo! Parks (`http://parks.yahoo.com`) and found state-by-state and international listings, plus an outdoor community message board and Net events section. Although the park listings seem sparse at this point, you can still browse the national parks list to find a park that might not be listed under its state. If you're looking for activity-based campgrounds, you can search Yahoo! Parks categories for parks and campgrounds that offer boating, camping, climbing, environment, fishing, hiking, mountain biking, and wildlife.

Here are some other online resources for locating the ideal campsite for your outdoor adventures.

➤ **National Park Reservation Service** (www.nps.gov) For general information on the U.S. National Park systems, and tips on preparing for your visit. You can preview park maps, gather campground reservation information and fees, and find out about senior travel programs like the Golden Passport programs. Or you can locate a park by name, region, or theme.

At the National Park Reservation Service, you can locate a campground or park and reserve your space online or get availability and contact information.

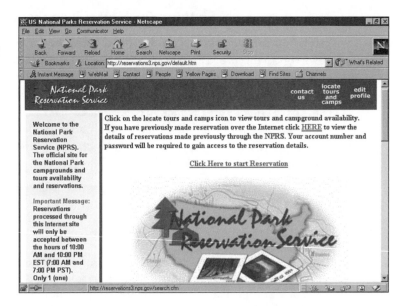

➤ **Reserve America** (www.reserveamerica.com) The one-stop reservation service for U.S. Army Corps of Engineers and U.S. Forest Service campgrounds. Campers can choose from more than 49,500 campsites at more than 1,700 federal campgrounds. Sites are available nationwide—from Alaska's Tongass National Forest to Florida's Lake Okeechobee and from California's Los Padres National Forest to the Knightville Dam in Massachusetts. The list of parks accepting reservations through an online system is growing, and as a one-stop-shopping site to find the perfect campsite, this is a great place to start. The search features help you locate campsites based on access for the disabled, tent sites, RV or trailer sites, tent platforms, car access, boat access, walk- or hike-in, or cruiser sites only. If you're after amenities, you can locate parks that offer playgrounds, showers, trailer dumping, organized programs, lake swimming, ocean swimming, pond swimming, pool swimming, river swimming, boat rentals, and boat launch—and even parks that allow pets.

The Least You Need to Know

➤ You can research and reserve rooms at inns and B&Bs in the U.S. and internationally.

➤ You can search for villas, apartments, and other furnished rental properties online.

➤ You can research hostel and Elderhostel information online.

➤ You can preview and reserve a campsite at a private campground or national or state park.

Part 3

Cruises, Package Tours, Group Travel, and Custom Group Tours

You just don't have the time to deal with the details of travel planning. Or you know you want to take a cruise, but you don't want to end up on the wrong ship. Well, there's a cruise for just about everyone—from singles to seniors to families to honeymooners. To find the cruise that's just right for you, and to hear what other cruisers think, go online.

If it's group travel you're looking for, go to the Net. New online planning systems and other group travel-planning tools can save time and eliminate the frustration of trying to coordinate plans for large (and small) groups of travelers. If your plans involve sports, educational, historical, or adventure travel, check it out.

This part of the book covers how to find the vacation package that's right for you. Or if you want to have a professional put a custom trip together for you or your special-interest group, you can find out how to do that in this section, too.

Chapter 16

Cruises, Cruises, and More Cruises

In This Chapter

➤ Making sense of the countless cruise options using online cruise directories and reviews

➤ Locating and selecting a travel agency or cruise consolidator to book your cruise

➤ If you want to take a cruise, there's a cruise for you: selecting your cruise based on lifestyle and budget

I can't say we owe it all to *The Love Boat* television series of the '70s and '80s (and now the late '90s!), but the popularity of commercial cruises has grown dramatically over the past 20 years. And according to surveys conducted by the Cruise Lines International Association, more than 60 percent of Americans say they'd love to take a cruise someday. That's a lot of people. And thanks to this great interest in cruise travel the various cruise lines are competing to get our business. That puts us in the driver's seat in terms of options, activities, and prices.

If you want to go on a cruise, chances are pretty good that you can find exactly what you're looking for in terms of fellow travelers, activities, sights, price, length of travel, and so on, and that you probably won't spend any more money than you would on your average land-based vacation. Many cruises are packaged with airfare and transfers, so planning your cruise can actually be a pretty simple process. Plus, you can easily take advantage of super deals and specials without the hassle of having to do all the legwork yourself.

With the exception of Carnival Cruises, you can't book a cruise directly through the liner. You have to go through a travel agent, and that means you don't have to worry about the nitty-gritty of travel planning. All you have to do is find the cruise that's right for you, and you're on your way to the ocean-going adventure of your lifetime. And thanks to the Internet, you can go online to find tips, reviews, recommendations, and profiles for almost every cruise available.

Online Cruise Directories Mean Smooth Sailing for Shoppers

Not all cruise ships are alike, and in fact, there are so darned many options, you may find yourself somewhat overwhelmed when it comes time to choose the one that's just right for you. Fortunately, though, finding a cruise that suits your lifestyle and budget is easy as pie on the Web. With directories, reviews from vacationers, and tips and advice on finding the right cruise at the right price, you can use this information and work with a travel agent to book the cruise of your dreams.

Cruise travel is hugely popular, and you'll find an endless array of options when it comes time to finding a cruise that fits your budget. But if you know how to use search engines and you know which cruise line directories can help you find what you're looking for, you can save time reviewing your options.

Say for example you're a fetching young, single professional with a week or so of vacation time coming up. When you're reviewing your vacation options, you say to yourself, "Yes, I would love to relax on the deck of a luxury cruise liner, have eight meals daily served to me by gracious hosts, and hit the decks at night to meet the man/woman of my dreams. But aren't cruises for old people? What if I board my vessel, only to find that I'm stuck playing shuffle board and bridge all day?" Come dinner time, you don't want to be seated with a bunch of East Coast snowbirds who want to know what a lovely guy/gal like you is doing alone on a boat like this. Your worst nightmare, huh? Or what if you're a 50-ish couple looking for a romantic, low-key high-seas adventure. You board your ship and discover hoards of screaming kids and stressed-out parents, or even worse, you find yourself surrounded by a mob of drunken fraternity brothers.

The Web makes the selection process easy by offering cruise directories that include reviews, an overview of onboard services, ship descriptions, photos, itineraries and activity plans, deck plans, menu options, and all the other information you need to select the cruise that fits your lifestyle. And because a good number of these sites are sponsored by travel agencies, it's a pretty simple procedure after you find what you're looking for to just click on over and send in an email request to be contacted by an actual human being, and sometimes even book directly online. So come aboard...they're expecting you.

After you've selected your cruise, visit the cruise line's Web site to preview deck plans of your vessel, like the Mandalay, Windjammer's (www.windjammer.com) queen of the fleet. This 236-foot barquentine was built in 1923.

You'll find plenty of helpful online cruise directories to give you the low down on what each vessel has to offer, even which one is best suited for you based on your lifestyle and budget. Here are some good starting points if you're new to cruise vacations, or just want to save time narrowing down your options:

➤ **National Geographic's Cruise Finder** (`www.cruisefinder.ngtraveler.com/`) A smart starting place. You can find the cruise that's right for you using the Tailor Your Cruise filter features in an easy-to-use system with data and reviews provided by Fielding Travel (see the next Web site review). After you've narrowed down your options, select the vessels you want to compare for a side-by-side breakdown of cost, features, lifestyle and atmosphere, ship ratings, room size, services, activities, and amenities. I like this interface more than the left-side/right-side comparison you get at the Fielding site. Although you can't connect directly to a travel agent from here to book your cruise, you can use this virtual travel agent to help you narrow your choices. After you've located the cruise line that meets your needs and budget, you can link directly with the operator's Web site to request brochures or get more information, call your local travel agency, or get connected with a preferred travel agency.

➤ **Fielding Worldwide Travel's CruiseFinder** (`www.fieldingtravel.com`) The data and rating source behind the National Geographic cruise finder feature, so for even more information on cruises, be sure to go straight to the source. After 18 years in the travel guide book business, this publisher has developed a Web site for travel professionals and cruise travelers to compare and review ships. Fielding's Crowsnest message board is a must-read, too, if you're looking for tips, advice, and reviews from real cruise passengers. You can post a question and get answers from other travelers, and every once in a while the expert staff at Fielding Travel will field your question, too!

➤ **Yahoo! Cruise Line Directory (www.yahoo.com)** From the home page, click **Travel** and then **Cruises** to start your search through a long list of cruise lines and travel agents that specialize in cruise travel. If you already know what cruise you want to take or which cruise line you want to set sail with, you can visit the Web site to request brochures, take virtual tours, see ship layouts, or get linked to travel agents specializing in that cruise lines' travel.

Or if you want to skip the directories, you can go straight to the source—the cruise line itself. Here's a list of the Web addresses for the major cruise lines:

➤ **Alaska's Glacier Bay Tours and Cruises** www.glacierbaytours.com

➤ **Alaska Sightseeing/Cruise West** www.smallship.com

➤ **American Canadian Caribbean Line** www.accl-smallships.com

➤ **American Hawaii Cruises** www.cruisehawaii.com

➤ **Cape Canaveral Cruise Line** www.capecanaveralcruise.com

➤ **Carnival Cruise Lines** www.carnival.com

➤ **Celebrity Cruises** www.celebrity-cruises.com

➤ **Clipper Cruise Line** www.clippercruise.com

➤ **Commodore Cruise Line** www.commodorecruise.com

➤ **Costa Cruise Lines** www.costacruise.com

➤ **Cunard** www.cunardline.com

➤ **Delta Queen Steamboat Co.** www.deltaqueen.com

➤ **Disney Cruise Line** www.disney.com/DisneyCruise

➤ **Holland America Line** www.hollandamerica.com

➤ **Norwegian Cruise Line** www.ncl.com

➤ **Premier Cruises** www.premiercruises.com

➤ **Radisson Seven Seas Cruises** www.asource.com/radisson

➤ **Regal Cruises** www.regalcruises.com

➤ **Royal Caribbean International** www.royalcaribbean.com

➤ **Royal Olympic Cruises** www.royalolympiccruises.com

➤ **Seabourn Cruise Line** www.seabourn.com

➤ **Star Clippers** www.star-clippers.com

➤ **Tall Ship Adventures Cruises** www.asource.com/tallship

➤ **Windjammer Barefoot Cruises** www.windjammer.com

➤ **Windstar Cruises** www.windstarcruises.com

➤ **World Explorer Cruises** www.wecruise.com

Working with Travel Agents and Cruise Consolidators

As budget travel aficionado Arthur Frommer says, "In the field of cruising, only the chump pays full price." Don't feel bad if you were chumped out by an uninformed travel agency or broker that didn't know (or tell you) where to go for the best price on your last cruise. With so many options and so many agencies, it's hard to know who you can trust to give you the best deal and put you on the right vessel. But most certainly, with the exception of Carnival Cruises, you *will* have to go through a travel agent or cruise consolidator to book your cruise. If you don't know an agent in your area, sometimes the cruise lines have preferred agents and can connect you with one.

Cruise travel is a little more complicated than other kinds of vacation options, so it is best to work with a travel agent. Plus, you're not likely to find a better deal doing all the legwork yourself, so look for a travel agency that has experience with a variety of cruise lines, that's willing to take the time to answer your questions and help you sort through your options.

Getting Help Choosing a Cruise

Besides poring over hundreds of flashy brochures and cruise catalogs, for the quick and easy way to choose a cruise, Fielding Worldwide's Web site (`www.fieldingtravel.com`) has helpful advice on what you should know before booking or embarking on any cruise. You'll find information on choosing a ship, choosing a cabin, dining room know-how, cruise line cuisine, how to avoid pigging out at sea, ship sanitation inspections, safety of life at sea, five hints for a hassle-free cruise, and seven ways to protect yourself from travel scams. You can also get expert tips on how to get through customs and info on port taxes, visas, passports, immunizations, pre- and postcruise packages, and really nearly everything you need to know about cruises.

Checking Out Travel Agents Before You Hire One

I talked about online security in Chapter 6, "Before You Buy...Protecting Yourself Online," and what to do to protect yourself when you go online to plan your trip, hire a travel agent, or purchase travel. First and foremost, when it comes to giving your money to anyone, you need to know who you're dealing with. It's probably a safe bet that the travel agency in your own home town, that's on the corner of State Street and Chauncey and has been in business for half a century or longer, is going to be around for a while. But one of the nice things about going online to plan your trip is how quick and easy it is to find specialty travel agents, or agencies that offer discounts, special packages, extra services, or something different from what you can find in your own home town.

A feather in the cap of any travel agency is membership in the Association of International Travel Agencies. You can visit the Web site at **www.aita.org** to get a listing of all member agencies and review what qualifies an agency for membership. Another way to check out a travel agent is to ask for references from previous customers.

Travel Agencies Turn to the Web to Service Customers

Is the Web going to put travel agencies out of business? No, probably not. But a good travel agency—and a travel agency that expects to compete and survive the online travel revolution—uses the Internet to help its customers get better deals and plan better vacations. One brick-and-mortar travel agency that's made the transition to using the Internet to service its customers is Lafayette Travel and Cruise. Visit its Web site at **www.laftravel.com** for a good example of how travel agencies are rolling with the changes of technology and making use of the wealth of travel information on the Web.

As I've mentioned before, if you're investing any amount of money that you'd hate to lose if something went awry, you should purchase travel and trip cancellation insurance. And don't buy directly from the cruise line itself. If the ship goes belly up, there goes your cash along with it. For tips on selecting the travel insurance policy that's right for you, see Chapter 6, "Before you Buy...Protecting Yourself Online."

One of the easiest ways to find a reputable and competent cruise specialist is to make use of the various cruise agent associations member listings at the Cruise Lines International Association (CLIA), at **www.cruising.org**, or the National Association of Cruise Oriented Agents, at **www.nacoa.com**.

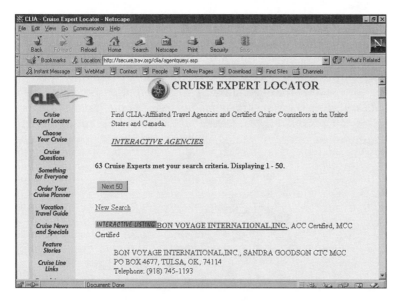

The CLIA Web site features member listings to help you locate cruise travel agencies in your area.

You can also check whether the agent or agency is a member of American Society of Travel Agents (**www.astanet.com**) or is a certified travel counselor. Being a member of one of these organizations or being certified doesn't necessarily mean the agent has cruise experience—it just means they abide by a set of rules and ethics set out by the member association.

Some Books to Get You Started

Besides what you'll find online, a wonderful guide to cruises is *The Complete Idiot's Guide to Cruise Vacations* by Fran Wenograd Golden, which can be found at bookstores or on the Web at **www.macmillan.com** and other online bookstores. It's highly recommended reading, as Fran offers first-hand tips and advice on the many, many options you have when it comes to booking the cruise vacation for you and yours.

Another great book to pick up if you're a first-time cruiser or if you're looking for a guide to choosing the cruise that's right for you, is Fielding's *Worldwide Cruises*, which is updated and published annually. It includes reviews of more than 160 ships and profiles of the top 61 cruise lines. You'll find it in all kinds of bookstores, or you can order on the Web directly from Fielding's at **www.fieldings.com/order/order.html**.

Finding Specialty Agents for Specialty Cruises

The first thing to look for in a cruise specialist is firsthand experience with the various ships, lines, destinations, and ports of call. And when you know what kinds of questions to ask and how and where to locate travel agents using the Web, you're ready to go out looking for agencies that specialize in your kind of cruise. There are cruise-only travel agents and then there are travel agents that handle travel arrangements beyond just cruises. Which one is best? Depends. Cruise-only agencies often bill themselves as discounters, so you need to take an ounce or two of precaution and check credentials before you book.

An Ounce of Insurance...

Trip cancellation/interruption insurance (TCI) covers you if an injury, illness, or accident happens before or during a cruise or vacation. Without insurance, you risk losing hefty pre-payments or the steep expense of emergency transportation home. With TCI and emergency medical evacuation (EME) coverage, you can rest assured that some or most of the money you pay for your cruise will be refunded if you have to cancel or cut the trip short, or if you have to be evacuated. Look for a policy that includes coverage for operator failure, too. Be sure to read the fine print, as some policies pay only if the operator stops all operation for 10 days in a row.

Check to see if the agency is a member of the Cruise Lines International Association (**www.cruising.org**) or the National Association of Cruise Oriented Agencies (**www.nacoa.com**). And if you want additional backup, check the regional Better Business Bureau agency where the travel agency makes its homebase and see if any complaints have been waged against it. In fact, if you plan on working with a travel agency for any kind of travel, there are many; you can locate the home pages for most of the many travel agency associations through the index maintained at the Travel Agency Association Web site (**www.travelagency.com**). And last, but not least, be sure to read the fine print before you close the deal.

Accommodating Passengers with Disabilities

Even though more and more travelers with disabilities are booking cruises, either as groups or as individual travelers, many still report minor inconveniences and even major problems with cruise line travel. Your best bet is to work with a travel agency that specializes in travel for the disabled and can guarantee that a ship's disability policies are in fact acceptable.

Got a Sick, Twisted Sense of Humor? If Not, Skip This Sidebar

It's not right to make light of health problems, but I must share a funny little story with you. I can't help myself. I stumbled across a page called Dialysis-at-Sea Travel Services, and with good-willed and light-hearted intentions asked a buddy if she wanted to take a dialysis cruise with me.

Now, I'm blessed to not have diabetes or any other serious health problems, but there is a good laugh here if you have a sense of humor. If not, skip this paragraph. Anyway, in a display of insensitivity and political incorrectness we laughed a bit, just because it sounds like an odd thing. Then my buddy wondered if there was such a thing as an incontinent cruise...not intercontinental cruises or even cross-continental cruises. Well, I didn't find anything specific to incontinence cruises, but my friend did remark, "Hmm. Gives new meaning to the term 'poop deck', huh?" Okay, sorry, sorry, sorry. I thought it was kind of funny.

Recently there's been an increase in the number of cruises and group tours that cater specifically to special-needs passengers. It's becoming easier to find travel agencies that specialize in meeting the needs of disabled travelers. One such place is the Society for the Advancement of Transportation for the Handicapped (SATH), at **www.sath.org/guide.htm**. You'll find information on special-needs accessibility for the travel-related industries...travel agents, tour operators, bus operators, hotels, airlines, railroads and cruise lines, terminals, stations, and related facilities. SATH actively represents travelers with disabilities, with the goal of promoting awareness, respect, and accessibility for disabled and mature travelers, and employment for the disabled in the tourism industry. SATH works for the creation of a barrier-free environment throughout all segments of the travel and tourism industry.

Finding the Cruise That's Perfect for Your Lifestyle

So, what are you? Don't you hate being put in a category? A demographic? Well, for the most part, it's for your own good. Unless you're a chameleon and can get along with anyone under any circumstances, you need to look for a cruise that suits your lifestyle. If you're single and looking for the love of your life on the high seas, you might not want to book a cruise on a senior adventure to Alaska. Go online to do your research, and work with your friendly travel agent to find the cruise that fits.

Seniors Cruises

If you're a member of the 50+ population and you're looking into cruises (or travel of any kind, really), you're a lucky dog. Not only are you a member of the largest demographic of Americans, you're a prime target for travel services and options designed just for you. See, travel suppliers have figured out that you've got "disposable income" and the time and desire to travel, now that the kids are gone and you're out and about enjoying your "golden years."

What this means is that not only will you find cruises designed with your tastes and activities in mind, there's plenty of competition for your business. And that means bargains, bargains, bargains for you. If you take the time to look around at all the options you have when it comes time to pick the cruise of your dreams, surely you'll find the perfect fit for you. If you belong to AARP or AAA, check out the deals offered through those clubs, and get ready to set sail on the cruise of your life-long dreams. Here are some good starting points:

➤ **Seniors At Sea (www.seniorsatsea.com)** Provides cruise opportunities for active seniors, aged 50 and over. Cruises are available on several cruise lines, including Holland America and Norwegian Cruise Lines. You can cruise to such places as Europe, Alaska, or the Panama Canal. You can take seminars on the area you are visiting, to learn about the builders of the Panama Canal or the geology of the Alaskan glaciers.

Seniors At Sea connects seniors with cruise options on the major cruise lines.

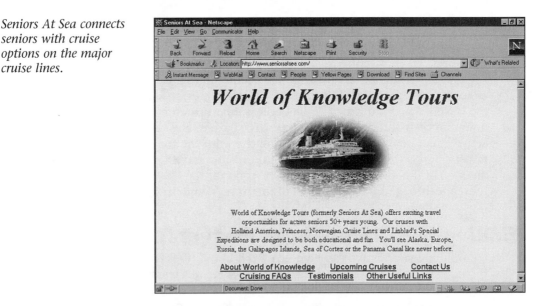

➤ **Escapade Cruises (www.singlescruises-tours.com/seniors.html)** Offers a senior cruise newsletter, as well as information about current discounted trips and which cruise lines offer AARP and other senior discounts.

➤ **50 Plus Travel (`aim-higher.com/50plustravel`)** Offers great ideas for destinations and cruises for folks 50 and older. Choose from many different lengths of cruises and a variety of destinations.

Singles Cruises

What could be more romantic than meeting your dreamboat on the high seas? It worked for Leonardo and Kate, so it will certainly work for you if that's what you're looking for. After all, life is just like the movies. But even if you're not going on a cruise to cruise for babes, plenty of ships set sail that have activities to meet your interests and lifestyle. If it's billed as a singles cruise, that doesn't mean you're going to be subject to turn-about dances or matchmaker ploys to hook you up with another passenger. What it does mean, though, is that you won't be charged a single-occupancy surcharge, and that you won't board a vessel teeming with screaming kids or love-struck honeymooners.

After all, single folks take vacations, too. And we are not a market that can be overlooked. You'll find lots of leads and singles-only cruise information online. Get a start at these popular sites:

➤ **Windjammer Barefoot Cruises (`www.windjammer.com`)** Singles cruises for the adventurous young luxury traveler. It's a bit on the pricey side, but worth every bit, as this top-notch cruise line promises balanced passenger logs on its singles cruises to increase your odds of meeting the Romeo or Juliet of your dreams.

➤ **Escapade Tours (`www.singlescruises-tours.com/index.html`)** A travel agency that specializes in singles cruises and travel. It works with cruise lines that offer lots of opportunities for singles to meet, and it can help you find special deals on single- or double-occupancy rooms.

➤ **Club Solo Vacations (`www.solovacations.com`)** Doesn't offer a lot of cruise options, but it does offer reduced prices for singles, as opposed to the surcharge you'll get slapped with if you want to book a cruise for solo travel. These cruises are designed by this club and Carnival Cruise lines to have activities and parties just for singles traveling alone or with friends.

➤ **Discount Travel Club (`www.singlescruise.com`)** Caters to singles with special services and discounts. Not only does this site have singles cruises, it also has links to non-cruise sites for singles. The site lists all the activities and amenities on its cruises.

Honeymoon Cruises

Almost any travel agent can help you plan a honeymoon cruise, and you're sure to find agents that specialize in honeymoon cruises that can help you find special services and activities for lovebirds only. Some of the bigger cruise liners even offer togetherness activities, like spa sessions, where you can rub your honeypie with mud.

Sounds like fun. I'd recommend going straight to the source—the cruise lines themselves—for the lowdown on honeymoon specials, and then call a travel agent to book.

If you go online to find a travel agent, you'll find virtual travel agency sites like Simply Cruises (**www.simplycruises.com**), which will plan all the details of your honeymoon for you, from airfare to the cruise itself. Simply Cruises also provides an online bridal registry so your friends and relatives can help with the payment of your honeymoon! Simply Cruises can also help you wrap the whole event together— ceremony, honeymoon, and all—with a romantic wedding at sea. By booking 180 days in advance, you can qualify for discounts.

Family Cruises

Not very long ago, the idea of taking kids on a cruise vacation seemed absurd or something that only the rich and famous would do. But now, travel suppliers try to be everything to everyone, and that means families too. After all, why not lasso the whole group rather than go after a honeymooning couple or just a couple of traveling companions?

Families that cruise together stay together, right? If you haven't thought about taking the whole gang along on a cruise, check out what's being offered. From kids activities to things to do together as a close-knit unit, more and more families are taking to the high seas as a fun and unique way to travel:

➤ **Disney Cruise Line (disney.go.com/DisneyCruise/)** Disney on water. Get a sneak peak of activities for children, characters, entertainment, and cruise features. Vacation packages are also available that include a land stop at the Walt Disney World Theme Parks. If nothing else, you'll get a kick out of the rockin' virtual video tour of Disney's cruise liner. (See Chapter 2, "Browsers 101," if your browser is not set up to view video.) Be sure to crank it up on this one.

➤ **Cruise for Families (www.onlineagency.com/cruisesforfamilies/)** An extensive family cruise site. You can find special deals for families or check out the activities that each cruise line offers for children. You can also read reviews on the different lines. It's a great site for families wanting to cruise.

➤ **Cruise Lines International (www.cruising.org)** Has a special section just for cruises for children. Click the **Something for Everyone** button and search for kid-friendly cruises. You'll find cruises that offer beach parties, ping pong, kids-only swimming pools, parties, games, language instruction and educational events, and a number of other fun things to do on board, in port, and on land. You'll get links to cruise lines and packages for family cruise travel, and find out about special deals and promotions.

Alternative Cruises

Vacations are much more relaxing and enjoyable when you travel with like-minded travelers. If you have special interests or a lifestyle that doesn't fit into the traditional categories of married, single, retired, family, disabled, or another demographic, going online to search for cruises that accommodate alternative lifestyles is a good place to start. You'll be connected with gay-friendly cruise lines and travel agents and can get the skinny on gay cruise charters. Here are a couple of starting points:

➤ **RSVP Vacations** (`www.rsvp.net`) Organizes charter cruises and cruise vacations for gays, lesbians, and their families and friends. To locate a member of RSVP's travel agent network to book your cruise, take a peek through the long list of international travel agents that specialize in RSVP vacation packages. Or complete a request form online, and you'll be connected with an RSVP travel agent.

➤ **Simply Cruises** (`www.gaycruisevacations.com`) Gay owned and operated, this offers quality travel programs with friendly gay groups on conventional cruise ships. You'll find a variety of interesting and exotic destinations. Along with its gay groups, Simply Cruises also represents RSVP Vacations, Atlantis Events, and Olivia Cruises and Resorts for exclusive gay charters and vacations.

You Can't Wait to Get to a Port to Check Your Email Inbox, Can You?

Sometimes you want or need to check your email, even when you're not supposed to be worried about such things. I had the darndest time locating a cruise line that offered Internet access as an onboard service. I know there's been talk of it, but it certainly isn't available on the majority of cruise lines. But if you're a true email junkie or are using email to stay in touch with the kids or the office while you're on the cruise that's supposed to take you away from it all, my suggestion is to wait it out between ports of call and check your email when you go ashore for excursions or shopping.

Say you're making plans for an idyllic Caribbean cruise, and one of your ports of call is St. Lucia. No problemo. Before you board the plane that takes you to your point of embarkation, just jump online and pay a visit to Net Cafe Guide (`www.netcafeguide.com`) or Cyber Cafe's (`www.cybercafe.com`) guide to Internet access cafes and providers across the globe. Of course, you'll save money if you have a toll-free global access number or a free email account with Hotmail or Yahoo! or another easy-access account, so you might want to take some time to set up a universally accessible account before you hit the high seas.

The Least You Need to Know

➤ You can save time by going online to select the cruise that fits your budget, schedule, and lifestyle.

➤ You can find specialty travel agents and tour consolidators for discounts and deals.

➤ You can go online to get the inside scoop and cruise reviews from other travelers.

➤ You can shop around for Internet-only cruise specials and discounts.

➤ You can use cruise line directories to do side-by-side comparisons of services, amenities, price, and lifestyle options.

Traveling in Style with Packages and Tours

> **In This Chapter**
>
> ➤ Finding out how packages and tours can save you time and money
>
> ➤ Picking and choosing options and services for your package
>
> ➤ How to steer clear of travel package scams, too-good-to-be-true deals and knowing how to spot a winner when you find it
>
> ➤ Using online resources to compare and research travel package options and prices

Travel packages and tours are ready-made trips that combine transportation, lodging, dining, and other travel services into a package, which you can buy at a single, set price. Packages can make travel planning much easier because they usually include all the major trip components. And even better, they are available for nearly every destination, interest, and activity you can think of.

From the lights of Broadway to the heights of Nepal, the perfect vacation package is probably all wrapped and ready for you. For an idea of what's out there, check out The Leisure Travel Network (www.travelfile.com), a specialized online directory of packaged travel.

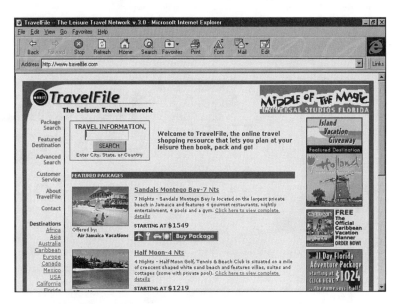

What's So Good About Packages?

Price, convenience, and peace of mind are what most people like about travel packages. The price of a packaged vacation is usually lower than if you purchase each service individually. This is because most packages are developed by tour operators who buy individual travel services, like lodging and air tickets, in bulk (at a low contract price) and combine them into a package.

For example, a tour operator might buy 300 rooms at a major hotel for the year. Buying so many rooms gives operators leverage to negotiate a lower price, so they get a better deal, and they can pass the savings on to you. It works the same way with the airlines and car rental companies, so the savings accumulate with each service added to the package.

All *you* have to buy is the package. All the homework is done for you. The routes, the hotels, the shows, the connections—everything—is worked out for you. And you can go up-scale, standard coach, or any class in between.

You pay one price for a package up front. You don't have to pay for rooms and sometimes not even meals as you go. Even tips can be included. That lets you budget more precisely for your trip and means you won't have to carry so much cash while you're on the road (except for shopping).

Airlines, resorts, and other travel companies also offer packages, and you'll enjoy the same benefits of better price and convenience if you book through them.

What Do the Experts Think?

Combine better prices with the convenience of knowing where to go, when to go, and how you'll get there and back, and it's hard to think of what isn't good about a travel package. Even expert travelers love them.

"I always recommend a package," says Dianna Ping, manager of Lafayette Travel and Cruise (**www.laftravel.com**), a 50-year-old travel agency that specializes in cruise, group, and individual leisure travel. "They can usually be customized any way the customer wants," she says. "You can purchase everything, or you can book just part of a package. And even if there aren't great savings, there's a lot more security and less trouble for my client."

Getting the Whole Enchilada

Typically, a package includes a combination of the following services:

➤ **Air transportation**   You usually get round-trip tickets with any necessary connections.

➤ **Lodging/accommodations**   Most packages are sold for a specified number of days, with lodging included for each night.

➤ **Meals**   Your package may include meals, whether at your hotel or during a planned activity. If you're on a raft trip, you might enjoy a picnic along the way. In Rome, you might dine by candlelight. The quality and type of meals included usually depend on the price and type of trip you're on.

➤ **Motorcoach**   Motorcoach, or bus, transportation is generally included in a package if you're on a sightseeing tour.

➤ **Rail service**   Getting you from Point A to Point B is crucial in a package. Count on at least some rail travel being included if you're going to Europe.

➤ **Car rental or limousine**   Depending on your price range, you may get a car or first-class shuttle service in a limousine.

➤ **Entertainment and activities**   Packages to places like Las Vegas generally include show tickets, and admission passes are standard for theme park packages and the like. Of course, if you're on a rafting trip, the price of seeing all that whitewater is included in your price.

➤ **Airport transfers** You'll never be stranded on a tour, but don't expect to always be swept away in style. Transfers guarantee a ride to and from the airport. Check ahead if it's a concern.

➤ **Taxes and port fees** If the package doesn't say these fees are prepaid, be prepared to shell out more cash, especially when entering or exiting an airport or sea port in a foreign country.

➤ **Tips and gratuities** If the package says these service fees are included, you won't need to tip the bus driver or the bellhop at your hotel. But if they are not included, be sure to leave appropriate gratuities for all services rendered.

The details of what's included in your package are spelled out in the promotional brochure. Prices are usually quoted per person. Be sure to review everything with your travel agent to ensure that you fully understand what you're buying.

Tours: Getting the Package Plus People

Although packages aren't always tours, tours are almost always packages. Tour packages provide all the benefits of a travel package, plus the services of a professional tour manager or escort who accompanies your group. Tours are generally developed around common interests and activities and are taken by groups of people who follow a preplanned itinerary together. You can find tours of all kinds and for all types of people. And you don't have to have a group to go along. The tour operator can put the groups together.

It's also possible to work with a travel agent to plan a custom tour for a group you already belong to. See more on that in Chapter 18, "Custom Group Tours."

Learning the Tour Lingo

The best way to learn about packaged tours is to review tour company brochures or to visit Web sites. And be sure to read the fine print. Here are some terms you should know (for a longer list, see the United States Tour Operators Association Web site at **www.ustoa.com/glossframe**.

➤ **Service charge** A fixed percentage automatically added to room and meal charges.

➤ **Tax** Fixed percentages set by the city, state, or federal government.

➤ **Ocean front** A room directly facing the ocean.

➤ **Ocean view** A room from which you can view the ocean.

➤ **Add-on fare** The cost of air travel that's not part of the tour. It can be "added on" to get you from one domestic city to the city where a tour package originates. For example, let's say my theater package tour of New York originates from Chicago. My airfare from Chicago to New York is part of the package. But if I choose to fly from Indianapolis to Chicago, that fare would be an add-on.

➤ **Voucher**   A document issued by a tour operator to be exchanged for accommodations, sightseeing, or other services. Hang onto your voucher. It's your ticket to ride!

➤ **Transfers**   Transportation between airports, city air terminals, rail stations, piers, and hotels.

➤ **All-inclusive price**   Usually includes land arrangements, including lodging and all meals, round-trip airfare, and all other transportation. Special services like spa treatments or manicures may be included if you're headed to a luxury resort, but usually these services are at extra cost to you. Be sure to read the description of exactly what's included in these packages.

➤ **Land price**   The cost for land arrangements only. Airfare is not included in the price.

Who Offers Package Trips?

Theme parks, resorts, sailing companies, airlines, cooking schools, adventure outfitters, museums, universities…all kinds of destinations and travel companies can be the centerpiece of a package. But the package is actually assembled and offered by a tour operator or packager. There are many, many companies like this—some good, some bad. Your travel agent is a broker for most reputable tour companies and will be able to help sort through packages options and find the best one for you. The travel agent is paid a commission by the tour company for his or her services, so you'll pay the same price as you would if you booked with the tour operator. I prefer to have my local agent assist me when I'm planning to go on a packaged trip.

The United States Tour Operators Association (USTOA) maintains a list of members that adhere to their financial and ethical standards. Definitely check out **www.ustoa.com** for the low-down on what to look for and expect in an operator.

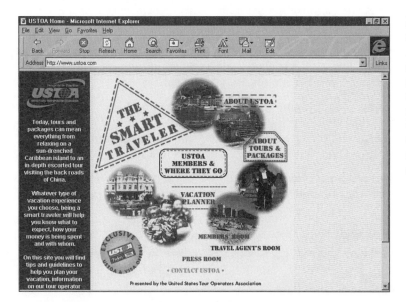

Members of USTOA are required to have a total of 18 references from industry sources and financial institutions. Formed to protect consumers' deposits in case of bankruptcy or fraud, USTOA also requires that members carry a minimum of $1 million of professional liability insurance.

It's very important to work with a reputable company. Remember that if it sounds too good to be true, it probably is. And you don't just want to protect yourself from scams. You want to make sure the operator who packaged your trip doesn't go out of business while you're traveling. If that happens, no one will honor your voucher, and you could be stranded! By the way, this a good reason to use a credit card—not cash, a debit card, or a check—for travel purchases. If the business closes or cancels your trip, you can dispute the charge and not have to pay if you didn't get what you paid for.

If you have a destination in mind, call directly and ask for the names of tour operators they work with. Or better yet, call your travel agent. Your agent will usually only represent operators he or she trusts and can help you sort through the many options available for your preferred destination.

Who Takes Package Trips?

People from all walks of life take advantage of package travel: the young and the old, the wealthy, families, singles, students and lifelong learners, mountain climbers, and sailors. You'll find trips designed for all tastes and budgets.

According to USTOA, its members move more than eight million passengers annually and account for annual travel sales of more than $4 billion. Chances are, you know someone who's booked a vacation package.

Finding and Buying Packages and Tours

I highly recommend that if you're in the market for a package or a tour, you start with your travel agent. If you haven't used one before, talk to friends for a recommendation. And don't just talk to one agent. Make sure the agent you use has experience with packages or tours. After you choose an agent, he or she can help you find and book your package or tour. Agents have loads of connections to tour operators and packagers that they trust, plus brochures you can take home and look over. Travel agents also get advance notice of new packages that will be on the market soon.

Make sure the operator or your agent has checked out the accommodations and other details of your trip. When you book a package, you're trusting their judgment, and you should always make sure you get the service you expect.

Going online is another way to find out what kinds of packages are out there and to do your homework on what kind of trip interests you. Even if you find a great package in Expedia's Deals section, check it out with your travel agent before you book. You might even hear about a better deal to the same place!

Here are some good online sources for finding an agent near you. You'll also find tons of great information on what to do if your trip is cancelled, what to expect on a tour, and who can help in the event of a problem:

➤ **National Tour Association** www.NTAonline.com

➤ **American Society of Travel Agents (ASTA)** www.astanet.com

➤ **USTOA** www.ustoa.com

214

➤ **Fodor's Resource Center**   `www.fodors.com/resource`
➤ **American Express Online**   `www.americanexpress.com` (Click the site map to quickly locate the travel service location directory.)

Proceed with Caution

Because packages require up-front payment, they're a magnet for scam artists. So use your head. No matter how tempting those ads in the Sunday paper might be, don't send money unless you're sure about the operator. Ask around. Call your state consumer protection agency or the Better Business Bureau. And your best protection is to go through your travel agent—someone you know. For extra protection, use a credit card.

Even the biggest tour operators can go belly-up—bankrupt, that is. And when that happens, it's unlikely that you'll ever see your money again. But if you book through a travel agent, that agent is responsible for your deposit and will seek recourse for you, and you won't pay any extra for the added security.

Old School Scams Catch Up with the Internet

What happened to the good old days when you only had to worry about telemarketers, direct mail and fax scams? Well, those weasley scam artists are coming after you online these days. One of the more publicized online travel scams are so-called instant travel agent programs. For a fee, victims pay for "training" and the title of travel agent to work from home and sell packages to other consumers, recruit other "travel agents" and then collect a share of the "new agents" earnings. Simply the classic illegal pyramid scheme in disguise.

The American Society of Travel Agents (`www.astanet.com`) offers these recommendations for avoiding scams:

➤ Be wary of postcard, phone, and email solicitations that say you've been selected to receive a "fabulous vacation."

➤ Never give out your credit card number unless you initiate the transaction and are confident about the company you're talking to. If someone calls or emails *you* with an offer, never, ever, ever give out your social security number, credit card information, or anything else unless you've carefully reviewed written materials about the offer. And even then, exercise caution.

➤ Insist on complete details in writing about any trip before making any payment! Details should include the total price and any applicable cancellation and change penalties. They should also include specific information on all components of the package.

➤ Walk away from high-pressure sales presentations that try to rush your decision or that require you to disclose your income.

➤ Don't trust companies that make you wait at least 60 days to take your trip.

Look for Guaranteed Pricing

Always read the fine print in brochures or online offers. Some tour operators may reserve the right to change pricing or change the package offerings, even after you've paid a deposit or paid in full. Look for operators that offer guaranteed pricing.

Choosing a Package or Tour That's Right for You

What kind of traveler are you? You need to know that before you meet with your travel agent. With the wide range of packages and tours available, pinpointing what you enjoy is fundamental to getting the most from your trip:

What are your interests?   Do you golf? Do you garden? Do you play a musical instrument? Do you dance? You can find a package that focuses on your favorite activities. Maybe you want to learn about art or architecture abroad. No problem. Theme packages, cultural tours, and adventures abound. Make a list of what you and your travel companion enjoy, as well as what you definitely want to avoid.

How experienced are you?   Are you a seasoned traveler? If not, you would probably like a tour. Having an expert along not only offers peace of mind, but also helps you get the most out of your trip. Good tour leaders are real gems who know about the out-of-the-way sights you'll treasure seeing. You'll also pick up lots of tips that can turn you into a smarter traveler for your next trip.

Where would you like to go?   Go ahead. The sky's the limit when you're planning. And who knows? There may be a very affordable package to your dream destination waiting for you. If you don't want to be too specific, at least have a general kind of experience in mind. A city? The beach? Mountains? Europe? Think hard about what you want and how you want to spend your travel time and dollars.

Are you a people person?   This is especially important if you're considering a tour. Know yourself, and then ask about the tour itself. Find out how much time you get away from the group. Can you explore on your own, or will you always be one big happy family? Do you like big families? How large is the group? How crowded will the bus be? Most tours provide a balance of time with the group and on your own, but make sure it's a good fit for you.

How active are you?   Can you walk a lot, or would you rather ride? Check out the way the tours are structured. Make sure you can keep up and you won't be too worn out to enjoy yourself.

What can't you live without?   Some friends of mine who are devoted Elderhostelers (read more about Eldershosteling in this chapter and in Chapter 15) have stayed in everything from dorms to old army barracks, and they get a kick out of it all. But not everyone would. Do you absolutely have to have a private bath? Fine. Make sure you get one. You can travel and tour in just about any style. Pay attention to your needs and tastes and choose accordingly.

Do you have special needs?   There are lots of specialty tours for people with disabilities and also rigid lifestyles. Let your travel agent know to find the trip that's right for you.

How much do you want to spend?   For most of us, this is the most important question. If you don't know, go online and do some research, because you can find tours in every price range. If destination is more important than price, tell your agent. If you have a strict budget, tell your agent. There are luxury packages and pretty basic ones, too. The more direction you give the agent, the better chance you'll have of finding a really great trip.

In *The Complete Idiot's Guide to Cruise Vacations*, Fran Wenograd Golden provides a helpful tool, adapted from the Cruise Lines International Association. I've adapted her tool further, so it's not so cruise specific. See which of these profiles in Table 17.1 fits you, and then pass the information along to your agent.

Table 7.1   Traveler Profile Guide

Profile	Description
The active traveler	On vacation, I like to choose from a wide range of activities. I like playing sports. I plan to stay fit on vacation. I'm interested in improving my game on my trip.
The adventurer	I've always wanted to visit the world's capitals and to see the sights. I like to visit places off the beaten path and see unusual things. I think it would be exciting to walk on a glacier, climb a mountain, or explore a volcano. I like to meet new people and learn about different cultures. I enjoy getting close to nature and wildlife.
The romantic	I like romaxntic dinners and dancing under the stars. I like doing new things with someone special. I like making friends on vacation. A breathtaking view, a full moon, and a quiet place to talk sounds absolutely sublime. I want our vacation to be something special.

continues

Table 7.1 CONTINUED

Profile	Description
The family vacationer	My spouse and I both work and never seem to spend enough time with our children. Even though we have different interests, our family enjoys vacationing together. With kids of different ages, our family needs a bunch of vacation experiences rolled into one. We need a restaurant that will satisfy all family members—burgers to continental. We are planning a family reunion and want a setting everyone can enjoy.

Finding Packages and Tours Online

The best place to start is from a travel directory or a booking site (you can read more about these in Chapter 7, "So, You Want to Be Your Own Travel Agent?"). Both have listings of tours and links to get you started. Online travel magazines, like Epicurious (**www.epicurious.com**) are other great resources. You can also start from travel association sites, like **www.ustoa.com**, and from travel and tourism bureaus. Fodor's (**www.fodors.com**) is another one of my favorite jumping-off points.

The Leisure Travel Network (**www.travelfile.com**) is a comprehensive directory of travel packages. This site is designed for consumers as well as travel professionals. You'll find lots of information on packages, and you can book directly from this site. (But that's something I don't really recommend.) The site is well designed with clear, easy-to-understand package descriptions.

Another good place to shop for tours and packages is at the Ambassadair (**www.ambassadair.com**) Web site. One of the more popular travel clubs, for an annual membership fee (you can apply online and perhaps even get a reduced fee!) you can sign up for luxury spa vacation packages, package tours and trips to North American and European destinations. The network of providers is extensive, so you're sure to find a vacation that suits your tastes and budget.

Destination Packages

If your vacation is just a sketchy idea at this point, and aren't sure exactly what destination you have in mind, definitely start with a travel directory or an online magazine. The Fodor's Resource Center (**www.fodors.com**) has a great section on tours that's broken down by group tours, packages, and theme trips. You'll find links to several tour operators, from super-deluxe Abercrombie and Kent safaris to the less exotic Vermont Bicycle Touring Company.

Epicurious (**www.epicurious.com**) has sections on the 50 best golf resorts, the 50 best ski resorts, and a link to Fodor's City Guides.

Adventure Packages

If you like adventure, check out Outside Magazine Online (`www.outsidemag.com`), which has an Active Traveler Directory with links featuring outfitters around the world. You can find sea kayaking and whale-watching tours, climbing schools in the Himalayas, walking tours and other active vacations, plus great articles and travelogues to wet your appetite.

The most comprehensive site for adventure travel is the Great Outdoor Recreation Pages (`www.gorp.com`). You'll find everything related to the outdoors and an online community that's as enthusiastic as you are. You can book from this site, too.

Don't Mess with Mother Nature

In 1996 nine people died on Mt. Everest in one day. Seven were travelers who booked an adventure to go to the top of the world. Two were highly experienced guides who lost their lives trying to save their customers. A tragedy any way you look at it, that disaster also pointed to the dangers of making wild places too accessible. When it comes to Mother Nature, a freak storm and life-threatening conditions can strike with little warning. So be sure you have the strength and skills to take care of yourself on an adventure tour. Are you accustomed to high altitudes? Do you swim well? Have you had a physical recently? How's your eyesight? Your endurance? Can you really carry your weight? The fact is, not everyone belongs on every adventure. So be realistic—before you book—for your sake and for the sake of others traveling with you.

Family Packages

Every theme park, water park, and amusement park is a prospect if you're in this category. But you have lots of other, quieter options, too. Go to the Travel section of Family.com at `www.family.go.com` and get some ideas on family vacations that won't break the bank. You can choose from Deals, Freebies, and Festivals, plus featured destinations that will provide plenty of ideas. For theme park packages, go to Fun Guide (`www.funguide.com`) or About.Com Theme Parks (`themeparks.about.com`) for listings of amusements around the world.

The Family.com travel section at www.family.go.com *has suggestions to make travel more enjoyable for everyone in the family.*

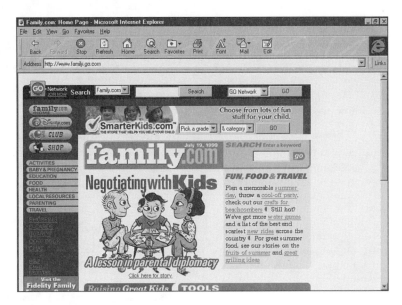

There also are some family-friendly tour operators you should look over. Grandtravel (**www.grandtrvl.com**) offers packages especially for grandparents and grandchildren to enjoy, and Rascals in Paradise (**www.rascalsinparadise.com**) specializes in family packages worldwide. Many resorts also offer special family packages. Work with your travel agent to check out all your family's options.

Gaming and Entertainment: Viva Las Vegas!

Las Vegas is the granddaddy of package deals, but it's not the only gaming and entertainment destination to check out. Gaming and entertainment towns are ripe with specials to get you there—they will even give you cash when you get off the plane! For Vegas, Lake Tahoe, Branson, Nashville, and similar destinations, go to their tourism bureau Web sites for more information on your entertainment options.

Cultural/Educational Packages

Looking to improve your brainpower? Make learning a vacation. There are many opportunities to learn as you travel—through museums, universities, and professional schools.

ShawGuides (**www.shawguides.com**) features a database of more than 3,300 career and recreational cooking schools, wine courses, golf, tennis and water sports, schools and camps, writers' conferences, photography workshops and schools, arts and crafts workshops, language vacations, educational travel programs, and artists' and writers' residencies and retreats. It's a uniquely detailed directory, and is a great site for travelers who want a trip that focuses on their interests and talents.

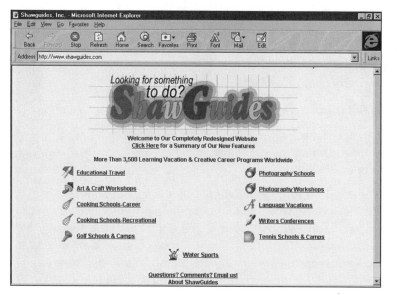

ShawGuides (www.shawguides.com) lets you search its database by state, country, U.S. region, global region, date, month, and focus.

Anther good place to look is your university alumni association. Many schools organize cultural tours you can join. Some of the biggest cultural institutions that sponsor travel include the Smithsonian (**www.si.edu/tsa/sst**) and the National Trust for Historic Preservation (**www.nthp.org**). Fodor's resource center has a good listing of sites like this.

Seniors Packages and Tours

Seniors, those 55 years and older, are one of the most prized groups of travelers today. Most packagers have specials for seniors, and there are many group tours available exclusively to this age group. You'll find terrific bargains as well as tours geared toward your interests and energy.

If you're a member of the American Association of Retired Persons (AARP), you're entitled to many travel discounts. Be sure you tell your travel agent that you're a member. If you're not a member, join! You can do it online at **www.aarp.org**. There are travel features and discounts featured on the site, too.

Elderhostel offers a totally unique travel experience to seniors. Promoting its "Adventures in Lifelong Learning," the not-for-profit organization sponsors education vacations in the United States and abroad. Generally offered at more reasonable prices than commercial packages and tours, Elderhostels often take travelers to university campuses and research stations to live and study for a week or more. You can check out an online catalog at **www.elderhostel.org**.

Elderhostel: A Golden Opportunity for Your Golden Years

Ernest and Roberta Deagan have been on 26 Elderhostel vacations. They're fanatics, more or less. But they say they meet others who have been on many, many more of these educational vacations.

"I usually choose by destination," says Mrs. Deagan. "But if it's not an interesting subject, why bother? We've done group tours, in London and Rome, but it's not the same. The Elderhostel trips are more about learning than about just seeing the sites. Almost all of them have about three different subjects, usually overlapping. Most of the instructors are experts—professors and scientists. We always learn so many things. It's a great way to really understand what you're seeing."

"The accommodations vary," Mrs. Deagan says, "But we don't mind. We recommend Elderhostel to anyone who wants to tweak their mind. Once you get used to them, going on a sightseeing tour is never as much fun."

Honeymoons

Planning that big trip? Many resorts (such as Sandals, at **www.sandals.com**), tour operators, and packagers cater to newlyweds. There are a wealth of packages just waiting for you. But do your homework first! Start with your favorite search engine and search on **honeymoon packages** for the widest selection possible. Other idea starters online include Bride's magazine (**www.brides.com**) which features a link to Epicurious Travel. Then, of course, check with your travel agent.

Special-Needs Tours

Some tour packages are specially designed for special-needs travelers. Mobility International (**www.miusa.org**) is a worldwide organization that promotes international access and distributes tip sheets on traveling abroad. You can find out more at the site. Also, visit Flying Wheels Travel (**www.flyingwheels.com**). This tour operator offers a wide range of escorted tours that cater to the special needs of people with disabilities.

The Least You Need to Know

➤ Travel packages and group tours are convenient and affordable ways to travel.

➤ You can go online to find a package for just about every destination, interest, or activity.

➤ A travel agent is important in booking travel packages and tours. Whether you use a virtual travel agent or the agency around the corner, rely on the agent's expertise to help with the details of your travel.

➤ You can get to know your tour operator or escort or hear from former customers when you visit the operator's Web site.

➤ Scams and too-good-to-be-true offers are creeping up on the Web. Read the fine print and know what you're buying before you lay down the cash.

Chapter 18

Custom Group Tours

In This Chapter

➤ Go online to check out tour operators and custom group travel agencies to find a match that's right for your group

➤ Use online destination guides and other travel sites to get ideas and details for custom group travel to save time and get the most from your travel agent

➤ Use online communication systems to stay up-to-date on planning activities and communicate important information to your group members without the hassle of playing phone tag or coming together for face-to-face meetings

➤ Build a travelogue Web site for your custom group travel or tour to show everyone at home what they missed out on

Chapter 17, "Traveling in Style with Packages and Tours," talks about the ins and outs and ups and downs of buying prearranged, all-inclusive travel packages. This chapter takes that concept a step further and shows you how to locate a travel agent or tour operator to help you plan a custom group tour for your special-interest group, such as a church group, an arts and entertainment club, a corporate group, a group of sports fans or participants, a family that wants to have a reunion, or any other club or member association. Technically, though, any group of 10 or more people with at least one common interest (we want to go somewhere warm, we want to see museums, we want to ride our bicycles) qualifies for the services of a travel agency in putting together a custom group tour.

You may be wondering what all this has to do with the Internet. Don't you just need to call on your local travel agent to handle the details? Yes and no. Even though you'll have to work with a travel agent or a tour operator to plan and book your group's custom tour, it doesn't hurt to do online research yourself before you even pick up the phone. You'll learn how to make use of online joint planning sites to coordinate and communicate with your group members if you're geographically spread out, or even just to coordinate and make accessible the details and itineraries for your whole group. You'll also learn how to build a travelogue Web site for your group, and learn how to post messages, photos, itineraries, reviews, links, and anything else that will help record your memorable trip experience.

If you're the group leader, or at least the person put in charge of getting the planning process started, you're especially in luck. In this chapter you'll learn how and where to locate a travel agent to handle your customized tour, and how to tap into online resources to assist your travel agent in researching the details of your trip. Although the agent you work with is already an expert in the field of group travel planning, it certainly doesn't hurt to do a little research yourself. You can also go online to meet people who share your group's interest and talk to them about their custom group tours.

Granted, you can often find prepackaged tours that relate to your area of interest. But what if all your group members are vegetarians and you have special needs outside of what's included in the prepackaged travel offering? Or what if you don't want to leave your lodging assignment to chance and want a guarantee of your room location? What if you're the travel coordinator, and you're looking to get a special deal or even a free trip as a reward for your planning efforts? These are considerations you need to think about if you've been given the task of coordinating your group's special travel plans.

How Many People Are Needed to Qualify As a Group?

Generally speaking, custom group tours are put together for groups of 10 or more people, up to as many as 100! The types of groups that make use of custom travel packages include church groups, reunion groups, arts and cultural clubs, organizations and membership associations, corporate incentive or convention travel groups, education or school groups, spectator sports enthusiasts, participation sports clubs or teams, and generally any group of people who have a special interest and a common travel agenda.

Discovering Tour Possibilities and Researching Ideas Online

After you've gathered interest from your group members on taking a custom tour, go online to see what other groups are doing and what kind of package possibilities are out there. It's also a good way to get a feel for the budget and how much you can expect to pay.

Chapter 17 lists lots of URLs, for some of the best tour packages and group travel ideas. Be sure to read through it to get started when you go online to locate ideas for your group's interest. Otherwise, go to Yahoo!, click **Recreation and Travel**, and then click **Tour Operators**. You'll get links to travel sites covering dude ranches, bear watching, educational and arts tours, auto racing (like NASCAR events), culinary interests, dog sledding, dolphin swimming, llama trekking, taking safaris, sea kayaking, and storm chasing. Now do you have some ideas?

Looking for Group Travel Ideas?

If you're looking for ideas for your group's travel plans, go to the Deja.com newsgroup community and do a keyword search to locate a traveler or special interest community. I saw this posting in `alt.food.wine`: "I need to organize a wine tour for about 70 people attending a conference in Santa Rosa in March 2000. I'm looking for a winery within 30–45 minutes of Santa Rosa that offers both a quality wine tour and premium wines. I'm also looking for a good restaurant for dinner for this group. Any suggestions?"

After you've narrowed down your travel activity, the next step is finding a travel agent to help you plan the details.

If you're still in the idea stage for your group's custom tour, going online is a great place to get ideas and feel out costs. You might want to start at a travel agency Web site that has information on package tours to get a feel for what's popular.

Depending on the level of specialization of your group's interest, though, you might need to do a keyword search to find a travel agent that can handle your trip-planning details. For example, if you're the group leader of a motorcyclists club and your group wants to take a motorcycle tour through the Midwest, stopping at James

Find a Tour Operator for Your Special Interest

Travel Roads (www.travelroads.com) specializes in adventure travel tours and can connect group leaders with tour operators for just about any kind of group tour you have in mind. You can also request brochures online, and learn about tour opportunities across the globe, covering nearly every possible activity-based travel. Art tour? Boar hunting? Ballooning? Walking tour of Ireland? Get your friends together and go online to get connected with a tour operator.

Dean's grave, Elvis's mansion, and the historic Hell's Angels Hideout in Indianapolis, you'd type in **motorcycle AND custom tours** in any search engine to get a link to a tour operator like Bosenberg's at **www.bosenberg.com**.

Locating the Right Travel Agent

Most travel agents you contact will tell you they can customize an existing package for you. But depending on the activity and level of specialization of your group's travel agenda, you'll want to work with a travel agent that has experience in planning many different kinds of custom group trips. And it's not always easy to find an agent around the corner, but you can go online to track down tour operators and travel agents that specialize in planning your group's kind of travel. Ask the agents you select what other trips they've planned and get names of references you can contact to find out how well planned the tour was.

How Much Lead Time Should You Give Your Travel Agent?

Depending on the level of detail and how complicated the travel itinerary is, most travel agencies like to have a lead time up to 9 or 10 months in advance of your group's departure date. Say you're going to France to tour wineries that specialize in Champagne and Merlot. The travel agent has to contact every winery along the way, make sure a tour is available, set up lodging to coordinate with the tour route, locate other attractions and activities, book flights and rail or bus transportation, and so on. Seems like a big headache, eh? That's why you're working with an experienced travel agent in the first place! Give your custom group tour planner plenty of lead time, plenty of ideas, and plenty of details about your group's preferences so you can work together to create the best trip possible for you and your group.

A good place to start is by looking for package deals that relate to your travel interests. Chances are, if you locate someone who coordinates educational tours to the Mayan ruins, they're probably willing to work with you to customize the trip based on your groups' interests and needs. If your group has a special interest and you think you won't be able to find an agent experienced enough to handle the intricacies and details, don't despair. There are plenty of travel agencies that can locate information and resources to plan any kind of travel for any kind of group—they are out there, believe me. If you have an extremely unique travel idea, be sure to let the agencies know when you start contacting them that you anticipate a considerable amount of research on their part. Travel agents don't get paid for the time it takes to research your custom tour, so be sure you're working with the right agency and that your group is committed to making the trip.

You should also take it upon yourself to bring the details to the drawing table. Not only will you help the agent get a head start on the planning process, but you'll ensure that no stone is left unturned.

Find the Right Agency and Stick to It

After you locate a travel agency to handle your custom group tour, stick with it. It can take a tremendous amount of work to put together custom travel itineraries. If you're just shopping around for the right agency, don't let the research begin until you've made a final decision on who to work with. If the agency can't convince you of its ability after an initial consultation, don't waste your time or theirs.

Human Contact: The Crucial Element

I haven't encountered any Web sites with interactive features that let you put together a custom group tour online. And there's a good reason for that—too many variables. If you do find a Web site that promises a custom group tour just by answering a few simple questions, I'd wonder if they weren't just selling you a package deal under the guise of a custom group tour. A custom group tour is just that—made special for you, considering your particular needs and interests.

That's why you should work with a travel agent who has experience putting together custom group tours. Most travel agents say they do custom group tours, but some really excel at this detail-oriented task. As the group leader and the person in charge of making it all happen, you'll be working closely with the travel agent, so spend a little time getting to know the agent and find out how to work together to plan the perfect custom group tour.

Remember, too, that just because it's a custom plan doesn't mean it will cost you an arm and a leg. The travel agencies are working directly with travel suppliers and have negotiating power that you, as a consumer, don't have access to. They simply can get a better deal, and you have the added advantage of security in knowing that if something goes wrong, you have someone to turn to for help. Plus, there are even bonus possibilities for you, the group leader. If you get enough people involved and bought into the trip, you might be able to travel for free! It's the travel supplier's and the travel agency's way of saying thanks for bringing together the customers.

Just the Facts, Ma'am

You can probably guess the basic questions your travel agent will ask when you call or email to inquire about putting together a custom group tour. Obviously, you'll be asked the number of people in the group, and the members' ages, interests, and menu preferences. Do any group members have special needs for special itinerary items? Are there any special points of interest you want to make sure you hit? How much money can you spend? How long can you go, and how much time do you want to spend on each leg of the tour? Take some time to anticipate the information your travel agent needs to know to best prepare your group travel package.

Your travel agent will also be able to locate a tour operator, guide, or escort for your travels. Travel agents are in the business of scouting out the right kind of person, who will be accredited by an official tour guides' organization. Depending on your travel plans, you want an experienced professional to show you the ropes, so draw on the advice and experience of your travel agent and let them make sure you've been paired up with the right escort, guide, or tour operator. Many of these folks have Web sites or brochures of their own, so be sure to ask your travel agent for more information or a Web address so you can get to know your guide before you arrive. You're going to be spending time with these folks, and you're relying on them to make sure your trip is all you want it to be, so find out a little something about them before you set off on your travels.

...And the Online Element

One of the finest examples of a custom group tour planning Web site is Group Travel Net (**www.grouptravel.net**), a travel agency-turned-virtual custom group tour planner. **www.grouptravel.net** is a travel planner's paradise. The site is full of the best travel links and online tools to help you plan your group's tour, plus current travel news and information and the inside scoop on special deals and packages.

The owners of Group Travel Net have been in the travel agency business for a long, long time and realize the potential to reach a wider audience outside their Lafayette, Indiana-based travel agency. Kendall and Beatrice Smith, owners of Lafayette Travel and Cruise, developed the site to help affinity groups and special interest groups create custom tours at reasonable prices, and down to the smallest detail, for memorable group travel experiences.

Besides the travel resources and custom group planning features, the site includes the online planning system described in the next section. This online tool makes it easier for the group members and the agents at Group Travel Net to communicate important trip information to its customers.

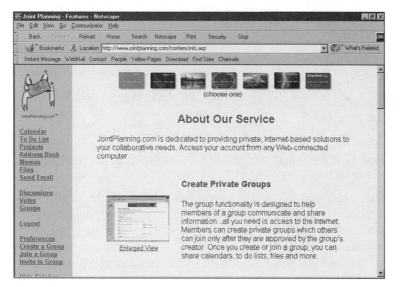

Joint Planning is an Internet-based communication and planning system that your group can use during the planning stages of your custom group tour.

Communicating with Your Group Via Online Planning Systems

Imagine trying to get your brothers, sister, their kids, a cousin in Iowa, an aunt in Chicago, a mother in Florida, and a significant other in New York coordinated for a trip. It's hard to keep track of your group members, but there are some online tools to help you communicate with your group and stay on top of the details to make the planning process a whole lot easier.

The best all-around online planning system I've run across is Bridgeline Technologies's Joint Planning system (**www.jointplanning.com**), a private, Internet-based solution for a group's collaborative needs. The tool works best if all your group members have Web access, but even if only a few have access to the Web, it's still a useful tool. You can even get your travel agent to participate and add updates as schedules and itineraries are confirmed! You can set up a free account that can then be accessed from any Web-connected computer. The following are some of the features of the system:

The Joint Planning online calendar and communication system can help keep your group members informed of upcoming activities and information concerning your travel plans.

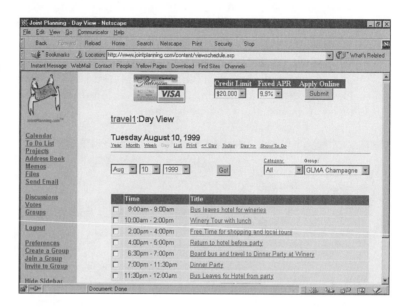

➤ **Creating private groups**   The group functionality helps members of a group communicate and share information. If you're the group leader, you can set up a private group and have your group members join to share calendars, to-do lists, itinerary information, and more. You and your group members will be issued passwords and usernames, so don't worry about prying eyes having access to your private group.

➤ **Using personal and group calendars**   You can maintain and view your personal and group calendars in one place by day, week, or month views. Your personal calendar is viewable only by you, but the group calendar can be seen by all members. Say you have some things to do around your house before you leave on your trip, like arrange for a housesitter, pay the electric bill, have the newspaper delivery suspended, or empty the fridge. You can use an online to-do list to make sure you remember all these pretrip details. For the group calendar, you can post meetings, due dates for payments, the trip itinerary, and info on when everyone is meeting to leave for the airport.

➤ **Using personal and group to-do lists**   You have the ability to maintain both personal and group to-do lists. You manage to-do items by assigning each a category and a priority level, and assigning tasks to different members of the group. You can view to-do items by group, category, or completion status.

➤ **Using personal and group address books**   What better way to keep in touch with your group members? Especially if the members are spread out across long distances, communicating via the Internet is a fast and cost-effective way to stay in touch. You can use Joint Planning to keep a personal address book and an address book for the group.

➤ **Using private group discussions**   Did you ever play the game "Operator"? Then you know how easy it is for information to get botched and scrambled. Using an online discussion board helps facilitate accurate communication among members. You have the option of receiving an email notification whenever there is a new discussion posting in one of your groups.

➤ **Sharing files**   You can share files with members of your group by uploading the file to the Joint Planning site. Members of your group can download the file to their hard drive to view or modify the file. The file-sharing feature saves you the hassle of having to email files between members of a group and facilitates collaboration on group projects and planning.

➤ **Voting**   Can't decide if you should go by train or bus to the third leg of your tour? You can use the voting feature to let the group make a decision. You can even have an open or secret ballot, and choose whether votes are anonymous. Maybe there's a member of the group who you don't want to go (ouch!). Let the group decide! You have the option to require all members to vote and to establish a voting deadline, and the group members are sent an email each time a new vote is created.

➤ **Passing memos**   You can use the memo feature to create a personal or group memo. This feature provides a place to store group procedures or something personal like your passport information or other official documentation.

➤ **Sending and receiving email reminders**   Departure date closing in? You can choose to receive a daily email to remind you of your personal calendar entries, to-do list, and new activity in your groups. You can also choose to receive email reminders of specific schedule entries.

➤ **Sending and receiving email**   You can use Joint Planning to send email to others in the group. Simply select the name of a group that you're a member of, and your email message will automatically be addressed to all members of the group. Each member of a group updates his or her own email address, so you don't have to wonder whether you have the correct addresses.

Creating Your Own Travelogue Web Site

Want to get really adventurous, before you even leave home? Why not build a Web site so that your group members can check in on the progress of the travel-planning process, and also have a nice travel diary pulled together after you return from the trip? Building a two- or three-page Web site is quite simple, and you can probably host it for free at your Internet service provider's Web site or on your organization or company's Web site.

Ideas of things to add to the Web page include bios of the group members, trip information, and contact numbers or email addresses for the tour operator, travel agent, and group members. You could include travel links of interest to the trip, currency converters if you're going overseas, links to destination information, photos (digital, if you get really, really adventurous, or scanned if you have access to such a machine), and a discussion board for your group members to add ideas. Questions, comments, or travel journal entries are other possibilities for your group travel Web site.

There's lots of online help available for building Web sites. A good starting place is CNET's Builder.com (**www.builder.com**). This site covers the basics of Web building, up to advanced techniques. You'll also be able to read reviews of other sites and get the lowdown on what makes a good Web site. Another good place for beginning Web site tutorials is Gettingstarted.net (**www.gettingstarted.net**). According to the folks at this site, "Building the Web is fun and it isn't hard to do. Gettingstarted.net is here to help you learn the basics through bite-sized tutorials and hands-on interactive lessons."

CNET's Builder.com is an online resource with beginner's resources up to advanced techniques for help on building your own Web site.

The tutorials are easy to follow, and in no time you'll be building your own Web pages! And of course, there are always off-the-shelf software programs like Microsoft FrontPage, which is essentially a point-and-click interface that helps you put together the elements of your Web site. No need to learn HTML programming—this stuff's what the computer people like to call "user friendly."

The Least You Need to Know

➤ You can locate travel specialists to help plan your group's custom tour.

➤ Besides information you'll get from your travel agent, you can go online to learn more about your destination.

➤ You can go online to preview tour operators and gather travel-planning information to share with your travel agent.

➤ You can use online planning systems to communicate with your group members and travel agent.

➤ Joint planning systems can be used during your travels to stay in touch back home.

Part 4

Traveler's Toolbox: Checklists and Planning Tools

This book's not just about going online to research your destination or buy airplane tickets. You also get the scoop on finding online travel tips, information sources, and tools, like locating passport and visa requirements and finding immunization information, packing tips, deals on meals, travel budget calculators, road condition reports, and currency converters. Plus, you'll learn how to combat jetlag, overcome motion sickness, and check your email on the road. The list goes on. And it's all online.

No matter what kind of traveler you are, this section helps you tie up the loose ends, the details, the things it's easy to forget to think about. Like watering the plants. And oh yeah, the dog…this part will help you find out which hotels are pet friendly and how to keep Rover calm and content in transit. You'll even learn how and where to shop online for all your travel gear and apparel needs.

ANDY'S SAILING, FISHING HOCKEY, AND MAGICIAN TOUR

Chapter 19

Travel Planning: Packing Tips, Traveler Tools, and Other Practical Matters

In This Chapter

➤ Learn how to fit the most stuff into the smallest suitcase

➤ Go online to find pre-travel checklists instead of relying on your own memory

➤ Save time locating house sitters, pet sitters, or kennels

➤ Get up-to-the-minute reports on traffic, weather, and travel warnings

➤ Take care of loose ends like paying bills, forwarding mail, and converting currency

Even if you've finalized most of your travel plans, you still need to spend some thought and attention on some practical matters. For example, if you've waited until now to figure out what to do about paying bills, watering the plants, feeding the dog, or getting the car ready for the big family road trip, you can go online to find lots of pretravel checklists and help to make sure you've got all your ducks in a row before you go. This can give you peace of mind as you board the plane or cross the state line, which is usually when you wonder whether you turned on the automatic cat feeder.

Taking Care of Practical Matters Online

If you visit only one Web site when you go online to plan your trip, make sure it's Fodor's Travel Resource center, at **www.fodors.com/resource**. I've mentioned the Web site in nearly every chapter of the book, so that should tell you something about the quality and quantity of information you'll find there. At Fodor's, you'll find tips for packing, traveling with pets or children, lodging, money and currency conversion, customs and duties, disabilities and accessibility, language, and lots and lots of other information. You'll find links to the best of the best on the Web, so be sure to stop for a quick tour of this invaluable online traveler's resource.

But just to shake things up a bit and to demonstrate how easy it is to find travel information online, go to Yahoo! and browse through the Travel category and Travel Tips subcategory. Some of the topics cover things to think about while you're on vacation, but you'll also find some valuable information on getting things ready before you go. You can locate valuable tips and tools at other search engines, too, like Webcrawler (www.webcrawler.com) or AltaVista (www.altavista.com). Just locate the travel category and look for a travel tips link or type in those keywords to run a search.

Making Arrangements to Pay Bills

You may have already heard about online bill payment and other online banking options. If you plan on doing this to manage finances while you're on the road, give yourself a month or two to test the system before you leave, and be sure to jot down your account username, password, and any other login information you might need to access your online account. Also take a few minutes to locate an Internet service provider (if you're not taking a laptop) in the area you're visiting so you know you have a place where you can go online to pay bills and check account information. See Chapter 22, "Staying Connected: Locating Email and Internet Service Providers" for the skinny on how to locate remote Internet service providers, like cyber cafés and libraries.

For monthly utility bills, student loan payments, car payments, mortgage payments, and other regular bills, you can usually set up an automatic payment deduction. At least two months in advance, check with your utility companies and other creditors to see if you can have your payment automatically deducted from your checking account. The trick here is to make sure you've got enough cash in your checking account to cover the charges. For a fee, your financial institution may also provide a bill payment service for credit cards and other variable-balance bills each month. If nothing else, locate a responsible, reliable friend or relative to handle bills while you're away.

What if you're lucky enough to be taking an extended vacation, say for more than a month? Well, there are plenty of places to go online to find the help you need to keep things in order while you're away. A great place to start for extended travel planning tips and checklists is the Sensational Sabbatical Suggestions personal Web page, maintained by a professor at Purdue University, who learned the tough way about preparing for extended travel. Visit Professor Allison Morrison's Web site, at http://omni.cc.purdue.edu/~alltson/sabbat.html. Even if you're not going on sabbatical or an extended vacation, there are some very useful pretravel checklists and considerations here that you can review before you hit the road.

Send Yourself an Email with Your Valuable Document Information

One of the niftiest travel tips I've come across is using email to record important travel documentation or paperwork. You should always keep photocopies of important travel documents, but a great backup plan is to send yourself an email with your passport and visa information, your itinerary, credit card numbers (and emergency phone numbers, in case your cards are lost or stolen), important addresses or phone numbers, prescription information, or just about anything else you might need when you're away from home. If the need arises, just go to a library, cyber café, or some other place where you can access your account to retrieve the information. This is just another good reason to set up a free email account with Hotmail or other email service provider, as it's a lot easier than accessing your regular account. Chapter 22 talks more about this, so stay tuned!

Forwarding Snail Mail

Snail mail is the term email and other Internet enthusiasts use to refer to the good, old-fashioned paper mail that's (usually) delivered by a postal carrier. And maybe I'm a dreamer, but I very much wanted to go online and find that I could complete a mail hold or mail forward request at the U.S. Postal Service Web site. No such luck. But you can download a change of address form, say if you're a snowbird or plan on being gone long enough to have your mail sent to a temporary address, you still have to sign it and turn it in to your local post office. To download a copy of a change of address form, visit **www.usps.gov/moversnet/coa.html**.

So, it looks like you might have to rely on a friend, neighbor, or house sitter to bring your mail in, unless you go to the post office and complete a mail hold request form. I've heard horror stories from vacationers who never received mail that was sent during a mail hold period, or who got letters or bills months later. Will your mail on hold end up in the dead letter office? Who knows?

If you really want to get your mail forwarded to you, though, there are services that can handle this (although it's typically provided for international destinations only). Be sure to check that junk mail is filtered out because you don't want to pay to have garbage forwarded to you. Mail Call Express (**www.mailcallexpress.com**) offers mail, voicemail, email, and fax forwarding services for a flat monthly fee. Another place to check out if you're an extended traveler or frequent traveler is Mail Network (**www.mailnetwork.com**).

Snowbirds and Extended Travelers, the Postman Only Rings for 60 Days

According to the U.S. Postal Service Web site, if you're going on an extended leave or heading south for the winter, you should notify everyone of your new address and the time period during which it should be used so you receive all your mail in a timely manner. Pay special attention to your magazine and newspaper subscriptions. The Postal Service will forward those items for only 60 days from the date of your move. After that, it's up to you to inform the publisher of your temporary new address. Also, pay special attention to financial institutions, which often request that their mail not be forwarded. Finally, when you fill out the change of address form, indicate a date to discontinue forwarding, and be sure to notify the postmaster at your old address if this date changes.

Finding House Sitters

Why impose on your neighbors, friends, or family members to take care of your house and pets while you're gone? Well, because you can and because it's often cheaper than pet boarding or hiring a professional housesitter to do those things for you. But with a professional service, you're guaranteed that the work is going to be done. How many times have you asked your niece or brother-in-law to take care of your things, only to return home and discover that someone completely forgot to water your orchid and it died? Or the housesitter forgot to bring in the paper or the mail, alerting your friendly neighborhood thugs that you're gone on vacation, and you return home to find all your prized lawn ornaments missing or smashed?

Well, if you do decide to go with a professional service, your best bet is probably to check regional information...the online classifieds of your local newspaper, or Yahoo!'s, or your favorite search engine's regional directories, where you can enter **house sitter** or **pet sitter** as the keywords. You'll probably find links to personal home pages of professional housesitters, or maybe even a company that provides house- or pet-sitting services for travelers. In larger metropolitan regions, there are plenty of companies that provide home or pet care services for the traveling types, so check out the online Yellow Pages (**www.bigyellow.com**), and look under housesitter, pet care, plant care, or a combination of those to find the type of service you're looking for. Whatever you do, make sure the person or company is bonded, licensed, and insured.

I've heard of one nationwide housesitting service, Home Sitters on Wheels of America. Essentially, the house- or pet-sitting service is provided by a roving RV traveler. The housesitter camps outside your house and enters only to water the plants, walk the dog, or bring in the mail and newspaper. Otherwise, they just hang out in their very own home on wheels, in your driveway, keeping an eye out for any suspicious activity. You can find them on the Web at **www.homesitters.net**, but you'll have to email or call for a quote on their rates. Rates are based on the length of the home sitting assignment, location, and complexity of the job. Be sure to check with your neighbors or neighborhood association first, though, to make sure you're not breaking any rules against RV parking. If you've ever seen the Chevy Chase classic, *Christmas Vacation*, you know what I mean.

To Fido or Not to Fido...

A family pet is often an important member of the family, and it can be quite an experience to share the joys of travel with your furry loved ones. Of course, the first thing you need to do is check with the place you plan on staying to find out the pet policies. If you absolutely must take your four-legged friends along and just can't find a place that allows pets, you can visit Web sites devoted to pet-friendly accommodations and destinations. There are even companies that make pet travel supplies and other goodies for taking the dog-and-pony show on the road.

When you bark, I listen, so for the scoop on taking pets along for the ride, check out these fun pet travel sites:

➤ **Travel Dog** (**www.traveldog.com**) Has regional directories of pet-friendly hotels, parks, and beaches, plus pet events, transportation products, and general pet travel supplies. Travel Dog also provides tips and advice on travel by plane and by car, and tips for staying at hotels. If you do have to put the pup in a kennel, you'll find advice on choosing the right one in your area. You can also locate pet sitters in your area and at your destination, in case you decide to go out for dinner, where I guarantee you won't be able to bring the pooch. There's also a forum full of tips and information from other dog owners who have experience traveling with pets.

➤ **Pets Welcome** (**www.petswelcome.com**) Lists thousands of pet-friendly lodgings in the United States, Canada, and France to choose from...just pick your state or region, select a city, and browse the free listings. Other helpful information on the site includes pet travel and medical tips, a list of emergency pet clinics, feature articles, a pet bookstore, and interactive maps so you can find—and print out—the exact location of your lodging. There's also an online forum to communicate with other pet owners. And if you can't take the pooch with you, or you just want to get away for the day or take Fido in for a makeover, you can visit the classified ads to look for pet sitters, boarding kennels, breeders, groomers, and pet-related products.

➤ **Fodor's Resource Center** (`www.fodors.com/resource/pets`) Has information on all types of petiquette travel issues. You'll find tips on how to calm your pet before departure, how to socialize and prepare Rover for meeting new people and seeing new places, and lots of links to Web sites that cover other pet travel issues. Fodor's even provides a pet packing list. Besides the animal itself, you should remember to bring along identification and health records, food and water from home, cleanup stuff, a bed or blanket, toys, medical stuff, and extras, like a flashlight for late-night walks.

Lookin' for a Waggin' Good Time?

Yep, there's a way you and your dog can enjoy the vacation of a lifetime: Take your pooch to Camp Gone to the Dogs. You can preview camp activities and schedules at `www.camp-gone-tothe-dogs.com` and get rate and deposit information. It looks like the camps fill up pretty fast, but it's darned fun just to visit the Web site, take a look at last summer's camp wedding (yes, it was a wedding between two dogs, with real dogs attending), or meet the teacher's pet. There are even testimonials (long and detailed) from camp attendees. That's right. Your dog can learn to read and write at summer camp. Actually, the testimonials are from pet owners, but you never know what a good dog is capable of.

Rick Steves' Web site (www.ricksteves.com/ tips/links.htm) is a great place for travel planning, packing, and predeparture tips.

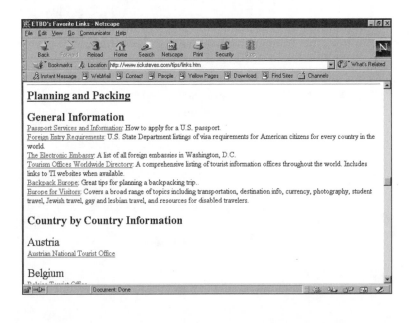

Finding Travel Checklists and Packing Tips Online

People love to share helpful information and advice, so you're sure to find plenty of resources online to help you prepare for your trip. For packing lists, tips for disabled traveler, safety considerations, and more, be sure to check out some of these Web sites. Of course, the way you prepare for your trip depends largely on where you're going, so if you don't find the information at these sites for your type of travel, go to a search engine and use keywords like **travel AND tips AND skiing** or **packing AND tips AND cruises**:

➤ **Tips 4 Trips (www.tips4trips.com)** Contains international travel tips, submitted by real travelers, just like you. You can get pretravel planning checklists and info on pretravel preparations, such as what to pack and how to pack, safety considerations, traveling with pets and children, and traveling with laptops. Regional travel tips include cold weather, warm weather, and U.S. and international weather considerations. There's also a cool message board, where you can post questions and get answers to life's deepest mysteries.

➤ **The Rec. Travel Library (www.travel-library.com/general/index.htm)** Has links to many useful travel-planning sites. You'll find links to Web sites offering packing tips, clubs and organizations for travelers, travel tips for less-developed countries, foreign languages for travelers, and travel guides for travel photographers, plus links to other online travel-planning tools.

➤ **Bardo's Travel Tips Page (www.mindspring.net/~phdietrich/traveltips.html)** For low-budget backpack-style travel, be sure to check out this site. Bardo's site covers the basics on getting the most out of your trip by taking the least amount of stuff with you. You'll get tips and advice based on real-life travel experiences, for packing, gear, transportation, money, safety, and responsible travel.

➤ **The Universal Packing List (www.henricson.se/mats/upl/)** Has lots of practical, funny advice on things to take care of before you take off on a short or long vacation. Other sections include information on clothing, money, documents, equipment, hygiene, health, electrical stuff, diving equipment, and climbing equipment, as well as comments from other travelers.

➤ **World Traveler (www.worldtraveler.com)** Has tips and advice on the art of packing, packing light, baggage requirements, safety tips, and more. You can also buy name brand luggage at discount prices at their online travel store.

World Traveler's Art of Packing Web site (www.worldtraveler.com/html/packing.html) offers great tips on deciding what to take and how to make it all fit.

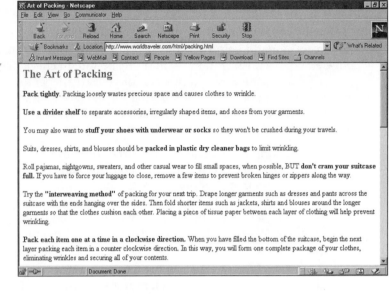

Art of Packing - Netscape

File Edit View Go Communicator Help

Back | Forward | Reload | Home | Search | Netscape | Print | Security | Stop

Bookmarks | Location: http://www.worldtraveler.com/html/packing.html | What's Related

Instant Message | WebMail | Contact | People | Yellow Pages | Download | Find Sites | Channels

The Art of Packing

Pack tightly. Packing loosely wastes precious space and causes clothes to wrinkle.

Use a divider shelf to separate accessories, irregularly shaped items, and shoes from your garments.

You may also want to **stuff your shoes with underwear or socks** so they won't be crushed during your travels.

Suits, dresses, shirts, and blouses should be **packed in plastic dry cleaner bags** to limit wrinkling.

Roll pajamas, nightgowns, sweaters, and other casual wear to fill small spaces, when possible, BUT **don't cram your suitcase full.** If you have to force your luggage to close, remove a few items to prevent broken hinges or zippers along the way.

Try the **"interweaving method"** of packing for your next trip. Drape longer garments such as dresses and pants across the suitcase with the ends hanging over the sides. Then fold shorter items such as jackets, shirts and blouses around the longer garments so that the clothes cushion each other. Placing a piece of tissue paper between each layer of clothing will help prevent wrinkling.

Pack each item one at a time in a clockwise direction. When you have filled the bottom of the suitcase, begin the next layer packing each item in a counter clockwise direction. In this way, you will form one complete package of your clothes, eliminating wrinkles and securing all of your contents.

Document: Done

WARNING

Women Travelers, You May Have to Watch What You Wear

Religious and cultural customs in foreign countries sometimes mandate acceptable and unacceptable clothing for travelers, particularly women travelers. In fact, in some countries, it's a downright insult for women to go out in public in a short-sleeved shirt or shorts. Even in countries where the dress code is a little more relaxed, some activities—like visiting places of worship—require cover-up clothing. Many restaurants, too, expect you to be dressed up, so be sure to visit Journey Woman's online magazine for women travelers (`www.journeywoman.com/ccc/default.html`) for culturally correct clothing advice. You can even get tips on what to wear in the country you're traveling to.

Travel Budget Calculators and Currency Converters

One of the first things you have to determine before you do much travel planning is how much you can spend on the trip. That usually determines everything else about the trip, but if you're still looking for ways to slash expenses, be sure to check out these Web sites:

➤ **Frugal Fun's 34 Ways to Slash the Cost of Your Next Vacation**
(`www.frugalfun.com/34waysvacation.html`) Helps you make sure your trip stays under budget. Get inside advice on discount air travel, negotiating and bartering for the right price, when and where to convert currency, when to visit museums and other attractions, how to save on international calls, and lots of other ways to save bucks on your trip.

➤ **Let's Plan a Trip** (`http://deaver.barry.edu/0461974/letsplanatrip.htm`) Has a travel budget worksheet and calculator to help you determine how much you can spend on your next family road trip. You can use a miles-per-gallon worksheet, determine a proposed budget for the trip, and learn how to stay within the budget when you get to your vacation spot. This exercise is designed especially for low-budget family travel to a national park, but the principles apply to other destinations as well.

➤ **Arthur Frommer's Budget Travel** (`www.frommers.com`) Has lots of tips and advice on finding great travel deals, plus budget tips to help you cut costs and get more for your travel dollar.

➤ **Rick Steves' Travel Tips** (`www.ricksteves.com/tips/moneytip.htm`) Has a lengthy and informative article titled "Changing Money Smart," that covers traveler's checks, using cash machines and ATMs, cash advances, changing money at banks, and carrying cold, hard cash. And because Steve is a budget traveler, you'll find other money-saving tips in the Travel Tips section.

Finding Up-to-the-Minute Reports

It doesn't matter how much in advance you plan your trip. It doesn't matter if you've chosen a travel time that's at the peak of the sunshine season. It doesn't matter if you got a map well ahead of time to plan a route around all the construction. These things don't matter because things can and do change overnight. Luckily, you can go online to get up-to-the-minute reports on things that affect your trip. This section offers some good starting points for last-minute information.

Weather Conditions

Uncle Jimmy used to tell me that if I wanted to know what the weather was like to put a rock in the yard. "If the rock gets wet," he said, "it's raining. If the rock turns white, it's snowing. If the rock is gone, tornadoes." Although Uncle Jimmy's method of watching weather is tried and true, it's not going to help when you need to know weather conditions in a remote location. But you can try another tried-and-true method for getting up-to-the-minute weather reports: Go online. Some online weather channels have extended forecasts, but I say the further into the future, the less accurate the prediction.

Even though weather predictions are correct only about half the time, it's good to know if there's even the possibility of a snow storm, tornado, or hurricane when you're getting ready to hit the road. Be sure to check out one of these sites, or go to a search engine and find regional weather information for your destination or your trip there:

➤ **USA Today's Weather (www.usatoday.com/weather/wilist.htm)** Has world weather reports, U.S. highway weather conditions, and a section on beach weather for the United States and Mexico. You can get the scoop on the UV index, tide conditions, marine forecasts, and observations and water temperatures.

➤ **The Weather Channel (www.weather.com/homepage.html)** Has weather reports and feature articles on weather topics of interest, like warnings of hurricanes and other severe seasonal weather. You can get forecasts for U.S. and international cities, plus weather conditions that affect golfing, travel, allergies, gardening, and beaches and boating. You can get the latest reports on rain, fog, and forecasts for two days out.

➤ **Intellicast (www.intellicast.com)** Has world weather reports, radar and satellite reports, plus an almanac that gives a month-by-month breakdown for typical weather across the country. If you're interested in learning more about the weather, take a peek at Dr. Dewpoint's Weather 101 online courses. This site is fun, easy to understand, and easy to navigate.

Intellicast has local and international weather reports, radar and satellite maps, and tips for golfers, sailors, and outdoor travelers.

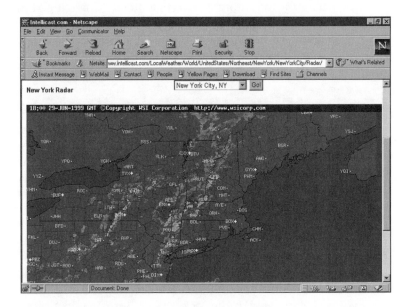

➤ **AccuWeather (www.accuweather.com/wx/index.htm)** Get up-to-the-minute international weather reports, or sign up for AccuWeather Direct, a customized local weather forecast and current conditions delivered right to you email inbox, whenever you want it. You also have the option of retrieving regional and national weather maps, as well as real-time Doppler radar and satellite images. Click on any regional or national button, and AccuWeather Direct retrieves the most current weather information. Signing up for email weather reports is easy as 1-2-3.

Road Conditions and Construction Delays

Most of the weather-reporting Web sites also include road condition information for major U.S. interstates. But for even more places to check on current road conditions and construction delays, start your search at your favorite search engine under the travel category or at Yahoo! Travel at (**dir.yahoo.com/Business_and_Economy/ Transportation/News_and_Media/Traffic_and_Road_Conditions**/). From there, you can check out sites like AAA's Road Condition Hot Spots (**www.aaa.com/road/hotspots/ hotspots.htm**) to get road travel information for the path you're following. Some official state Web sites include inclement weather reports, and you can locate those Web sites through Yahoo!, too.

Travel Safety Warnings

The U.S. State Department (**travel.state.gov/travel_warnings.html**) issues travel advisories and safety warnings for countries around the globe. The State Department issues travel warnings when it decides, based on all relevant information, that it's safest to avoid travel to a certain country. If you're looking for travel safety information, you can't always trust what you find at tourism or visitor's information Web sites, as they probably don't want you to know about civil unrest or potential traveler safety concerns.

The Least You Need to Know

➤ You can find packing tips and checklists for any type of travel online.

➤ You can get advice from travelers just like you at traveler's resources Web sites.

➤ You can locate housesitters, pet sitters, or bill-payment services online.

➤ You can go online to get up-to-the-minute weather, road, and safety conditions before you leave.

Chapter 20

Finding and Shopping for Travel Gear and Accessories

In This Chapter

➤ Shop at travel supply stores you know and trust online

➤ Hunt for bargains and special deals on hiking, camping, fishing, and other outdoor activity gear

➤ The inside scoop on where to find bargains and discount sites for travel gear and accessories

➤ Find specialty items at online retail stores

So you've made it through the planning and reservation steps to get ready for your dream vacation. Now that the easy part is out of the way, it's time for some really tough questions to be answered. What are you going to wear? How much "stuff" should you take? What special accessories are you going to need on your journey? Do you have regulation-size carry-on luggage? Do you need special equipment for camping, hiking, or outdoor adventures? Remember that it's not where you go or what you do—it's how good you look when you're there. So, if you need to do a little shopping for your travel adventures, just stay seated at your computer. All the goods, gear, and get-ups for your trip can be found on the Web.

Besides the convenience of shopping from the comforts of your own home, you'd be surprised how much more stuff you can find online than in conventional malls and stores. From electrical adapters to water filters, ponchos to walking shoes, it's all on the Web for your shopping convenience.

You can order backpacks, mosquito nets, travel books, and sleep products at www.walkabouttravelgear.com. *The site also contains a helpful list of links and resources.*

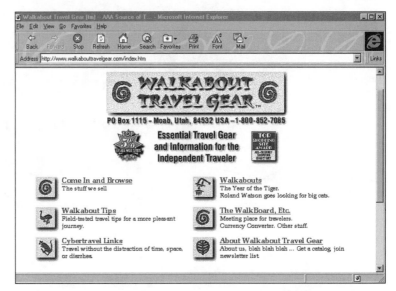

I'm even willing to bet a shiny nickel that if I tried hard enough, I could find just about any travel-related accessory or bit of apparel that I could ever need for almost any travel-related adventure. If you've shopped online at all, you know there's a lot of stuff for sale on the Web, and if you're looking for something that's hard to find, the Web is a good place to start looking. It sure beats hauling out the yellow pages to call specialty stores when you may not even know exactly what you're looking for or even all that's available.

Some Essentials for Online Shopping

Shopping on the Web allows you a convenient way to compare prices, gather warranty information, and get advice and tips from real users of the products. Plus, the stores are accessible 24 hours a day, so you shop when you want and at as many stores as you feel like visiting. And even if you don't make the sales transaction online, you can still preview the product, gather telephone numbers and ordering information, or request a catalog.

If you do want to do some cybershopping to save time, to get started on your online shopping spree, you'll need your credit card, as most sites require them for purchase through online shopping systems. Most sites give you the option to order a catalog, place an order over the phone, or send a money order or cashier's check to process and ship your order. But half the fun of buying things online is the convenience and speed with which you'll get your goods delivered when using a credit card. Plus, it's fun to brag to your friends that you did all your travel planning and accessory shopping online.

Besides the time you can save, another plus to using your credit card for purchases is the added protection you get from your credit card issuer. In the event that you have a problem with an online merchant, you'll usually only have to pay up to $50, and your credit card company will cover the rest. But whatever you do when shopping online, always read through the customer service or FAQs section of online merchant sites to check out store policies before you buy. That way, you'll know what your options are if you have to return or exchange the goods.

At a reputable online store, you should also expect to find shipping prices and options, security and privacy statements, and other things you need to know when placing your order online. Although it might seem like you're getting a good deal shopping online, you still have to be a savvy shopper and take the time to read the "fine print" before you buy. Are there shipping costs? Handling costs? Re-stocking fees? There are sometimes hidden costs. The more time you spend looking into the customer service policies and general business practices of the merchant, the more secure you'll be that your order is safe and you're getting a good deal.

Confirming Orders Placed at Online Stores

If the merchant you're buying from doesn't send you an automatic email order confirmation, just print out the confirmation page that appears after you've placed the order and put it in a safe place. (You can do this from your browser menu bar.) Many online merchants automatically send an email notification that your order has been received, including the order and confirmation number, total cost, and other purchase information. Print the email message, too, and keep it with the Web page printout after you've placed your order and a confirmation screen appears.

There used to be a much more widespread suspicion that sending personal data or credit card information over the Internet was dangerous or that some geeked-out hacker could steal your information as it traveled across the lines. Well, to tell you the truth, I'd rather give my credit card information over the Web than to some of the sketchy characters manning gas stations, restaurants, and oil change operations. No offense to the people who serve us in these capacities, but in my many years of owning and using a credit card in traditional face-to-face situations, I've never had a problem anywhere except through a particular gas station in a suburb of Chicago. But that's a long story.

The reason I'd rather send my information across a secure online ordering system is that no one actually ever sees my credit card number. The data is scrambled through an encryption process (Secure Sockets Layer or secure HTTP) making it impossible for bleary-eyed hackers or miscreants to steal my information. And as e-commerce and online shopping continues to grow at an amazing rate, the online merchant community is making strides to improve the secure ordering system so that every merchant who sells online meets a strict set of standards. Not to mention credit card companies aggressively pursue and investigate any allegations of credit card fraud. After all, they have a big stake in making sure they aren't left footing the bill if you dispute the charges.

So rest assured. With online merchant certification entities ensuring that the merchant you're dealing with meets a set of standards and upholds the proper security measures to see that your credit card information is sent only to the people who need to see it, and the backup of your credit card company, online shopping is just as safe as any other place you use your plastic.

Online Tips for Avoiding Scams

Deals that seem too good to be true often are just that, so don't let yourself fall for scams or fraudulent activity on the Web. The Federal Trade Commission (`www.ftc.gov`) and the Online Better Business Bureau (`www.bbb.org`) offer tips on keeping scam artists at bay. For reports on the latest online scam operations, check out the National Fraud Information Center (`www.fraud.org`), and if you do have to file a complaint, contact one of these agencies that track online scams. Besides these online gatekeepers, there are a number of travel newsgroups and forums that would like to hear about your experience, too, so share your story of misfortune with others to warn them of the scam. See Chapter 5, "Online Travel Communities 101," for a list of travel-related newsgroups and forums.

As discussed in Chapter 6, "Before You Buy...Protecting Yourself Online," the best way to know you're shopping at a secure site from a reputable merchant is to look for a few tell-tale signs:

➤ Upon entering the ordering system of the site, you are presented with a dialog box that tells you you're entering a secure site and shows you a secure site certificate.

➤ The Web site offers Secure Sockets Layer technology. You know this is the case when your browser displays a locked padlock or key symbol in the lower-left corner. You can also look at the location bar of your browser (where `http://www.companyaddress.com` appears), and if you see `https:`, you know you're at a secure site.

When you shop at L.L. Bean and other secure ordering sites, you'll see a locked key pad in the lower-left corner of your browser, as seen in this figure, which lets you know your credit card information is being scrambled.

➤ The merchant has included contact information, customer service information, return policies, guarantees and warranty information, and user or customer testimonials. Keep in mind, though, that these aren't as reliable as a Better Business Bureau certificate or an endorsement from another online security regulating entity.

➤ You can pretty much count on big-name retailers like L.L. Bean, The Gap, Amazon, and Borders to be on the up-and-up. An online merchant like Bubba's Beanie Babies has less at stake in terms of bad publicity, plus who knows Bubba ain't gonna slip away in the night with your dough? Moral of the story is to use some common sense.

In any case, follow your instincts. The same principles apply to shopping online as to real-world shopping. If you walk into a store and you just get a feeling that the store is not a place where you want to spend your money, turn around and walk out the door. Say, for example, there's a "NO REFUNDS. NO EXCHANGES." sign. Move on. If nothing else, shop with the tried-and-true established online sites for your travel gear and accessories. And look for sites that offer numerous ways to place your order, including toll-free ordering systems and printable/faxable order forms, and sites that let you request catalogs through email or over the phone. You may also want to ask around and get advice and tips from your friends that shop online. Learn from their mistakes, or get the inside scoop on great sites they've shopped that you may not know about.

foulweathergear.com features secure ordering and clearly states its policies on shopping security and privacy. The site also makes it easy to contact the company to place an order by phone or to get in touch with a representative if there's a problem with your order.

Read the Customer Service Policies for Return Information, Guarantees, and so on

A reputable online merchant should have an easy-to-find and easy-to-understand customer service section at its Web site. It's important to read through this so you know what the return policies are, how long you have to return items, whether there's a restocking fee, what your return shipping charges are, and how returns are credited. You should also find information on any gift shipping and wrapping services that are offered. If the store policies aren't clearly stated and the merchant doesn't offer a phone number for customer support, move on to another site.

What Are Cookies and Should You Eat Them or Throw Them Away?

In case you skipped Chapter 2, "Browsers 101," one thing you'll come across when shopping online are cookies. Cookies are bits of data that a Web site sends to your hard drive when you enter a site. The site checks the cookie after it's been placed to see what pages you visit, how much time you spend online, whether you buy some-thing and what you buy, so that the next time you visit, the site will feed you infor-mation based on your preferences and shopping habits. Seem a little creepy that online stores know so much about you?

Actually, cookies are used to customize your shopping experience, similarly to the way that if you're a regular customer at local stores, the clerks recognize you and you don't have to show ID to write a check, or your favorite bartender knows that you like it shaken, not stirred. Some online stores require you to allow cookies to be set in order to shop at their store, so unless you have a major problem with bits of data being sent to your hard drive, just accept the cookies and go about your shopping. For more information on cookies, take a peek back at Chapter 2.

Shopping for Travel Wear? Pay a Visit to the TravelSmith

TravelSmith's got it covered when it comes to travel gear. An established seller of leisure and business travel wear and accessories, TravelSmith's online storefront is a near-perfect example of what an online merchant should be. No, I'm not trying to butter up the staff at TravelSmith in hopes of getting my very own Indispensable Black Dress. But if you haven't shopped online before and you're looking for travel wear that "helps you travel lighter and smarter," **www.travelsmith.com** is a good place to get your feet wet.

At **www.travelsmith.com** you'll find men's and women's clothing and accessories, designed and tested by real travelers. Wrinkle-free, easy to clean, durable, and com-fortable clothing makes a real difference when you're on the road. After all, you're on vacation, so do you really want to spend time ironing or running to the drycleaner? I don't even like to do those things when I'm not traveling.

With a home base just outside San Francisco, the world hub of Internet activity, TravelSmith even has a toll-free number staffed by "outfitting advisors" who can answer questions about travel gear and what works best in the area you're visiting. This information is available online, too, as the good folks at TravelSmith have com-piled a thorough and thoughtful list of travel links to help you plan your trip and pack your bags.

TravelSmith's Weather page includes a list of about 200 world cities, listing average temperatures and average rainfall amounts. And what if you're going on an African safari? The easy-to-use destination weather guide takes you through a series of ques-tions and then compiles a packing list, complete with fabric recommendations, styles, and items to keep you comfortable, cool, and camouflaged on your adventure.

The weather conditions at your destination of choice dictate what you need to pack for your adventure. TravelSmith's Weather guide gives you the lowdown on average temperatures and rainfall, plus a five-day forecast.

TravelSmith also carries a line of luggage and travel accessories, and has just about anything you'll need on your trip. The site also offers same-day shipping and a no-questions-asked 100% guarantee. For travel gear and travel wear online or catalog shopping, TravelSmith gets two thumbs up.

Top Picks for Online Travel Shopping Sites

Besides the top sites listed in this section, you might just want to check out some other online storefronts. Fortunately, you've got those neato-torpedo search engines and Web directories to get you started on an online travel gear shopping expedition.

Let's start with finding general travel gear and accessories, like luggage, inflatable pillows, and wrinkle-free clothes. I usually like to start my online shopping expeditions using whatever my favorite search engine happens to be that day. Generally, I find there are hundreds of general travel accessory sites being added to search directories every day, and you can expect to find a breakdown in categories of specialty sites dealing books, luggage, maps, outdoor gear, and equipment and software.

Is Your Carry-On Too Big?

The Leather and Luggage Goods Manufacturers Association site (`www.llgma.org`) provides a list of carry-on baggage size requirements for U.S. domestic airlines. The list recommends that you check for up-to-the-minute regulations, as the airlines' rules can change without notice. The site lists carry-on baggage program information for American, Delta, TWA, America West, Northwest, United, Continental, Southwest, and US Airways. The site also includes safe travel tips, travel Web site links, industry news, and a wealth of travel-related information not necessarily related to luggage or leather.

Of course, at any time, you can type in search keywords (see Chapter 3) to find exactly the item you're looking for. If you're using Yahoo!, you can also go into the general Yahoo! category **Home**, and then select the subcategories **Business and Economy**, **Companies**, **Travel**, and **Luggage and Accessories** to find a long list of sites offering everything from automatic plant waterers to cruise wardrobes and mosquito nets. The beauty of the Web is that you'll find just about anything you're looking for, and most likely you'll come across ideas and items that you hadn't even thought of before.

Here are some of my favorite online travel-supplies shopping sites:

➤ **Family On Board** (`www.familyonboard.com`) Has just about everything for those cozy family vacations, including kids' and adult luggage, car seats, car console organizers, trunk organizers, travel cups, puzzles, games, and maps and atlases. You'll also find a wide selection of kids' tapes, sun shades, motion sickness medicine, and potty supplies. The site offers secure online ordering, toll-free phone ordering, and a faxable order form. (Unfortunately, they don't sell "clue pills" to help kids know when enough is enough.)

➤ **Tropi-Ties** (`www.tropi-ties.com`) Has everything for beach travel, including resort wear, bags and totes, sandals, hats, kids' stuff, footwear, and watches. Even though I felt like I was trapped in the middle a Bud Light spring break commercial with all the bikini glamour shots, if you're headed to the sands and shores, this site is worth checking out.

Throw Away Your Underwear When Done

Just because you're going on a big trip doesn't necessarily mean you need a big suitcase or backpack. First, consider where you're going, how long you're going to be there, and what you'll need. When it comes to choosing the right size of luggage, even though they say it doesn't matter, size does count. A carry-on that slips under your airline seat or into the overhead compartment can save you the time and hassle of getting your bags out of baggage claim, if your bags arrive at all. And a smaller bag means less weight to move around and less hassle in general.

I read a tip in a traveler's forum from a woman who takes her tattered underwear on trips, and simply throws them away when "done," instead of hauling around dirty underwear or washing them out at night. But if you really are attached to those special briefs and bikinis, you can pack enough for the whole trip and take along a small container of soap to wash them out at night—nylon underwear dry much faster than cotton. Or you can just buy underwear, t-shirts, and other inexpensive items when you get there.

➤ **Travel Products (www.travelproducts.com)** Really has all your travel supplies covered, from maps for exploring museums to bike and car travel accessories. Organizers, plant care, motion sickness remedies…you name it, they've got it. A thorough, well-researched travel links list is another good reason to stop at Travel Products before you hit the road. Secure ordering, search features, responsive customer service, and a great product selection are some more good reasons. Even though they don't carry luggage, they have all the travel accessories you'll need. Check it out!

➤ **AOL Shopping** (AOL keyword: **pets** and **travel**) Membership in AOL certainly has its advantages, including discounted prices and a two-year extended warranty on all goods purchased through its online megamall, Netmarket. In the travel supply department you'll find run-of-the-mill luggage, backpacks, camcorders, cameras, compact hair dryers, and so on. If you have the patience to wait for images and pages to download, shopping at AOL is available to members and nonmembers, although AOL users get a distinct price advantage. If you're not a member of AOL and want to browse the online retail stores, go to **www.aol.com/shopping/pets.html**.

➤ **World Traveler Discount Luggage and Travel Goods** (www.worldtraveler.com) Claims to have the best prices on name-brand luggage, and a quick trip through some other suppliers' sites makes me think they just might be right. Besides getting awesome prices and special deals, if you buy certain brands of luggage, the shipping is free. World Traveler also sells travel clothing, travel accessories, briefcases, and more. The site also offers secure ordering, intuitive navigation, and lots of product information.

➤ **1-800-LUGGAGE** (www.1800luggage.com) Just like the name implies, this site is all about luggage. Carrying most major brands of luggage and business travel cases, this discount luggage warehouse has a mother lode of luggage to sell. Even though the site doesn't feature an online order form or secure ordering, it does provide a toll-free number and an online request form that you can send to have a luggage salesperson call you. Although the site boasts a guarantee of the lowest luggage prices, I did find a better price on a specific item at www.worldtraveler.com. Fluke or not, if you do find a better price within 30 days of your purchase, 1-800-LUGGAGE will refund the difference.

➤ **The Traveler Shop** (www.travelershop.com) Carries pretty much the same line of travel goods you'll find at the other online storefronts, including a full line of Samsonite luggage goods and an emphasis on business- and golf-related travel. The site even sells cigars and cigar accessories online.

➤ **Le TRAVEL STORE** (www.letravelstore.com) Owners say that in 1976, when the store opened, it was the first retailer in the known universe to call itself a travel store. In one convenient location Le TRAVEL STORE (www.letravelstore.com) offers all the travel gear, travel books, and travel services travelers need to plan a big trip. Designed for like-minded international, independent travelers, Le TRAVEL STORE now enjoys an international customer base and is one of the few U.S.-based online retailers that doesn't mind dealing with the hassles of international shipping.

Lighten the Load a Little

When you're on a trip or vacation, especially if you're overseas, it can be a good idea to have your purchases sent home via FedEx or UPS to avoid customs hassles, to have less baggage to carry around, and to have one fewer thing to worry about when packing for the trip home. If you're like me, you always end up taking more stuff home than you had when you left, plus fragile items are probably safer being shipped than staying in your luggage.

Shopping for Specialty Travel: Hiking, Camping, Sailing, Adventure Travel, and Roughin' It Travel Supplies

All this talk about travel and spending time online, and really there's no place on Earth I'd rather be than at the mall on a Friday night. Unfortunately, though, duty calls, and sometimes I'm in need of a specialty travel item that I just can't find at the mall, so it's off to the Web I shop.

I run across things shopping on the Web that I just never imagined existed. The Web offers both merchants and consumers the chance to sell and buy hard-to-find items that aren't carried in traditional mall-based stores, which is good news for you if you're looking for a specialty item, or just a favorite catalog item, like those L.L. Bean boots that have gotten you through every rainy season since you were knee-high to a grasshopper.

Save Money by Buying Used Equipment

At Excite Classifieds (`www.classifieds2000.com`) you can find good deals on used sporting goods and hiking and camping supplies. Activity categories of used items for sale include everything from rock climbing to scuba diving and surfing, and wake boarding to snow shoeing, and just about everything else in between. Check out your local newspaper, too. Many papers in larger cities (and more and more towns and smaller cities, too) now have online classifieds and it's easy to find what you're looking for. Just type in the keyword of the item you're looking for and if there are any listings, the handy search tools will help you find it.

Here are some cool online specialty travel gear shops for you to check out if your travels call for accessories and apparel that you just can't find at the local corner shop.

➤ **Patagonia** (`www.patagonia.com`) In all my years on the Web, I don't think I've ever been as impressed with an e-commerce Web site as what I've found at Patagonia. The good folks at Patagonia have taken online stores to a whole new level, and I go there from time to time, just to have a look around. Even if you're not shopping for outdoor adventure gear and accessories, this site is a must-see. Connect with other campers and hikers and get expert advice from Patagonia employees at the Patagonia Guide Line, an outdoor information service started by a few Patagonia employees who wanted to share their knowledge of the outdoors. The Guide Line is staffed with Patagonia employees who are product users and have years of outdoor experience. If you want to talk to someone in person you can call the Patagonia Guide Line, or send an email that will be answered by one of Patagonia's outdoor experts.

➤ **REI (www.rei.com)** Has an easy-to-use online shopping system that features products from its catalog, as well as its outlet store. Sign up for the REI Gearmail and be the first to hear about new online products, sales, and special events. The site even has a Learn & Share section where you can get tips and advice from other campers and outdoor enthusiasts.

➤ **L.L. Bean (www.llbean.com)** Features a simple online ordering system and a catalog quick shop system that lets you shop for an item by entering its catalog number. You can also sign up for LLB-Mail for email notification of sales, new gear, and more.

➤ **Cabela's (www.cabelas.com)** A must-stop if fly fishin' is your game. For easy online ordering, to request a catalog, or to preview products, Cabela's online retail site has product information, specials, and interesting tidbits for all you outdoorsy hunter and angler types.

➤ **Foulweathergear.com (www.foulweathergear.com)** The folks here know that even a little bit of foul weather really can ruin your day. When you're out on the high seas, comfort and protection from the elements are top concerns. But high-performance sailing gear isn't just something you can find at your run-of-the-mill department store or even outdoor gear specialty stores. Fortunately for all you maties out there, finding a dinghy jumpsuit with an elasticized waist is just a matter of stopping at **www.foulweathergear.com**. Nice design, easy-to-use, secure site with monthly specials, contests, and helpful links to sailing-related sites.

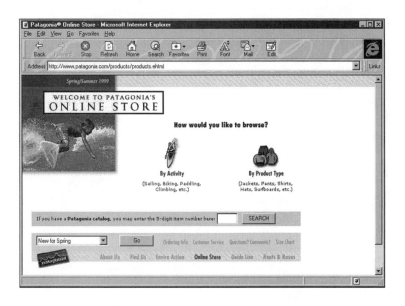

At www.patagonia.com, you can browse by activity or by item and learn about the company's environmental activism efforts. Exquisite design and cool photography make a trip through this Web site a pure pleasure.

The Least You Need to Know

➤ You can use search engines or travel product directories to find luggage, travel accessories, and specialty travel gear online.

➤ You can get tips and advice from travel gear experts at online stores and in newsgroups.

➤ Shopping online can save you time and sometimes money, and it's a good way to comparison shop and check out store policies before you buy.

➤ Hard-to-find items aren't so hard to find online. And you can sometimes even buy used equipment online.

Chapter 21

Going International? Planning Ahead for Paperwork and Safety

In This Chapter

➤ Find out about shots, boosters, documentation, and other essentials for entering and traveling safely in foreign lands

➤ Don't wait until you get there to find out about government travel warnings—go online for up-to-the-minute reports

➤ Learn how to stay safe and where to get help if you need it

➤ Go from dollars to pesos in seconds flat with online currency converters

➤ Get up to speed on the native tongue and gather foreign language information

➤ Know when to shake hands, stand up, bring a gift, and other customs in foreign countries

Although one big reason we go on overseas vacations is to add adventure to our lives, there are certain kinds of adventure most of us want to avoid on international trips. For example, you don't want to find out at the airport that you don't have the proper paperwork to leave the country. And you don't want the week you planned to spend on the sunny Riviera to instead be spent seeking shelter from heavy rains and cold winds. Or, even worse, you don't want to find out that the country that had once seemed so friendly to Americans is suddenly in the midst of political upheaval (although you could end up being rescued by a sexy revolutionary, and the two of you could go on to save the country from its despotic leaders and further the cause of democracy...okay, so that only happens in cheesy movies and trashy novels with Fabio on the cover, but you get the point).

Anyway, all these potential "adventures" can be avoided with just one thing: information. You can get information by asking the right questions and knowing where to get the answers. How can you be sure you have the correct documentation? Do you have all the immunizations you need? Can you drink the water? Do you know enough of the country's language to get by in an emergency? Is it safe to travel to that country? These are just some of the questions you need to think about before embarking on an international adventure.

What's the Best Time to Visit?

Preview Travel's Destination Guides by Fodor's (which you can find by going to `www.previewtravel.com` and then clicking **Destination Guides**) contain detailed information about a variety of popular international locations. You can find such information as "local highlights," "best times to visit," "suggested itineraries," and maps, pictures, current weather, and exchange rates. This can be a one-stop source for almost all the necessary information you need to travel.

Preview Travel is an online booking agent, but its Destination Guides by Fodor's are a concise source of information for several world destinations.

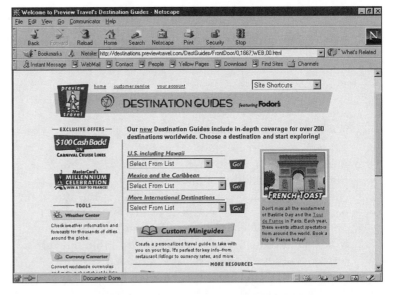

Online Resources for Immunizations, Documentation, and Other Essentials

Immunizations and Other Health-Related Issues

Chapter 24, "Health, Wellness, and Online Information," covers general health and wellness information and resources, and you'll even find some of these same Web sites listed there. But in case you didn't plan on reading that chapter (shame on you), you can make sure that you have all the proper immunizations and paperwork by checking out the following sites:

➤ **The Centers for Disease Control (CDC)** (`www.cdc.gov/travel`) Can help you determine what health precautions you need to take before leaving on your trip. The site is easily organized into regions of the world. Be sure to check this out before leaving on your trip.

➤ **The International Association for Medical Assistance to Travelers (IAMAT)** (`www.sentex.net/~iamat`) For the most complete medical information for traveling overseas, you can become a member of IAMAT. Membership is free (though donations are appreciated), and you get complete listings of immunization requirements, along with updated travel health warnings, listings of English-speaking doctors worldwide, and many other benefits.

➤ **Shoreland's Travel Health Online** (`www.tripprep.com`) Provides a wide range of useful information on all travel matters, beyond just health-related information. The site lists health concerns in individual countries, including required and recommended immunizations, climate-related health warnings, contact information for medical emergencies, and links to international health Web sites, including the CDC, the World Health Organization, and the government health departments of individual countries. The information on individual countries is thorough and easy to read. You should definitely check out this site before traveling overseas.

Passports and Visas

One of the first things you should do if you're planning international travel is get a passport. You need a passport in order to travel to any country outside the United States (with the exception of Mexico and Canada, where an original birth certificate or a valid driver's license will suffice), so if you don't have one yet, or if you have one that needs to be renewed, you can get the passport application forms and information online at the U.S. State Department Web site (`travel.state.gov/passport_services.html`). Remember, though, you still have to apply for your passport in person and it takes several weeks to process your application, so give yourself enough time to receive your passport before your departure date. Passport renewal takes time, too, so don't get caught with your pants down. Passports are processed faster in the fall and winter, when there is less international travel.

Shoreland's Travel Health Online is misnamed. This site contains some of the most complete international travel information you can find on the Web.

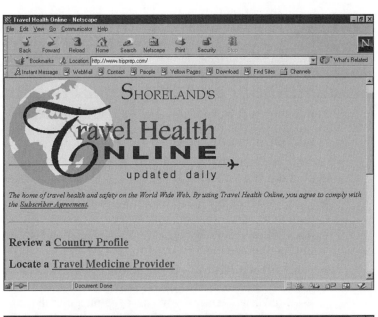

The U.S. State Department's Passport Services Web site gives you all the information and forms you need to apply for or renew your passport.

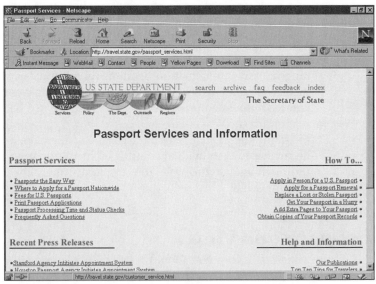

Some countries require visas and others don't, so to find out if you need one, check out **www.travel.com.au**. Click the **Travel Tools** icon, and then **Visas**. Then you can type in your countries of origin and destination to get the most updated visa information. Shoreland's Travel Health Online (**www.tripprep.com**) also lets you know how long you can stay in a country without a visa and other requirements and laws specific to different countries.

Waited Too Long to Apply for Your Passport? Shame on You!

If you waited too long to get or renew your passport or visa, you might want to check out G-3 Visas and Passports (**g3visas.com**). At this site, you can download PDF versions of passport application and renewal forms, as well as instructions sheets for the forms (see Chapter 2, "Browsers 101," if you need help downloading and working with PDF files). G-3 Visas and Passports specializes in expediting visa and passport applications under tight time constraints, for a fee of course. You can also use its free database to find out whether the country you are traveling to requires a visa. The fine folks at G3 Visas also put together a handy-dandy links page to guide you through other international travel-related Web sites.

Finding Safety Tips and Travel Warnings Online

I love a cliché, so let me say an ounce of prevention...could mean the difference between a safe and happy trip or a disastrous danger-filled adventure. Besides doing things like making sure you lock your hotel door and hiding your stash in a secure money belt, you need to think about things like protecting your passport from would-be thieves and knowing what the laws are before you unknowingly break a law and land yourself in jail. If you've ever seen Midnight Express, you know how awful an experience like that can be.

Go online to get tips and advice from experienced travelers before you hit the road. And if you're going to a country that has a tendency to erupt in violence, check government travel warnings when you make your plans and right before you leave. Situations can literally change overnight, so to protect yourself, spend a little time online gathering reports before you land in an unfamiliar and potentially unfriendly land.

Common Sense Safety Tips

The last thing you want to deal with on your travels is getting mugged, thrown in the pokey, or even worse, being hijacked or kidnapped. If you arm yourself with common sense and do a bit of pre-trip preparation, you can avoid safety and security dangers. A good place for travel safety and security information is the Armchair World's well-informed traveler section at **www.armchair.com/info/security.html**. Here you can read about passport safety tips, airline security and seat selection, hotel security, guarding against thieves, what to do if you're arrested, and how to survive if you're kidnapped or taken hostage.

Now, don't get yourself in a tizzy over the possibility of being kidnapped or some other dramatic incident on your trip. More common crimes like pickpocketing are what you need to be aware of, so do a little reading and go about your travels with confidence and common sense at your side.

Another good place for travel safety advice is Travel Health Online (**www.tripprep.com**). The individual country listings include detailed sections on crime and terrorism, insect and climate concerns, traffic and aviation safety, and embassy locations. This is the most concise source for a wide variety of information on individual countries.

If your travels take you to Europe, check out the travel tips at Rick Steves' Europe Through the Back Door site (**www.ricksteves.com/tips/menu5.htm**). There's a whole section on health and safety, including everything from avoiding thefts and terrorism to "toilet tips."

Government Travel Warnings

To find government travel warnings, go to the U.S. State Department Web site (**travel.state.gov**) and click the **Travel Warnings/Consular Info Sheets** icon. This is the most up-to-date and complete source for information on travel warnings issued by the U.S. and other countries. Also, Travel Health Online (**www.tripprep.com**), in addition to providing great health information, provides useful information on individual countries' political climate and relations with the United States.

Finding Foreign Language Information

No one wants to be seen as an ugly American, and there are few things more embarrassing than seeing Americans in other countries acting like buffoons because they can't find anyone who speaks English (see the message board at **www.ricksteves.com** for some humorous, but also educational, anecdotes of ugly American sightings). To avoid creating such international incidents, and to help create a more positive image for Americans around the world, you can get some useful information from the Web. At the very least, keep handy a few basic phrases that you know you will need. At Travlang (**www.travlang.com/languages**), you can get a few basic phrases in more than 60 languages, plus sound files to give you the correct pronunciations. Fodor's Resource Center also provides lists of useful phrases. That site's language section is divided into categories based on social situations, like At the Airport and Dining Out. If nothing else, you should learn to ask for the bathroom.

You can also order a common phrase dictionary from an online bookseller, usually found under the Reference Category. You'll find many different types of foreign language books, from basic phrase books to more detailed dictionaries and textbooks. Many of the publishers have their own Web sites, so you can check these out to see which book is right for your needs. For example, Lonely Planet (**www.lonelyplanet.com**) offers a series of low-cost phrase books that can help travelers with the necessities when speaking a foreign language. These books have a logical format with pronunciation and grammar help and some advice for memorizing vocabulary. The books even include help with, let us say, the more intimate types of social situations not represented in more formal language books. Also check out the Fodor's Living Language series (**www.fodors.com/language/home.html**) for a variety of language learning materials, from beginning to expert levels.

Or maybe you should buy an electronic handheld or pocket translator. There's a wide variety of these products on the market, from such brands as Franklin, Lingo, and Language Teacher. Some only translate English into one language, and others translate many languages. These products also vary in the number of words and phrases they contain in their memory. You can order them online at **www.101language.com**, **www.languageteacher.com**, or **www.pygmy.com**, or at any other online electronics and computer store. (Personally, I find a small pocket-sized book of phrases much more convenient to refer to. With most electronic translators, you have to enter a word or phrase on a tiny keyboard and then wait to get the translation, which is too time-consuming when you all you want is to ask the waiter for your check.)

If you want to get really adventurous, take a foreign language course, either in the comfort of your own home through a book, tape, CD software, or video, or at a language school. Amazon.com, again, offers a wide selection of language resources. 101language.com (**www.101language.com**) specializes in language learning tools, and carries books, tapes, CDs, software, and videos to help you learn more than 100 languages. For a list of intensive language schools across the country, check out **www.studyabroad.com/simplehtml/languages/bylang.html**. Also, the famous Berlitz language school has its own Web site at **www.berlitz.com**. Here you can find Berlitz courses in your area; order Berlitz books, software, and audio tools; or just find helpful hints for learning a foreign language.

And trust me, most native speakers appreciate any effort you make to speak their language. It's up to you how much of the language you feel that you need to know in order to be comfortable in another country or in the social situations you might encounter. I took four years of German in college before taking a trip to Germany. While in that country, I had only one opportunity to even use my German language skills, and that was after begging a clerk at the train station in Hamburg not to switch to English, so that I could feel that all those college credits actually amounted to something. Perhaps knowing in advance how pervasive English is in the country you are visiting will help you decide how much language instruction you might need. A good way to find out is to post a question in a travel newsgroup and hear from other travelers how much an American needs to know to be prepared for a foreign language situation.

Learning About Customs in Other Countries

Besides language faux pas, there are many other ways to screw up and make the United States look bad while you're in another country. For one thing, things we take for granted are completely different in some other countries. For example, in some countries, it's not proper to leave tips in restaurants (I found this out personally, and embarrassingly, in Spain a few years ago, after being chastised for doing so by a restaurant manager in Seville). Before leaving for your trip, learn a little bit about the customs of the country. Here are some sites to help you out:

➤ **About.com (formerly The Mining Company)** (`www.about.com/travel`) Offers an impressive extensive list of world culture sites, including individual country and region guides. This will give you some basic information on the customs of the country that you're planning to visit.

➤ **Rick Steves' Europe Through the Back Door** (`www.ricksteves.com`) A must-see site for anyone traveling to Europe. You can buy Rick's European travel books here, but the site is also loaded with tips that you won't find at more conventional travel sites. You can read excerpts from Rick's books, a monthly newsletter, and individual country information. The real gems of this site, however, are in the Travel Tips and Tricks section and The Graffiti Wall message board. The Travel Tips and Tricks section gives a wide range of obscure tips, from communicating through gestures and international terms to the best bargaining techniques. The Graffiti Wall contains thousands of great tips tested by international travelers, including a rather racy section titled "Hedonism." (Check out the section "Ugly American Sightings" for definite don'ts in European travel.) And if you have any questions, you can post them here and get good, friendly feedback. This is an entertaining site even if you're not planning a European vacation.

➤ **Lonely Planet's The Thorn Tree Bulletin Board** (`www.lonelyplanet.com/thorn/thorn.htm`) You can also post and follow questions about world travel. The site is organized by country and region, so it's easy to find help on your specific destination. The Lonely Planet site itself is also useful for a wide range of general travel help and resources.

The departments of tourism in most countries have their own Web sites. You can usually find them by typing the name of the country and **tourism** into your favorite search engine. Also, the individual country profiles on `www.tripprep.com` usually have links to these sites as well. Or check out the Tourism Offices Worldwide Directory (`www.towd.com`).

Hear What Other Travelers Have to Say

You can check out message and bulletin boards on travel sites to find tried-and-true advice for world travelers from those with experience. Many of the little tidbits you get here can save you a lot of trouble, or lead you to an exciting adventure that you hadn't thought of before. Even if you just read postings and messages and don't register to post your own two-cents' worth, you can learn a lot from other travelers.

Using Online Currency Converters

Foreign currency can often seem like Monopoly money—its different sizes, colors, and denominations don't seem as real as the dollars and cents we're used to. If you don't keep track of how many dollars and cents you're spending translates to, you can easily bust the budget. And if you don't have your wits about you when you're standing in line, getting ready to pay for something, you run the risk of getting ripped off by seedy merchants that prey on dumb American tourists. Not that you're dumb, but if you don't know how to convert currency, you're definitely at a disadvantage, so don't set yourself up for being ripped off.

To Euro or Not to Euro?

The Euro, the new currency adopted by the European Commonwealth as of January 1999, will cause confusion for travelers planning to visit Austria, Belgium, Finland, France, Germany, Ireland, Luxembourg, Netherlands, Portugal, and Spain over the next few years. The new currency won't be available until January 2002. In the meantime, the exchange rates for these countries' currencies have been fixed relative to each other, and retail outlets have begun listing prices in both the Euro and the native currency. After July 2002, the old money will no longer be accepted in these countries. So, for a couple of years, travel in these countries may be a bit confusing when it comes to currency conversion, but after 2002, it should be a lot easier.

Check out www.ricksteves.com and click the **Travel Tips and Tricks**, then **"The New Euro Currency"** link. Also see the tips page at www.travel-travel-travel.com and click the **New Euro Currency** link for more on the new currency.

Also, the currency market fluctuates, sometimes drastically and quickly. And to make things even more complicated, your local bank, your credit card company, and money exchange booths at airports, hotels, and train stations all give you a different exchange rate. How do you make sure you get the best exchange rate possible?

Getting the Most Bang for Your Buck

According to the good folks at Fodor's Resource Center, you'll most likely get the best exchange rates by using plastic. Even though fees charged for ATM transactions may be higher abroad than at home, Cirrus and Plus exchange rates are extremely competitive because they're based on wholesale rates offered only by major banks, rather than the lower exchange rate offered to consumers. Credit- and charge-card purchases also are exchanged at very reasonable rates, and you have the added protection of using a credit card.

Several Web sites can help you accomplish this:

➤ **Fodor's Resource Center** (`www.fodors.com/resource/`) Once again, Fodor's provides the most concentrated source of information and links on all travel-related money matters. You can find answers to questions about credit cards, debit cards, and traveler's checks, and the relative merits of each. There are also links for daily updated exchange rates, ATM locations around the world, and even a photo gallery of world currencies.

➤ **Olson and Associates** (`www.oanda.com`) Offers a variety of financial information for the world traveler. It forecasts trends in currency exchanges to help you predict the ideal time to make your exchange. A useful currency converter calculates the most recent exchange rates for a variety of currencies. It even factors in the differences between credit card, bank, and exchange booth rates. Its best feature is a printable cheat sheet that figures different values for you. You can carry around this handy reference in your wallet or purse so you don't have to fiddle with a calculator or, Heaven forbid, figure the math in your head.

➤ **Xenon Laboratories** (`www.xe.net/ucc`) Xenon, a developer of Internet-based financial services, offers a universal currency converter free of charge. The simple two-step process converts dollars to your currency of choice in seconds flat, and helps if you want to be kept up-to-date on current rates. Just sign up for the free email notification of changes in rates.

Staying Connected to the Currency Market

If you have your own personal Web site that you plan to access while traveling, you can put your own customized currency converter on your site, thanks to Xenon Laboratories (**www.xe.net/ucc**) and OANDA (**www.oanda.com**). Xenon doesn't charge for this service, but **www.oanda.com** charges a monthly fee, unless you put a banner ad for Olson and Associates on your site—and then it's free! With your own currency converter, you can include only the currencies that you need for your trip. Also, by putting this on your own Web site, you can make your Internet time more efficient.

It's Your Duty to Make Claims in Customs

If you're like me, you're going to load yourself down with souvenirs and goods you picked up along the way on your international adventure. Most of the stuff you bring back you just can't buy in the states, right? Well, before you go spending a ton of cash on goods in foreign lands, remember you're going to have to make a claim at the airport when you come back to the country, and if the value of your purchases exceeds a certain dollar amount in a certain time period, you have to pay a duty on those goods. To find out the latest regulations for customs and duties, see the U.S. Customs Web site at **www.customs.ustreas.gov/travel/index.htm**. And for all you lovely Canadian neighbors to the north, you can read up on Canadian customs regulations online, too, at Revenue Canada: I Declare (**www.rc.gc.ca/~paulb/pamphlet/rc4044e.htm**).

The Least You Need to Know

➤ U.S. government offices, like the State Department and the CDC, have Web sites that contain the most up-to-date information on immunizations, health risks, passport and visa requirements, and government travel warnings.

➤ You can use online currency converters to create cheat sheets that help you keep track of how much you are spending in U.S. dollars.

➤ A number of online language resources can help you learn a few useful words and phrases for when you're traveling in non-English-speaking countries. Many of these sites also give you useful cultural background to avoid making embarrassing mistakes.

➤ You can find the tourist information site for your country of destination to get some of the basics to plan for your trip.

➤ Get the latest customs and duty information online at government Web sites.

Chapter 22

Staying Connected: Plug In and Log On from the Road

In This Chapter

➤ Sign up for a free email account for easy access from the road

➤ Find a place to check your email and surf the Web, in the largest of cities to the wide open Outback

➤ Use personal digital assistants and other hardware to stay connected on the road

The World Wide Web is just that—worldwide. It is surprisingly easy to access the Web from almost any location around the world. Everywhere, from the urban centers of Tokyo to the Australian Outback, is wired to the Internet. And often, it can be cheaper—and certainly faster—to send emails and Web postcards than to send letters and postcards through snail mail. And how often have you bought postcards while on a trip, and not gotten around to sending them until you return home (if you send them at all)?

Although staying connected is easier than it has ever been, there are still some tricks you need to know before you go on your trip. First of all, if you don't have an email account, you need to get one! Then, where do you find Internet access, and how much does it cost? You'll be surprised at how much free access is out there. If you take a laptop, you may solve part of your problem, but where can you hook up? And what extra hardware do you need to stay connected in other countries? And finally, how might a handheld personal digital assistant (PDA) provide solutions to your connection problems?

There Is Such a Thing As a Free Email Account

If you don't have an email account yet (and if you don't, what're you waiting for?), there are many places you can get free email to keep in touch with friends and family while you're home or away. If you have Internet access through a local service provider, email is included with your monthly service. But if you plan on checking your email while you're on the road, you'll have to do a little bit of legwork to get into your account from a remote location. But if you sign up for a free Web-based account, all you have to do is get on the Web and go to the free email provider's Web site to check your mail. Here are some options you might want to consider:

➤ **Hotmail** (www.hotmail.com) The first Web-based email provider. Like all free email providers, Hotmail makes money by placing banner ads on its pages rather than charging you money to have an email account. One of the benefits of Hotmail for travel is that you don't have to reconfigure the computer you use with your POP or SMTP addresses every time you go to a new terminal. Instead, you just log in through the Hotmail Web site. All you have to do is enter your username and password—by far the easiest and quickest way to check your inbox.

SMTP@#!*POP$@!

Who wants to spend vacation time trying to reconfigure *anything*, especially something that requires you to know what the heck SMTP and POP mean! Leave that mumbo jumbo for the geeks of the world. If you're the curious type though, SMTP stands for Simple Mail Transfer Protocol, and it's understood by all networked computers hooked up to the Internet for the storing, retrieval, and sending of email. POP stands for Post Office Protocol, and it's the old–time way to send and receive email, but it's been made obsolete by SMTP. You may still run into the term, though, from time to time.

➤ **Yahoo! Mail** (www.yahoo.com) Yahoo! is not only a search engine, but it's also a free email provider. Yahoo!'s email service is Web based, just like Hotmail's. Just go to the Web site and sign up!

➤ **Portableoffice.com** (www.portableoffice.com) Offers more than free email— it offers a "Portable Folder" to store your computer files while on vacation, a calendar, a bookmark file, and your own personal chat room and message board. This service provides many of the average computer user's needs, and, best of all, it's free!

➤ **Lonely Planet eKno (`www.ekno.lonelyplanet.com`)** Offers a package of services to keep you connected while traveling overseas. It provides low-cost international phone cards, phone service, voice mail, Lonely Planet guidebook access, and free email. Check out `www.ekno.lonelyplanet.com` to see exactly how this service works. You can set up a free email account, but you do have to plop down your credit card number for a pre-determined charge for international calls. If you don't make any calls, you won't be charged, but the service does claim to have pretty good rates, so check it out if the package looks like it's the right fit for you.

There are many free email providers besides these, and more are popping up all the time. Even though they're free, you can still shop around to find the one that offers what you need for your trip.

Why Not Make Your Own Travel Web Site?

If you're going on vacation and you plan to surf the Web frequently, you might want to make yourself a Web site that contains links to all the sites you want to check regularly. This way, especially if you have to pay for computer time at cyber cafés and other locations, you can make your Internet use more efficient. You can even install your own customized currency converter on your site (see Chapter 21, "Going International? Planning Ahead for Paperwork and Safety"). And this also gives you more time to do the things that you should be doing while on vacation, like sightseeing, eating, and just plain relaxing.

You can also include on your site emergency contacts and other important information that you don't want to lose. If you have access to a scanner or a digital camera and photo–editing software (like PhotoShop), you can post pictures of your trip on your Web site for all your friends and family to enjoy. Most Internet service providers also offer free space to post Web sites, so this won't cost you anything extra. It's usually included as part of your home Internet service. You can also get free Web space at `www.geocities.com`, among other sites.

Where to Check Your Email or Surf the Web

One of the easiest places for checking your email on the road is an Internet (cyber) café—little coffee houses that provide you with a computer and an Internet connection, and for a fee, let you check and send email or surf the Web. And it's easy to go online before you leave to get a list of cafés in the area you're visiting. Many of the cyber café directories list locations, maps on getting there, rates to use their computers, and whether or not you can plug in your own laptop and use their Internet connection.

But besides cyber cafés, you'd be surprised over some of the other places that have Internet access, and often times, it's free of charge. Libraries, post offices, Internet vending machines, department stores…the list goes on. Here are some options for staying connected on the road, and some Web sites to visit to find exact locations in your travel zone. Later in the chapter I talk about plugging in your laptop, so if you're taking one along, be sure to read that section for the skinny on hooking up and logging on.

What About Internet Access in Far-Flung Countries?

Val, a world-traveling friend of mine, recently returned from Africa and Southeast Asia. She explained to me exactly how easy it was to stay connected in countries where one wouldn't expect it, along with some advantages to staying connected that might surprise you: "It was ridiculously easy to get Internet access in far-flung countries. In Thailand, I hooked up every night in my hotel. And in Nepal—get this—it's most people's primary means of communicating. I often communicated with people I met while in Nepal to compare trekking routes, prices, and that sort of thing. The telephone and mail delivery were unreliable. The thing that was so great about checking my email in cafés and hotels in Nepal is that those were the only businesses that were ever air conditioned, probably to keep the computers comfortable."

It's Easy Access at Cyber Cafés, Libraries, and Hotels

Getting Your Java (and Email) at Cyber Cafés   The easiest places to find Internet access are the cyber, or Internet, cafés that populate most major cities. Some of these amount to nothing more than a kiosk in a public place, but most resemble traditional cafés, offering coffee and snacks along with Internet access. At all these places, you have to pay for Internet access by the hour, and it can often cost you from $5 to $8 per hour. Many world travelers find that cyber cafés usually have employees who speak English well, probably because they have such a large English-speaking clientele. Also, some countries use a different keyboard from the one you are used to—take a couple minutes to adapt before writing your email. Finally, some Internet café terminals may be infected with computer viruses. It would be a good idea to warn any email recipients not to open unknown attachments to your messages.

The Internet Café Guide (**www.netcafeguide.com**) maintains a constantly updated list of Internet cafés around the world. The makers of the site also offer a handy book to take on your vacation. Both the site and the book offer helpful tips and advice for staying connected while on vacation, including a list of questions to ask if you plan on using a cyber café.

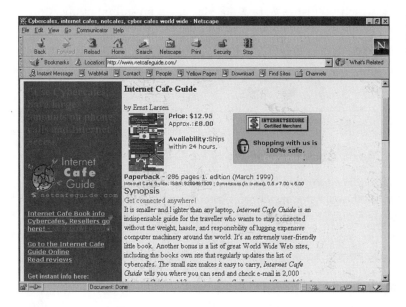

The Internet Café Guide offers a complete list of cyber cafés worldwide.

Essential Information That's Easy to Forget

Most of us know our street address, but do you know your SMTP address? Jusin case, here's a great piece of advice I found at the Internet Café Guide (`www.netcafeguide.com`): "Bring a note of your username, password, POP and SMTP address (in the email client), and the FTP address you use to transfer files to your site. It's incredibly easy to forget these if you have them installed so you don't have to remember them daily." Without this information, you probably won't be able to access your email or make changes to your Web site.

Many cyber café owners have worked together to form The Cyberstar Cafe Network (`www.cyber-star.com`), which publishes CyberCafe Magazine, an online publication providing information, locations, profiles, and articles on cyber cafés worldwide.

Want to Learn More About the History of Cyber Café Culture?

Café Magazine, a net publication (`www.blackapollo.demon.co.uk/cafindex.html`), covers the worlds of traditional cafés, cyber cafés, and the culture surrounding them. Although the magazine is published infrequently, the articles are interesting and insightful.

Besides cyber cafés, you can often use a public computer at a library or hotel. If you're traveling on business especially, hotels that cater to the business traveler often have business centers, complete with fax machines, dataports to plug in your laptop, or PCs that are connected to the Internet. Here's what to expect if you're looking to libraries or hotels to stay connected on the road.

➤ **Libraries Aren't Just for Books Anymore**   Most major metropolitan libraries offer Internet access. This service is usually free, but don't always count on that. Many world travelers are surprised when they have to pay to use services in public libraries. It's best to go to public libraries early in the morning, because lines very quickly form around the library terminals later in the day.

➤ **Finding Hotels with Internet Access** Most modern hotels have dataports in the rooms for modem connections, but if you're not taking your own laptop with you, this service is useless. The best way to find out if the hotel you plan on staying at has Internet access available for guests is to email, call, or fax the hotel and ask. On the Web, there are several good international hotel guides, but many don't list Internet access as a feature, so hotels may offer it even if they don't advertise it. Local Hotels (**www.localhotels.com**) can connect you to many local hotel and reservation Web guides around the world. Some of these local Web guides let you know about Internet access, but it does take some digging. Most sites, like The Hotel Guide (**www.hotelguide.com**), let you know if the hotel rooms feature dataports.

Don't Fry Your Laptop! Look Before You Plug In!

Make sure you're plugging into a dataport. You can do serious damage to your laptop if you accidentally use a phone line that's not meant to be used with a modem. More about that later in the chapter....

Sugar-Free Keyboards

Check out travel Web site message boards, like Rick Steves' Graffiti Wall (**www.ricksteves.com/graffiti/index.htm**), for useful information and helpful hints not only for finding Internet access, but also for avoiding potentially troubling situations. At The Graffiti Wall, for example, one poster recommends packing a towel or moist towelettes to wipe off the public keyboards at cyber cafés in case the last customer who ate a sticky croissant at the terminal you're using wasn't very tidy!

Locating Off-the-Wall Public Access Resources

Even if you can't find Internet access at a cyber café, library, or hotel, don't lose hope. Many other locations, some you might not even think of, can give you access, often even for free! Wherever there is civilization, there is Internet access. Sometimes, where there is little civilization, there is Internet access. Check out some of these off-the-wall places to get online.

➤ **Retail electronic stores, computer stores, and department stores**
Many of these stores offer free Internet access as a way of demonstrating their computers' capabilities. Basically, it's a sales tactic that you can use to your advantage. Most stores that offer this service advertise it with window signs or banners within the computer department. A word of warning: You might have to wait in line, and you might even have to deal with a sales pitch before you can log on, both of which can seriously cut into your vacation time.

➤ **Kinko's** The Kinko's copy (and so much more) store you know and love has branches in Australia, China, Japan, Korea, the Netherlands, the United Arab Emirates, and the United Kingdom. You can go to the Kinko's Web site (www.kinkos.com) to find the exact locations of these international branches. At Kinko's, like at cyber cafés, you have to pay for Internet access, and you don't get the benefit of coffee or pastries.

➤ **The local post office** Post offices in many countries offer Internet terminals, either for free or for a small charge. Again, the lines for these terminals can be long. In fact, many countries are discontinuing this service because of the crowding it has caused.

➤ **Overseas offices of U.S. companies** If you're really desperate to log on, and you just can't find any of the more conventional sources for Internet access, you might want to give this one a shot. Several travelers have described situations where they've walked into the offices of recognizable American companies, very politely explained their situation, and asked for assistance. Sometimes, especially if the office is populated by expatriate Americans, they might be happy to see a friendly face. This, of course, does not always work. But I emphasize that you should only use this method in an emergency or the most extreme situations, and be prepared to be disappointed.

➤ **Internet vending machines** It sounds crazy, but it's true. Internet machines are popping up all over the place. My world-traveling friend Mike describes his experience coming across one of these in the Australian Outback: "There are a lot of weird things in Australia, but the weirdest were the Internet vending machines I encountered deep in the Outback. Roughly the shape and size of a Pac Man video game, this machine advertised the opportunity to 'surf the Internet!' for only $2. Even some of the most remote roadhouses on some of the most remote roads had at least one dusty machine occupying a corner of the room." These machines, however, can be somewhat unreliable, and they usually come with a disclaimer stating that they are not responsible for lost signals. Still, if you're in the middle of nowhere and you want to hook up, this can be a great opportunity.

Plugging In Your Laptop

To avoid many of the minor hassles associated with finding Internet access, you might just want to take a laptop computer with you, complete with your own Internet and email accounts. As I said earlier, most modern hotels have dataports for modem connections, but you might want to check ahead to make sure.

If you do take your laptop, you will have to make some minor modifications. First, you probably will need a phone jack adapter. These run about $60, and they're available at most consumer electronic stores. Many international airports also carry these, so you may be able to wait until the last minute to make this purchase. Check out the World Wide Phone Guide (**kropla.com/phones.htm**) to find out all you need to know about connecting your modem around the world.

Also, voltage and electrical outlets differ from country to country. As with any electrical appliance you might bring, you may need a voltage converter and plug adapter. Most laptops are dual-voltage, meaning they work at both the U.S. standard 110 volts and at the 220 volts used in most other countries. However, there is a wide variety of plug shapes around the world. The World Electric Guide (**kropla.com/electric.htm**) gives you pictures of all the plug types in the world, plus answers to all travelers' electricity questions.

Some more technologically savvy travelers like to carry other laptop accessories in case of emergencies. For example, Road Warrior International (**www.warrior.com**), offers a product called Modem Saver, which tests telephone lines to see if they are analog or digital (your modem won't work on a digital line). It also tests for dangerous power spikes in the phone line that might fry your modem. Also, in case such a modem-damaging event were to occur, some travelers carry extra modems. Use your own discretion as far as how much you want to invest in these gadgets. Another neat product is the Road Warrior Telecoupler II, which allows you to connect your modem to any telephone, so you don't have to monkey with different phone line adapters.

You can also shop for laptop accessories and computer hardware needs online at places like Computer Discount Warehouse (**www.cdw.com**) and eCOST (**www.ecost.com**).

*Road Warrior
International provides
a variety of products to
make your laptop travel
ready.*

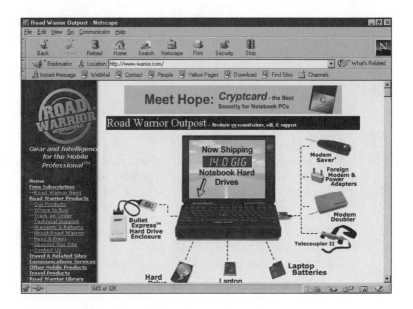

Computers So Tiny They Fit In Your Hand

If a laptop is too bulky or expensive, or if you're worried about it getting stolen, then a compact, handheld PC, also known as a Personal Digital Assistant (PDA) may be what you need to stay connected while on vacation. The appeal of a handheld is its size and connectability. There are plenty of makes and models, and depending on your budget and what you plan to use your PDA for, you may want to shop around and read reviews and comparisons of the various PDAs on the market. CNET has a thorough product review section, including user reviews and editor test-drives. Go to **www.computers.com** and click the **handhelds** icon, or use the pull-down menu and select **handhelds**. Then under options, click **all handheld reviews**, or click the link that takes you to a review of the Top 5 models.

Just like people, some PDAs are stronger, faster, and smarter than others. But if you don't need a lot of power or don't require a color monitor, why spend the money on bells and whistles you aren't going to use? Expect to pay between $100 and $600 for a PDA, with the higher-end models featuring tools like handwriting recognition, full Web surfing features, and super-dooper audio capabilities.

Handhelds are made by a number of manufacturers like Hewlett-Packard, 3Com, Compaq, Casio, NEC, and Phillips. If you want to go straight to the maker's Web site, you can connect from the CNET site. But for an impartial review of the product, be sure to check out what the CNET editors and real users of the products have to say, or go to your favorite computer product review site. And be sure to shop around. After all, isn't that what your Momma told you to do?

Going, Going, Gone

If you want to try your hand at online auctions, the CNET site has an easy-to-use auction feature, complete with step-by-step instructions on how to use the system, plus quick and easy links to product information so you know more about what you're buying and what a reasonable asking price may be. To access the CNET online auction, go to **www.computers.com** and click the **Auctions** link, and then the type of product you're looking for.

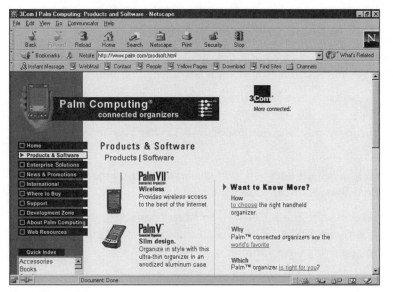

The PalmPilot Web site from 3Com lists the features and benefits of the different Palm organizers.

Trusty, Little Handheld to the Rescue

Mike Langberg, a staff writer for the Mercury News (**www.mercurycenter.com/svtech/news/indepth/docs/tt061399.htm**), describes a situation where his handheld proved indispensable. Mike experienced a travel nightmare: While flying from San Jose to Atlanta, thunderstorms caused him to miss his connecting flight at O'Hare Airport in Chicago. "When I arrived in Chicago and realized my connection was history, I went to a pay phone and called United reservations to book the next available flight. I then tapped the screen of the wallet-sized handheld to access a slimmed-down version of the Official Airline Guide site on the World Wide Web. After entering the route and date, I was looking at a list of United flights from Chicago to Atlanta on Monday morning. Now I could tell the agent which flight I wanted, rather than expressing a vague desire for the next available departure."

The Least You Need to Know

➤ If you don't already have an email account, get one before you leave on vacation. Many companies offer free email service.

➤ Internet access is available in major cities around the world, sometimes even for free. Look for cyber cafés, libraries, and other sources of access while traveling, or plan ahead by checking out international cyber café and Internet access listings.

➤ If you're headed to a remote location, you can sometimes connect through Internet vending machines or the local post office.

➤ A laptop computer may be the easiest way to keep connected. If a laptop just isn't feasible for you, a PDA may be an affordable, portable solution for your connection needs while on vacation.

➤ Go online to read computer experts' reviews of products before you spend a dime.

Chapter 23

Are We There Yet?!

In This Chapter

➤ Find tips online to keep the kids (and you) happy (or sedated) in transit

➤ Save time and money by reading online magazines for kids and family travel

➤ Find message boards to gather ideas and get real-world advice from other families

➤ Discover cool and whacky places to eat before you hit the road

➤ Get your car ready for the road, and lining up roadside assistance, just in case

Before we departed on family trips when I was a kid, my parents used to make bets on how long it would take for someone to ask "Are we there yet?" a mile? an hour? just outside the city? Depending on the actual distance to our destination, the answers to the dreaded question ranged from "No dear, not yet." to "Don't make me pull over!" or "No dear. If you ask one more time, Mommy will turn this wagon around and you won't have to wonder how long 'til we get there. You'll be asking 'How long until I'm not grounded anymore?'" (Actually, my Mom never said that, but she might have been thinking it.)

Short of canceling your trip or sedating your kids to keep them calm on a long road trip or airplane ride, there are some things you can do to keep kids (and adults) happy and occupied during transit...games, nonsugar snacks (who wants a car full of kids jacked up on Pixie Sticks?), stopping every two hours to exercise and burn off excess energy, sing-along songs, and so on. Or keep them busy with a delightful game of roadkill bingo. Everything you need to know is online, and if you're looking for books, games, or toys, you can buy those online, too.

Finding Online Tips for Keeping Everybody Happy in Transit

You can find tips and resources for traveling with kids in a variety of places on the Web:

➤ **Family travel Web directories**   A good place to get started, from here you'll find links to sites ranging from personal home pages, family travelogues, guides to family-friendly destinations, special discounts on hotels, trip planners, and more. A good place to get started is the Family Travel Files Web site (**www.thefamilytravelfiles.com**). Here you'll find a directory of family vacation spots, advice, and an ezine with personal travel articles.

➤ **Online parenting magazines**   You can read magazines for free! Online you can find articles from regular print publications, so if you don't already have subscriptions to the popular parenting magazines, check out magazine directories in Yahoo! or your favorite search engine directory, or do a search with the keywords **parenting AND magazines**. And just like regular magazines, there are plenty of ads to help you make smart buying decisions. A good example of an online parenting magazine that covers family travel is ParentsTalk magazine (**www.parents-talk.com**). Click the **Families, Food & Travel** icon for family travel tips and advice.

➤ **Family travel Web sites**   You can meet other parents and get advice through message boards, chat rooms, forums, and online newsletters. Some family travel Web sites sell books, games, and toys. A popular family travel Web site is the Family Travel Forum (**www.familytravelforum.com**), which has message boards, destination reviews, and tips and advice for family travelers.

➤ **Family travel newsgroups**   You can post messages using email, sign up for notification of responses to your posting, and read others' advice and tips for traveling with kids. A popular travel newsgroup is **rec.travel.misc**, which can be accessed through the Deja.com newsgroup Web site at **www.deja.com**. (See Chapter 5, "Online Travel Communities 101," for the scoop on newsgroups.)

➤ **Online bookstores**   Many bookstores online specialize in children's books. For a wide selection of children's books, check out Amazon.com at **www.amazon.com**, and either click through to the Children's book listings or use the search engine to locate titles specific to travel.

➤ **Online travel stores**   Many of the travel supply and accessory stores online sell kids' travel supplies. You can also buy earplugs and noise reducers for yourself (see Chapter 20, "Finding and Shopping for Travel Gear and Accessories"). The Rand McNally Web site (**www.randmcnally.com**) has a travel supplies section with plenty of games and activities designed to keep the kids occupied in transit. From the home page, click **Online Travel Store**, **Departments**, and then **Kid's Travel**.

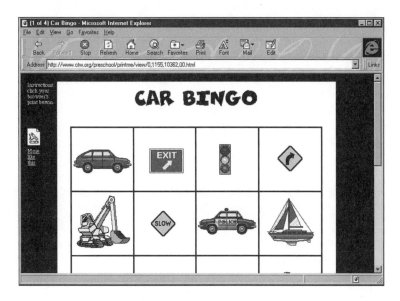

The Children's Television Network Web site at www.ctw.org features games, books, tips, and tales for keeping kids happy in transit.

What About Keeping the Driver Happy?

Here's an idea for keeping you happy in transit: Books on tape. Visit Books on Tape (**www.booksontape.com**) for a selection of more than 4,800 classic and popular book titles. You can even rent the tapes for 30 days for about half the price of buying. Heck, I saw some titles in the kids' section that I wouldn't mind hearing, like *Alice in Wonderland* and *The Wizard of Oz*. You can even rent tapes at Cracker Barrel restaurants and return them at another location along the way. For a list of locations, visit the Cracker Barrel Web site at **www.crackerbarre-locs.com** and click the **Locations** icon. And here's a books on tape safety tip: If you're going to use headphones to listen to books on tape or any audio cassette or CD, always keep one ear uncovered. It's the law!

Top Sites with Ideas and Games for Kids

One of the best things about going online to do travel research is learning from other people's travel mistakes. Not only do you get to gloat in another person's discomfort and pain, you get to add to your knowledge-base on being a perfect parent. If you're taking a long road trip or going by plane for the first time with the little monsters, be sure to go online to get ideas and games that are designed to keep the kids quiet and you sane on your adventures. Here are some sites to get you started.

➤ **About.com (formerly The Mining Company (`www.travelwithkids.about.com/`)** A good place to start, you'll be impressed by the extensive list of family travel links, including state-by-state guides of family-friendly attractions and lodging, top-rated family vacations, advice about car travel with a teen who wants a crack at the wheel (yikes!), and suggestions on keeping all ages happy in cars and on planes.

About.com has lots of family travel resources, including regional and state travel guides and tips for traveling with kids and infants.

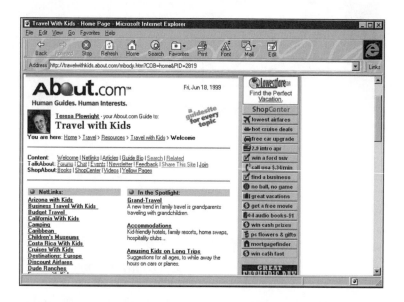

➤ **Fodor's Resource Center (`www.fodors.com/resource/children/`)** Once again, Fodor's online Resource Center earns my vote for top site for online information and links to family travel resources. The Resource Center's Children and Travel section is a comprehensive guide to road and air travel for kids of all ages. For road travel, you can find tips and advice on choosing a destination, preparing to go, and things to do when you get there. For air travel, Fodor's advises that you check with the airline you're flying on to find out about discounts for children, safety seat requirements, special meals for babies and children, and even a guide to letting kids fly solo to Grandma's.

➤ **Disney's Family.com Travel (`www.family.go.com/Categories/Travel`)** Leave it to Walt and company to come up with some real winners when it comes to keeping kids happy, even in the car. You'll find travel tips as well as lists and links to family-friendly cities and attractions, including Disney World. The site even provides a free trip planner to help you develop your vacation. You can also read destination, city, and attraction reviews from other parents and kids.

➤ **Family Travel Forum**
(www.familytravelforum.com) A nicely
put-together site that provides all kinds
of resources for parents. You can search
related sites by child's age, destination, or
interest. You can subscribe to an online
newsletter, read message board postings
from other parents, or visit the family
travel shop. And you can get the latest
scoop on the best family vacation deals.
Much of the information on the site is
free, but you can also become a member
of the forum for a low annual fee, which
gets you coupons, discounts, insider tips
on travel deals, and more.

➤ **Parentsoup** (www.parentsoup.com/
library/kbk503.html) An online parents'
community and resource center that
offers articles, tips, and advice on kids'
travel. You can also buy books and toys,
join a chat room, or post a question to a
message board.

➤ **Parents Q&A** (www.parentsing-qa.com/
cgi-bin/detail/travelvacations/)
A general resource guide with links
to books, publications, fact sheets,
CyberMoms chat rooms, and other kids'
travel information. Be sure to check out
the fact sheets that give tips on airplane
travel, games to play, child safety issues,
health issues, and more.

➤ **Rand McNally Travel Store Games
and Activities Department**
(www.randmcnallystore.com) You can
pick up a volume of "My First Backseat
Books" or get the kids involved with trip
planning with a copy of "Trip Tracker
Travel Journal and Gamebook." The site
offers online or toll-free phone ordering,
as well as fax and mail ordering.

Listen to Mother's Advice

At Disney's Family.com Web site
(www.family.go.com/Categories/
Travel) you'll find plenty of
resources for family travel. You can
find out what other people in your
region have done on vacation, and
get the scoop on where to go, what
to do, and how to save a few bucks.
On the message board, one mother
posted a review of a trip to the
Children's Museum in Indianapolis
(a great museum... check it out at
www.childrensmuseum.org):
"What we liked: We just love the
Indianapolis Children's Museum.
There is so much to see and do that
you just can't miss it. We've been to
several other children's museums
and none of them compare....What
the kids liked: Our three-year-old
still raves about the train exhibit...
and the carousel ride....Our eight-
year old took rock-climbing lessons.

At this site you can also read information people have posted on what
a given vacation costs and what
they didn't like.

The Baby's Screaming, The Baby's Screaming!!!!

Traveling with kids is tough enough, but traveling with an infant or a toddler is another scary story. Infants can't entertain themselves for hours on end with a video game. But then again, unless they're crying, you're not going to get much trouble from them—they are, after all, pretty much stuck where you put them. You can go online to find tips and products to get ready for traveling with infants. Here are some places to get started:

➤ **ParentTime Online Magazine (www.pathfinder.com/ParentTime/homepage/ homepage.all.html)** A good place to start your search on travel with kids ages 0–6. You'll have to use the site's search engine to find the latest article installments, but that's easy. Just type **travel** in the search box, and you'll get a long list of resources at ParentTime online. There are also chat rooms, bulletin boards, links to sites where you can buy toys and books, and more.

➤ **Preview Travel Tips and Advice (www.previewtravel.com)** Preview Travel, a popular online booking site has tips and advice on all sorts of travel-related topics. For the inside scoop on family travel, go to the **Tips and Advice** section and click **Family Travel**. I found a good article on traveling with infants on long flights and an article on making family travel more enjoyable.

➤ **Travel Tots (www.traveltots.com)** The tips and products at the Travel Tots Web site can help you and your munchkin have a more enjoyable trip...across town, across the country, or around the world. The Travel Toy Packs are chock full of goodies for when you hit the road, and include both boys' and girls' packs, infant and toddler packs, and small travel games and art activities for older children. You'll also find classy backpacks for Mom and Dad, insulated bottle warmers, a babysitter memo board, Travel Buddy Bear, Travel Snuggie Blankie, travel first-aid kit, and more. You can order online at the site.

➤ **The Triplet Connection (www.tripletconnection.org/atwti.html)** You think you've got it bad? Try flying with twins or triplets. For a taste of triple trouble, check out the questions and advice on flying with multiples at this site. Actually, all the people who posted advice said the airline personnel and fellow passengers were extremely helpful, but even so, what an undertaking!

What Does the FAA Say About Safety Seats for Children?

Because plane crashes are statistically infrequent, the Federal Aviation Administration (FAA) does not *require* children to use safety seats, although it recommends that all children who fly, regardless of age, use a certified child safety restraint (CSR) system, usually called a car seat. Air turbulence can mean bumps and bruises for the little ones, so keep them safe with a CSR. Check with the airline you're flying to find out exactly what the requirements are for traveling with children, and whether you should bring your baby's car seat or if one will be provided. Some airlines even offer seat-size bassinets. You may want to bring a car seat anyway, just in case your rental car agency doesn't provide one, although most do.

Finding Great Roadside Restaurants and Stops

Trying out local restaurants on your road trip adventure is a great way to break up the monotony of fast-food restaurants, and it's a good way to introduce your kids to regional foods, like grits or fried green tomato sandwiches. For a directory of road trip restaurants, check out these sites:

➤ **Diner City (www.dinercity.com)** A directory of diners across the United States and Canada, presented by state and regional areas. You can read reviews from other travelers and get directions to your diner of choice.

➤ **Eat Here (www.eathere.com)** I talked about this site in Chapter 11, "Takin' It to the Streets: Traveling by Car, RV, or Motorcycle," but in case you skipped that chapter, here it is again. Do a search for restaurants by type of food served or by state, highway, or food type.

➤ **CitySearch (www.citysearch.com)** After you've got your travel route planned, visit CitySearch for restaurants in the areas you're traveling through.

➤ **USA Star I-95 Exit Directory Online (www.usastar.com/i95/food.htm)** All restaurants, diners, and fast-food establishments located within 1/2 mile of an I-95 exit are listed by state. You can find listings along the entire length of I-95 from Maine to Florida and back. The site lists both fast-food and local establishments.

Planning Ahead for Roadside Assistance

The obvious choice for roadside assistance is getting a membership in AAA, but there are many other motor clubs like Shell Motorists Club and JCPenny's MotorPlus. Not only do auto travel clubs provide 24-hour roadside emergency service, you can get customized maps and itineraries and just about any road travel resource you need, as well as discounts at many hotels and attractions. You should also check with your auto insurance provider to see whether roadside assistance is covered under your policy, and if so, whether it applies to out-of-state travel. Check your vehicle warranty, too. Many car manufacturers offer roadside assistance coverage under regular and extended warranty plans for newer models of cars.

Are You Already Covered for Roadside Assistance?

You can go online to find out if your vehicle's warranty provides roadside assistance. Go to your favorite search engine and search with the keywords **roadside AND assistance AND mercedes** (or whatever your model of car happens to be, although newer models are more likely to offer this kind of warranty). Then visit the manufacturer's site and locate warranty information for your car. Or if you own a brand new car, an easy way to look up roadside warranty information is to go to Edmunds (**www.edmunds.com**) or Kelley Blue Book (**www.kbb.com**) and click through the new car information section to find warranty information for this year's models.

To find tips online to get your vehicle ready for the road and learn what to do if there is an emergency, visit these sites:

➤ **Learn2.com Road Trip Survival Guide (209.24.233.206/survival/ sur_road.html)** Tips and advice to get your car ready for the road so you don't even need roadside assistance, unless of course, you do something idiotic like lock your keys in the car or run out of gas. It's fun and entertaining, with links to other valuable life lessons.

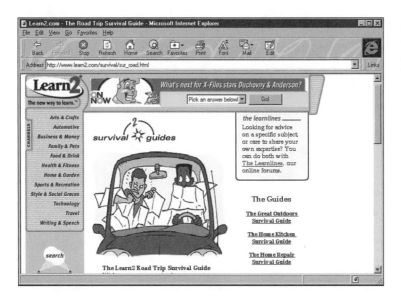

At Learn2.com's Online Learning Center, you can get quick tips to get your car and yourself ready for a road trip.

➤ **AAA (www.aaa.com/news12/buttons/trafficf.html)** You can read and print AAA's online articles and travel safety advice. Recent postings include these articles on driving safety, choosing a vehicle for family safety, sharing the road with trucks, summer driving on slippery road trips, and winter advice for young drivers to name a few.

How About a Site for Sleepy Eyes?

Driver fatigue is one of the leading causes of accidents, but do you know the signs of fatigue? Check out AAA's Foundation for Traffic Safety (**www.aaafts.org/Text/wakeup.html**) and take a driver fatigue quiz to learn about how to stay alert when you're behind the wheel.

Or check out the new S.A.M. (Steering Attention Monitor) Web site at **www.sleepydriver.com**. This site sells a device called a Steering Attention Monitor, which is a small, computerized, electronic device that monitors corrective movements of the steering wheel with a magnetic sensor. When lack of normal wheel movement is detected, you're alerted by an alarm that's automatically reset as soon as normal steering motion is restored. It's not intended to help you drive longer—just safer. If the alarm goes off, you should pull over at the first safe place and take a rest, especially if there are little ones on board.

The Least You Need to Know

➤ You can find family travel tips online using online magazine forums, message boards, chat rooms, family travel Web sites, and newsgroups.

➤ Many Web sites have game ideas for kids to play in transit, and many sites sell kids' books, games, and toys for use in the car or on a plane, plus tips on things to do before you hit the road.

➤ You can involve your kids in travel planning and go online to research destinations and sites along the way.

➤ You can research family-friendly hotels, attractions, and restaurants.

➤ You can go online to find cool and interesting roadside oddities and restaurants for a more exciting road trip adventure.

Chapter 24

Health, Wellness, and Online Information

In This Chapter

➤ Listen to the Boy Scouts—making pre-departure preparations for safe and healthy travel

➤ Prepare for life's little surprises with travel health insurance, and knowing what it does and doesn't cover

➤ Know what kind and when to get shots and other immunization requirements and disease information

➤ Fight back against jetlag and motion sickness

➤ Keep the bugs away and stop an upset tummy with healthy travel products like mosquito nets and water purifiers

➤ Find what's up with doc in your destination

Those darned Boy Scouts sure know what they're talking about when they say "Be prepared." Knowing what activities, foods, and drinks to avoid are the first steps to having a safe and healthy travel adventure. You also need to know about other health risks at your destination. The next step is getting the proper health insurance coverage and immunizations, and knowing what medical resources are available in the area you're visiting. After all, nothing ruins a vacation like a bad case of yellow fever, so take some time to prepare for a healthy trip before you hit the road, and don't add insult to injury (or illness) by finding yourself uninsured or unprepared if disaster strikes.

Although a good deal of the information in this chapter deals with health concerns in international destinations, you still need to prepare yourself for life's little bumps, bruises, and bugs when you're traveling in the good old U.S. of A. And don't think that it's only "underdeveloped" or exotic destinations that are high risk. Ticks in North America spread a lot of disease, and you can suffer the woes of sunburn, heat-stroke, sprained ankles, diarrhea, and poison ivy just about anywhere. Spending a little time online looking into travel health issues is a quick and painless way to plan for healthy travels, regardless of your destination.

Pretravel Preparations

No one wants to spend vacation cooped up in bed, sick with an upset tummy, or in the hospital recovering from a near-fatal snake bite. Besides having to cut your trip short and return home to recover from unforeseen health problems, your regular health insurance might not cover your medical expenses. Or what if you're not permitted to cross the border because you don't have current vaccinations? Well, there are plenty of online resources and pretravel checklists to help you prepare for your journey. You can even go online to find medical care providers in the town or country you're visiting.

Depending on your travel destination, you'll need to think about health and wellness precautions and taking measures to prevent illnesses or insurance woes from raining on your parade. If you're working with a travel agent or tour operator, that person should give you health and wellness precaution information. If you're planning your own travels, you need to do some legwork yourself, but it's actually pretty easy to find up-to-date information to get ready for a safe and healthy trip.

General Travel Health Web Sites

Besides some of the Web sites listed in this section, you can start your travel health research at your favorite search engine or travel directory. At any search engine, just use the keywords **travel AND health**, and you'll get matches with Web sites covering healthy air travel, safety precautions for the outdoors, international medical directories, disease information, immunization requirements, and tips to help prepare for safe travel. Here are some of the most comprehensive Web sites to get you started:

➤ **Lonely Planet's Health Check** (`www.lonelyplanet.com/health/health.htm`) Covers the ABCs of pills, ills, and bellyaches. You'll find tips on predeparture planning, keeping healthy, women's health, and diseases and ailments, and a long list of health links. With a bit of knowledge and basic precautions, you can eliminate most health hardships, except maybe a little jetlag, upset tummy, or a heel-full of blisters (but, as you'll see at the site, you can take measures to avoid even those ailments).

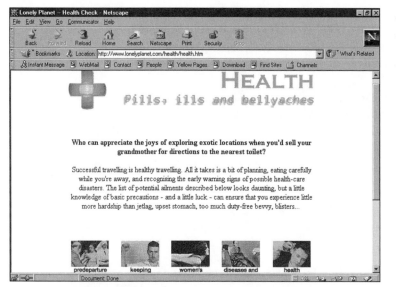

Lonely Planet can help you with predeparture travel planning to help you get ready for a safe, healthy vacation.

➤ **Fodor's Resource Center** (www.fodors.com/resource/health/) Have you bookmarked this site yet? The Resource Center's health section covers health tips for any type of traveler—campers, international travelers, hikers, skiers, and beach bums. You'll find links to what to do for snake bites, how to remove a tick, how to recognize and treat exposure to poison ivy and other poisonous plants, and how to filter and purify your drinking water. The site also has a checklist for what to include in a first aid kit, and a link to Active First Aid Online (www.parasolemt.com.au/afa/) for instructions that you can print out and take on your trip. Fodor's also has a whole section (www.fodors.com/resource/disabilities) on precautions and travel planning resources for disabled travelers, for preparing for emergencies, making sure there's adequate accessibility, and learning about insurance issues.

➤ **The Great Outdoor Recreation Pages** (www.gorp.com/gorp/health/main.htm) Lots and lots of links to sites covering travel health issues, like overcoming the seven enemies of survival (boredom and loneliness, pain, thirst, hunger, fatigue, fear, and temperature extremes), and related articles on wilderness survival skills, waste disposal ("the inside scoop on how to poop"), preventing heat exhaustion, dehydration and heat stroke, and how to plan a safe river trip. You can even purchase travel health and safety supplies right from the GORP travel gear online store.

➤ **The Travel Health Information Service** (www.travelhealth.com) Courtesy of Dr. Stephen Blythe, provides links and resources on food and water precautions, insect avoidance, diarrhea treatment (one of the most common travel ailments), and tips on traveling with medications. You'll also find tips for special travel situations, like traveling with AIDS patients and pregnant women, particularly in international situations where there could be limited health care and an increase in exposure to disease or infection.

➤ **The Medical College of Wisconsin International Travelers Clinic**
(`www.intmed.mcw.edu/travel.html`) A lengthy and comprehensive list of links
to Web sites covering aircraft cleanliness and hygiene (yuck!), global emergency
services, city health profiles, travel warnings, and a directory of travel medicine
providers.

➤ **Travel Health Online** (`www.tripprep.com`) Health information and country
profiles from Afghanistan to Zimbabwe, a directory of travel medicine providers
around the world, and in-depth articles about travel-related ailments, treatment
guidelines, and emergency preparation.

Getting in Shape Before Your Trip

Sightseeing, camping, or sitting on a plane or in your car for hours on end may not
seem like terribly grueling activities, but any change in your daily routine can be
stressful and will require your body to meet unusual challenges. You don't want to
find yourself pooped out before the day is done, so if you don't already, consider
starting an exercise regime before you leave for vacation so you have increased
energy to make it through the long, long days of leisure and activities. Stretching,
walking, swimming, and bicycling are great ways to get in shape and increase your
endurance. And keep up the good work on vacation, too. The GORP Web site has
a section on travel health issues (`www.gorp.com/gorp/health/main.htm`) and tips
on maintaining your endurance.

Travelers' Health and Medical Insurance

I talked about getting travel insurance and why you need it to protect your travel
investment in Chapter 6, "Before You Buy...Protecting Yourself Online." Besides the
dollars and cents that need to be protected, you also need to consider medical and
health coverage in case you're injured or become ill on vacation. This is especially
true for international travel because whether you're out of the country for three days
or three months, accidents can happen. And if you're not properly covered or are too
ill to return home, you could find yourself in big trouble. Remember, too, that you
can't purchase travel insurance after you leave the country and start to feel sickly, so
it's a good idea to spend some time researching different policies and find one that's
right for you and your traveling companions. If you're a solo mom traveler and you
become ill, you might want to look for coverage that pays for interim child care.

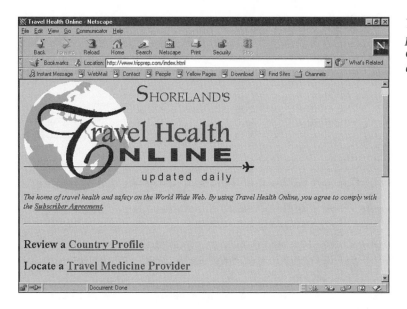

You can review a country profile or get information on preventive medications at www.tripprep.com.

There are two things to think about here: medical insurance and travel assistance. Although your current health insurance may provide some coverage, you need to look for supplemental travel insurance that provides medical evacuation (getting back home or to a hospital to recover) or emergency services, as well as access to a network of providers (who speak English) and provide around-the-clock care. Don't skimp on your policy or purchase a plan based solely on the premium price. Read the small print carefully, and get advice from other travelers or your travel agent.

And if you really think you don't need insurance, you're a gamblin' fool. At the very least, all travelers should join the International Association for Medical Assistance to Travelers (IAMAT), which is a nonprofit organization that gathers and distributes worldwide health information to assist travelers in locating qualified medical care overseas. Visit IAMAT's Web site at **www.cybermall.co.nz/NZ/IAMAT/**, and be sure to make a donation if you join—free membership means a little help from its members keeps the boat afloat.

Here are some starting points to locate the type of travel insurance and travel assistance coverage you need. Again, ask around, post questions in newsgroups or message boards, or call a local travel agent to get expert advice on reputable insurance carriers who meet your travel coverage needs:

➤ **Champion Insurance Advantage** (**www.champion-ins.com**) One of the most frequently recommended plans I've come across in my online research, although you'll need to check it out for yourself and compare to other providers' policies. It provides health, accident, and emergency evacuation coverage.

➤ **Traveler's Emergency Assistance** (**www.tenweb.com**) Provides worldwide medical assistance, medical referrals, medical expense advances, and prescription medication assistance, plus other medical assistance program features.

➤ **Highway to Health** (www.highwaytohealth.com) Offers travel insurance, plus other medical services, like doctor and hospital information and doctor network services.

What Are the Main Causes of Travel-Related Illnesses and Injuries?

According to Dr. Stephen Blythe at Travel Health Information Service (www.travelhealth.com), most travel-related maladies are not caused by skiing accidents, parasites, or bacteria. The major cause of deaths and injuries requiring medical evacuation (being returned to the United States or to a properly equipped medial facility) are automobile accidents and alcohol-related mishaps, usually involving water activities. Water-skiing or yachting on a full belly of booze is not recommended. Take precautions to avoid car accidents, Dr. Blythe says, by wearing your seatbelt, avoiding rural roadways after dark, and using common sense when mixing alcohol with pleasure.

A Tough Pill to Swallow, Plus a Shot in the Arm

For some international destinations, no immunizations are necessary, but the more tropical or close to the equator you go, the more precautions may be necessary. You need to allow plenty of time to take care of shots and preventive medication, as some immunizations need to be followed by a booster. You'll also need to document your shots on an international health certificate that you can get from your doctor or state health department. It's also a good idea to look into health warnings for the area you're headed to long before your trip to find out exactly what's required for entry into the country or what precautions you need to take to combat malaria and other dreaded diseases. Here are some government warning and travel health information sites you should check out at least two or three months before you're set to depart:

➤ **Centers for Disease Control** (www.cdc.gov/travel) Has long lists of disease-related topics to think about. They include childhood immunizations required for entry, a geographic map of disease outbreaks, health recommendations by region, summaries of sanitation inspections of cruise ships, and U.S. State Department information on nonmedical issues like civil unrest, crime, and natural disasters. You'll also find food and water precautions and a traveler's guide to preventing typhoid fever.

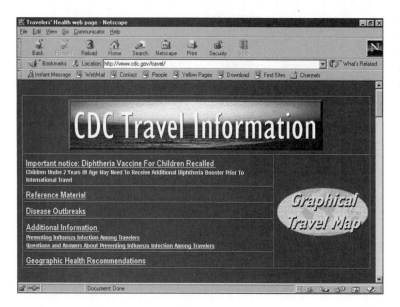

The Centers for Disease Control Web site provides information on disease outbreaks and health concerns for any travel area.

➤ **Travel Health Information Web (www.travelhealth.com)** You should check out this site for practical tips on everything from water purification, to safe food handling, to combating insects.

➤ **Travel gear sites** If you're going to an area where malaria or insect-borne diseases are an issue, you'll want to get a hold of essential travel supplies like mosquito bed nets and DEET to slather all over your body to keep those pesky and sometimes dangerous varmints away. You can get just about all your safe and healthy travel supplies online at Walkabout Travel Gear (**www.walkabouttravelgear.com**) or Magellan Travel Supplies (**www.magellans.com**).

Staying Healthy On the Way

So you've gathered all the facts and information you need to get ready for your trip. You've booked your flight or cruise, or prepped the car for your journey, and now you need to think about all the mishaps and maladies that can happen while en route to your destination. Here are some Web sites where you can learn about air travel health issues, including combating jetlag and motion sickness:

➤ **Healthy Flying with Diana Fairechild (www.flyana.com)** A must-stop for any air traveler. Here you'll get the inside scoop from a veteran flight attendant who gives you the down and dirty on airplane air quality, airline meals, crew fatigue, dehydration, jetlag, fear of flying, lost luggage, and lots of information on safe, healthy air travel.

You can get an insider's perspective on safe and healthy airplane travel at www.flyana.com.

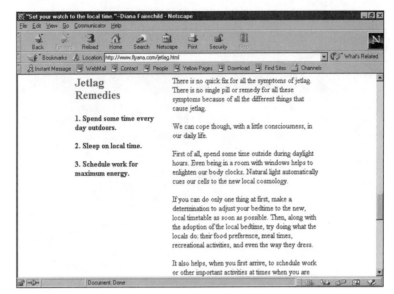

➤ **Travel Products (www.travelaccessories.com)** There are lots of different remedies for car sickness and motion sickness on boats, so check out this site to get the scoop on ways you can reduce or eliminate travel motion illnesses. There are even supplies specially designed for kids' travel.

Staying Healthy After You Arrive

One of the most common tips for staying in tip-top shape when you arrive at your vacation spot is "don't drink the water." That can even be true of traveling within the United States, as even the slightest change in water quality can give you an upset tummy. So, for that reason, you should only drink bottled or purified water or carbonated beverages, like beer or soda, and stay away from ice cubes.

Be careful of what you eat and drink, and bring yourself up to speed on some basic precautions for avoiding food poisoning and illnesses. I've listed some general travel health Web sites here, and most of the ones listed in the preceding sections also have information or links to other Web sites dealing with staying healthy when you arrive. But in the event that you become ill or an accident happens, you should be prepared by locating medical facilities and emergency numbers in the area you're traveling to, so I've also provided a link to health care provider information for just about any country in the world:

➤ **Travel Health Online's Directory of Travel Medicine Providers (www.tripprep.com/clinics/clindex.html)** Lists, by country, doctors and other health care providers specializing in health needs of travelers. You can visit the site to find a listing of hospitals and physicians in your destination, including some emergency numbers.

➤ **The International Society of Travel Medicine** (`www.istm.org`) Provides links to travel medicine clinics worldwide.

➤ **CyberDocs** (`www.cyberdocs.com`) If you travel with a laptop and plan on having it with you when you break your leg, through CyberDocs, you can consult a physician from the nearest phone outlet. Actually, if you need medical advice while you're on the road, it's as easy as going online to virtually visit with a U.S.-trained, board-certified doctor. Physicians are available by appointment to address your medical needs through interactive keyboard chat or audio- and videoconferencing.

➤ **Global Emergency Medical Services** (`www.globalmed.com`) Provides online medical consultation for minor medical problems without appointment, 24-hours per day, seven days per week, using keyboard interaction. Other types of services include medical consultation and advice, prescriptions for minor ailments, medical information services, emergency birth control, and emergency refills of prescriptions.

I'm on the Highway to Health

Even classic rockers should check out this site. Highway to Health's City Profiles (`www.highwaytohealth.com`) provide detailed information about local hospitals, clinics, airport clinics, pharmacies, and health care providers. It also sells travel insurance, so take a look to see if they have a policy that's right for you.

So now that you've gotten the scoop on just about everything you need to know to be a smart and savvy traveler (or at least where you can go online to gather facts and information) it's time to pack those bags (not too full, remember) and hit the road for the trip of a lifetime. Safe and happy travels to you all!

The Least You Need to Know

➤ You can research travel health concerns online and gather tips on preparing for unexpected illnesses or injuries.

➤ You can get up-to-the-minute disease outbreak information to prepare for safe and healthy travels.

➤ You can find travel health insurance providers online.

➤ You can buy travel health products online, like water purifiers, first aid kits, and mosquito nets and repellents.

➤ Travel safety is an issue anywhere you go, even if it's a trip to Grandma's.

Speak Like a Geek: The Complete Archive

alt   A newsgroup category on alternative subjects that may be considered bizarre, inappropriate, or obscene.

Amadeus   A GDS that is an essential sales tool for travel agencies, which represent the core of Amadeus's users. More than 136,000 travel agency terminals are connected to Amadeus.

America Online (AOL)   A popular online information service and Internet access provider. Almost half of all Internet users connect by using AOL.

AOL   *See* America Online.

article   A message posted in an Internet newsgroup.

auction site   An online site where you bid to buy goods, or where you state a price you're willing to pay and then wait for a travel agent or tour operator to bid on it.

audio file   A music or sound file that you can download or play from the Internet, using certain browser plug-ins.

Bookmark   In Netscape Navigator, an archive of Web site addresses that has been saved in your browser. When at a site, you choose **Add Bookmark** in your browser, so that the browser saves the site and you can easily and quickly return to that site. For example, if you make travel arrangements on Travelocity, you can bookmark the site to make it easier to retrieve flight or other information before your trip. *See also* Favorites.

cache   A place where a browser stores Web documents that have been retrieved. The cache may be on the hard disk, in memory, or a combination of the two. Documents you return to are retrieved from the cache rather than from the remote site, which cuts down transmission time.

Channels The most popular topics in Deja.com.

chat A system that allows people to communicate by typing messages. These messages are sent and received as you type them. The most popular Internet chat system is Internet Relay Chat, but there are other Web site–based systems, too. The most popular way for people to chat is through online services like AOL.

comp A newsgroup category on computer science, software sources, and information on hardware and software systems.

computer reservation system (CRS) An online-based network of computers that connects travel agents and travel suppliers in real-time for making reservations and travel purchases.

cookies Pieces of data that a Web site puts on your computer. If you become a member of an online reservation site, for example, you'll need to set your browser to accept cookies so you don't have to re-register every time you visit the site.

cross-post To post a single message to several forums at the same time.

currency converter An online calculator that lets you enter an amount and a currency to convert, and then displays the converted amount.

cyber café A coffee shop where you can use the café's computers to log on to the Web and read or send email.

cyberspace The area in which computer users travel when navigating a network or the Internet.

dial-in connection A connection that you can access by using a modem and dialing into a computer through a telephone line. When you're connected, your computer acts like a terminal connected to the service provider's computer.

directory A category-based listing of information that you can click through to find information before starting a search using keywords. *See also* search engine.

domain name A name given to a host computer on the Internet.

Domain Name System (DNS) A system that helps one Internet host find another so it can send email, connect FTP sessions, and more. The DNS basically translates words into numbers that the computers can understand.

download To transfer something from the Internet to your computer. For example, you can download software to your computer and then run that software on your own computer. Whenever you visit a Web page, you download to your computer the pictures and files that make up that Web page; these pictures and files end up in your cache. *See also* upload.

email   An electronic mail message that is sent from computer to computer over the Internet, online services, or a company network.

email alert   An email message that is sent to alert a person of something of interest. For example, you can sign up for email alerts to tell you when a special travel bargain or airfare is available.

emoticon   The techie name for small symbols created using typed characters, such as :) and ;-). You tilt your head to the left to view them. *See also* smiley.

encryption   Scrambled data that cannot be read or understood by unauthorized recipients. Secure Sockets Layer is one such type of technology.

FAQs (frequently asked questions)   A list of commonly asked questions at a Web site, newsgroup, or message board. This is a good place to start if you're visiting for the first time or looking for basic information.

Favorites   In Internet Explorer, the term used for the Bookmarks list. *See also* Bookmark.

File Transfer Protocol (FTP)   A protocol that defines how files transfer from one computer to another across the Internet. It is usually abbreviated FTP and can also be used as a verb to describe the act of transferring files. For example, "I FTPed to the system to get a file."

filter   Search criteria that allow you to narrow results. For example, if you're looking for a hotel and you want results only for hotels with tennis courts or swimming pools, selecting this as a criterion will filter your results.

flame   An abusive newsgroup or mailing list message. Things in a newsgroup you can do to get a flame are to ask dumb questions, offend people, not read the FAQs, or simply get on the wrong side of someone with an attitude. Also, if you abuse a mailing list and send out an irrelevant message, you can get flamed. When these things get out of control, a *flame war* erupts.

followup   A message generated in response to another message that is broadcast for all to see. If differs from a reply, which goes through email to a single user.

form   An interactive document that lets you type information into different fields. This kind of document can be used to fill out a survey, purchase an item, or search a database.

forum   Similar to an Internet newsgroup, an online bulletin board or discussion group.

frame   An independent subwindow or pane within the main browser window.

freeware   Software that you can download from the Internet and use for free.

FTP   *See* File Transfer Protocol.

Galileo An example of a GDS. It is a consortium of European airline sites and is located at **www.galileo.co.uk**.

GDS *See* global distribution system.

global distribution system (GDS) A system that provides online distribution, marketing, and sales tools. Examples are Amadeus, Sabre, Galileo, and WORLDSPAN, which provide information to travel professionals around the world.

handle Your online nickname, much like a CB radio handle. My online handle, for example, is Hooliana.

History list A list of Web documents that you've visited in the current session or previous sessions. You can return to a document by simply selecting it from the history list.

home page A Web page on the World Wide Web. A collection of these Web pages at one site is referred to as a Web site. *See also* Web site.

host A computer connected to the Internet. A service provider's computer or one with a permanent connection is a host. Dial-in terminal connections are not hosts. *See also* server.

HTML *See* Hypertext Markup Language.

hyperlink A word, a phrase, or an image on a Web page that you can click on to jump to another location on the Web.

hypertext A system of links in documents that help users move between areas of the document by clicking links. The World Wide Web is a hypertext system.

Hypertext Markup Language The basic coding system used to create Web documents.

IAP *See* Internet access provider.

icon A small picture or image on the computer screen that you can click to run a program. An icon can also be an image on a Web page that you click for a link.

IE A common abbreviation for Internet Explorer.

Internet When spelled with a small I, this refers to any network connected to another. The Internet is one example of an internet. It is a global network of computers, and it is the system on which the World Wide Web operates, as well as email and newsgroups.

Internet access provider (IAP) An Internet service provider.

Internet Explorer (IE) A commonly used Web browser from Microsoft. *See also* Netscape Navigator.

Internet Relay Chat (IRC)   One of the most popular chat programs. Internet users can chat with other users in their choice of IRC channels.

Internet service provider (ISP)   A company that provides services for dialing in to the Internet.

IRC   *See* Internet Relay Chat.

ISP   *See* Internet service provider.

Java   A programming language that allows programmers to create a single program that can run in many kinds of operating systems. Browsers, such as Netscape Navigator and Internet Explorer, both have built-in Java interpreters.

keyword   A word you type into a search box on a site, such as a travel site, that describes the information you're trying to find. For example, you could go to your favorite search engine and type **bed AND breakfast** to find Web sites and Web pages that contain these keywords.

link   Another term for hyperlink. *See* hyperlink.

log off   To tell the computer that you've finished your work and you don't need to be online; the opposite of log on or log in. The procedure is normally fairly simple and involves typing a command, such as **exit**, or clicking a **Disconnect** button.

log on   To access a computer to use its services, normally by typing a username and a password. This makes sure that only authorized people can use the computer. A synonym is *log in*.

login   The ID and password that you use to log on to a computer or a network.

lurk   To read newsgroup or mailing list messages without responding to them. Other users don't know you're there, but in a chat room, other users can view a list of everyone present in the chat room. It's a good idea the first time you visit a chat room or want to post something in a newsgroup to lurk for a while to get a feel for the members and the subject being discussed.

lurker   Someone involved in lurking.

mailing list   A list of email addresses that a single message can be sent to by entering one name as the To address. An example is a travel club mailing list. Also, discussion groups have mailing lists, where each message sent to the newsgroup is sent to everyone on the list who subscribed to be notified via email of any followups to a posting.

Microsoft Internet Explorer   *See* Internet Explorer.

Microsoft Network (MSN)   A major online service that was launched when Windows 95 was released. It is also known as MSN. Its online travel site is Expedia, one of the most heavily trafficked travel sites.

mirror site   A copy of another site. This provides an alternative location so that if you can't get into the original site because it already has too many users, you can go to the mirror site to get exactly the same information.

misc   A newsgroup category addressing themes that don't really fit into any of the other headings or that include themes from multiple categories.

modem   A device within, or added externally to your computer that converts digital signals from your computer into analog signals for transmission through a phone line or cable service and vice versa.

MSN   *See* Microsoft Network.

navigate   To move around the Web using a browser.

navigator   A program to help you find your way around an online service. One feature of these programs is that you can use many applications, such as writing email offline and then quickly going online to finish the task.

Netiquette   Internet etiquette, the correct form of behavior to use while working on the Internet and newsgroups.

Netscape Navigator   The Web browser made by Netscape that helps you get onto the World Wide Web. It is part of a package of Internet tools, called Communicator.

newbie   A new user. The term either refers to a new Internet user or a user who is new to a particular area, such as a chat room or a newsgroup.

news   A newsgroup category concerned with the newsgroup network, group maintenance, and software.

news server   A computer that gathers newsgroup data and makes it available to newsreaders.

newsgroup   A worldwide discussion group or message board on the Internet in which people post and read public messages. There are thousands of newsgroups, covering every topic imaginable, including many on travel and travel-related topics.

newsgroup reader   A piece of software that allows you to participate in newsgroups by letting you read and post messages.

offline   The opposite of online; not connected.

online   Being connected to the Internet or an online service.

online service   A service, such as America Online, that has information, sites, and services you can access through your computer and modem.

online transaction   A financial transaction conducted over the Internet or online service. When you pay for something, such as an airline ticket, using a credit card on a Web site, you've performed an online transaction.

opt-out policy   A policy that gives you the option to say that you don't want to receive certain services or messages from a Web site. For example, when you sign up for an online travel directory, you might be asked whether you want to be sent email from that site, and if there's an option you can check saying you don't want to receive email, then there's an opt-out policy. An opt-out policy also often means that if you cancel or discontinue membership or customer status at a Web site, the site won't sell your personal information.

password   A combination of characters and numbers that you create that identifies you as the person you say you are. Passwords are used to make sure that you are the only one who can access a site with your personal information, such as address, phone number, email address, or credit card numbers.

PDA   A small, handheld portable organizer that can include a date book, address book, email, to-do list, memo pad, calculator, and game applications. Also known as a personal digital assistant.

Personal Digital Assistant   *See also* PDA.

plug-in   A piece of software that works with your Web browser to help you view or listen to music, pictures, or movies.

point of presence (POP)   A connection to a local service, without dialing long distance.

Point-to-Point Protocol (PPP)   A protocol computers use to connect to the Internet, through phone lines.

POP   *See* point of presence.

post   To broadcast a message to an entire forum, such as a message board or newsgroup.

posting   A message sent to a newsgroup.

PPP   *See* Point-to-Point Protocol.

protocol   A set of rules that governs the format of data that is exchanged by computers.

RealAudio   A popular plug-in that lets you play audio files from the Internet and listen to them on your computer. The newest versions are RealSystem and RealSystem G2, which also allows you to view video files.

RealPlayer   A popular plug-in that lets you play audio and video files from the Internet and see and listen to them on your computer. *See* RealAudio and streaming media.

rec   A newsgroup category on hobbies and recreational activities.

reload (refresh)   A command that tells a browser to retrieve a Web document again, even though you have it in the cache file. Internet Explorer uses the term *refresh*, and Netscape Navigator uses the term *reload*.

Sabre   A GDS used by professional travel agencies that provides schedules, availability, pricing, policies and rules, reservations, and ticketing for more than 420 airlines, 40,000 hotel properties, and 50 car rental companies. This system also powers popular travel sites like Travelocity.

sci   A newsgroup category covering special knowledge of research or application of the established sciences (not astrology or science fiction).

search engine   A site such as Yahoo! or Lycos that searches the Web and tells you where to find the information you're looking for. This is also known as a *search site*.

secure site   A site that uses encryption technology or a standard SSL so that all confidential information you put into a form is kept confidential. On most secure sites you'll notice an icon in your browser that looks like a closed lock. *See also* encryption and Secure Sockets Layer.

Secure Sockets Layer (SSL)   The technology standard used on the Web to ensure that confidential information sent over the Internet, such as credit card information, addresses, or phone numbers, remains private.

server   A program or computer that services another program or computer (client). *See also* host.

shareware   A version of software that you download from the Internet or an online service to your computer. You can try it out for free for a trial period. After using it for a certain length of time, you're supposed to pay the author of the program a registration fee.

Shopping cart   *See* virtual shopping cart.

Simple Mail Transfer Protocol (SMTP)   A protocol used to transfer email between computers on a network.

site   *See* Web site.

smiley   A symbol in email and newsgroup messages used to convey emotion or simply to provide amusement. ;-) The term first referred to a symbol that looked like a smile, but now it refers to just about any small symbol created with text characters. You create smileys by typing various keyboard characters and can then view them by tilting your head to the left. For example, :-(means sadness. The technical term for a smiley is *emoticon*.

SMTP   *See* Simple Mail Transfer Protocol.

soc   A newsgroup category that discusses social issues, socializing, and world cultures.

spam   Unsolicited email that is sent to large numbers of people without any regard to whether those people want to receive that mail. The term first referred to a single message sent to a large number of newsgroups. It comes from the Monty Python Spam song, based on that much-loved processed meat, in which the word spam is repeated endlessly.

SSL   *See* Secure Sockets Layer.

start page   A term used in some versions of Internet Explorer to refer to the home page.

streaming media   A kind of media that lets you view and listen to audio and video files from the Internet while they're still downloading to your computer. Without streaming media, you have to wait until the entire file downloads before you can listen to or view the file. This could sometimes take a half hour or more.

surf   To travel from one site to another on the World Wide Web.

talk   Similar to chat, a more private program that lets two or more Internet users type messages to each other. The text is immediately transferred to the other user. AOL Instant Messenger (which is available to non-AOL users) and ICQ are the two most popular forms of talk. *See also* chat.

Telnet   A program that lets Internet users log in to computers other than their hosts. As a verb, to use Telnet to access a distant computer.

thread   A chain of messages on a particular topic.

TRUSTe   A governing organization of the Web that sets voluntary rules that member Web sites choose to follow. These rules have to do with the privacy of information gathered from you when you visit Web sites.

upload   To transfer information, such as a file or program, from one computer to another. *See also* download.

URL (uniform resource locator)   A Web address, such as `www.travelocity.com` or `www.grouptravel.net`. In most recent versions of Internet Explorer and Netscape, you don't need to type `www`. In the location bar, you can type just `grouptravel.net`, for example.

Usenet   A large network connected to the Internet, the user's network, and the newsgroups distributed through this network.

Usenet newsgroup   *See* newsgroup.

username   A name that identifies you to a Web site. Usernames and passwords are typically used together to make sure you are who you say are. For example, when logging on to many travel directories, you have to provide a username and password that you established during your first visit. Sometimes also called *user ID* or *login*.

video file   A file that you download or play from the Internet that has video in it.

viewer   A program that displays or plays computer files that you find on the Web. For example, RealSystem G2 and Adobe Acrobat are viewers.

virtual shopping cart   A service offered on Web sites that lets you keep a list of all the things you're possibly going to buy. When you're ready to buy, you can throw away the things you don't want, pay for the ones you do want, and leave some in your shopping cart for your next visit. Most online shopping sites, such as Amazon.com, offer this function.

virus   A program created by Internet hackers or terrorists that uses different techniques to duplicate itself and travel between computers. Viruses can either be simple nuisances or cause an entire computer or network to have serious problems.

W3   *See* World Wide Web.

Web   *See* World Wide Web.

Web browser   Software that lets you get onto the World Wide Web, view Web pages, and go from site to site. Two examples are Internet Explorer and Netscape Navigator.

Web forum   A discussion group on a Web site.

Web page   A single page on the World Wide Web. Web pages are put together to form a larger Web site. *See* Web site.

Web server   A computer system that makes Web documents available to browsers. The browser asks the server for the document, and it transmits the document to the browser.

Web site   Many Web pages are put together at a location on the World Wide Web to help you get information, view audio or video, shop, or do many other different activities. *See* Web page.

Web surf   *See* surf.

World Wide Web   The most popular part of the Internet, made up of Web sites and pages that are hyperlinked together.

Worldspan   A travel GDS providing airline, hotel, and car rental information and searches. Many well-known Web sites, such as Internet Travel Network, are powered by this system.

WWW   *See* World Wide Web.

Index

X–Z

Web Site Index